'Eating disorders begin in adolescence during a critical transformational period of brain development. Approximately a third of patients have a protracted form of illness often with a complex formulation that involves many systems. This book fills an important gap as it has a focus on the psychological and interpersonal rather than the medical aspects. It offers a rich resource with a wide-ranging collection of expertise in the understanding of the process of the development of a confident adult identity. It includes a wide range of strategies to target the core symptom of loneliness and loss of self-security which is at the heart of this illness.'

Janet Treasure, *King's College London*

'This is a very comprehensive text that provides an analysis of the role of self and identity processes in the development, maintenance, and recovery from anorexia nervosa. The edited volume incorporates diverse theoretical perspectives on identity and a large number of accomplished identity scholars have contributed. A must-read for researchers and practitioners in the field.'

Tegan Cruwys, *University of Queensland*

'This important book brings together a number of highly influential academics and clinicians working in the field of anorexia nervosa. In the first book of its kind, the volume covers the important issue of identity in anorexia, the way in which it may contribute to both the development and the maintenance of the disorder. In this groundbreaking book, Fox, Williams and their co-authors provide important insights into this most challenging eating disorder, where our understanding is still limited, and treatments are at best, only partially effective. Linking the concept of identity to emotions such as disgust and shame and to the concept of the anorexic voice, the authors offer profound and original insights into how anorexia develops and what makes it so hard to recover. Strengths of the book include the consideration of neurodiversity and gender identity, both important aspect of the condition. Underpinned by theory and research evidence, and supported by insights from experts by experience, the book offers crucial ideas that are already leading to improvements in psychological treatments for anorexia nervosa, offering hope to sufferers and their families. It will offer new insights to seasoned eating disorder experts as well as those new to the area.'

Lucy Serpell, *University College London*

'We cannot fully understand anorexia nervosa without understanding the role of identity. This book explains why, and what can be done about it. By examining identity through multiple lenses, this volume offers a comprehensive overview of anorexia that integrates theory, research, clinical practice, and lived experiences. Filled with invaluable insights, it is an essential resource for clinicians and researchers alike.'

Matthew Pugh, *University College London*

Feeding the Self

Feeding the Self brings together leading scholars, clinicians, and lived-experience authors to place self and identity at the heart of how we understand and promote recovery from anorexia nervosa (AN).

Spanning developmental, social, cultural, and clinical lenses, the volume maps how identities are formed, threatened, and reclaimed within families and peer groups, under stigma and loneliness, across gender roles and gender identities, and in diverse cultural settings. The chapters examine the anorexic voice; self-conscious emotions; gender-role norms; transgender and non-binary experiences and gender-affirmative care; global and cross-cultural perspectives on body ideals, acculturation, and meaning; autism and identity in relation to AN; and the lived experience of AN, highlighting the role of narrative identity and hope. Clinical sections translate these insights into practice, covering a range of therapeutic approaches (including psychodynamic, cognitive behaviour therapy for anorexia nervosa [CBT-AN], Maudsley Model of Anorexia Nervosa Treatment for Adults [MANTRA], and Specialist Supportive Clinical Management [SSCM] approaches; compassion-focused therapy; body-neutral and functionality-based methods; and innovative approaches such as chairwork and VR-supported exposure).

For clinicians, researchers, trainees, and policymakers, this book offers a rigorous yet compassionate reframing of AN; not merely as a set of symptoms, but as a lived experience shaped by stories, relationships, and identities – and, importantly, as a condition from which new and meaningful identities and lives can emerge.

John R. E. Fox is Professor of Clinical Psychology and Programme Director of the Sheffield DClinPsy programme. He is Co-Editor-in-Chief of *Psychology and Psychotherapy: Theory, Research, and Practice* and has over 20 years' clinical and academic experience in eating disorders.

Marc O. Williams, DClinPsy, PhD, is Clinical Psychologist, Senior Lecturer, and Co-Editor-in-Chief of *Psychology and Psychotherapy: Theory, Research, and Practice*. His expertise spans eating disorders and climate change related mental health.

Feeding the Self

Identity and Recovery in Anorexia Nervosa

Edited by John R. E. Fox and Marc O. Williams

Routledge
Taylor & Francis Group
LONDON AND NEW YORK

Designed cover image: © Getty Images

First published 2026
by Routledge
4 Park Square, Milton Park, Abingdon, Oxon OX14 4RN

and by Routledge
605 Third Avenue, New York, NY 10158

Routledge is an imprint of the Taylor & Francis Group, an informa business

British Library Cataloguing-in-Publication Data
A catalogue record for this book is available from the British Library

ISBN: 9781032742137 (hbk)
ISBN: 9781032720524 (pbk)
ISBN: 9781003468189 (ebk)

DOI: 10.4324/9781003468189

Typeset in Times New Roman
by Deanta Global Publishing Services, Chennai, India

Contents

Chapter 1

Introduction to the Book

Marc O. Williams and John R.E. Fox

Introduction

Anorexia nervosa (AN) is a serious and complicated condition that continues to elude satisfactory treatment in many cases. Its physical features are the most obvious and command urgent attention from family, loved ones, and professionals alike. Beneath the obvious can lie a hidden world of anxieties and preoccupations, from which only some concerns – weight, shape, food – rise to the surface. This book delves beneath that surface, into the psychological undercurrents that may sustain AN and contribute to its emergence. We anchor these concerns in the concept of *identity*. In doing so, we aim to explore how identity can be both starved and fed by the experience of AN and how nourishing a fuller sense of self may be key to recovery.

Contributors include researchers, clinicians, and experts by experience, some of whom speak from more than one of these perspectives. Our hope is to highlight the importance of identity-based approaches to treatment and to bring attention to identity as a promising area for theoretical and empirical exploration. By placing identity front and centre, we aim to advance more inclusive care that sees the person behind the AN, recognising their unique sociocultural experience and lived reality.

Identity and Anorexia Nervosa

Young people face the task of fashioning a unique sense of self, or identity, that is continuous over time, across situations, and forms in a social context (Erikson, 1968). McAdams (2008) later built on this, suggesting that identity is shaped by constructing a life narrative that draws on both past experience and future aspirations, filtered through cultural meaning systems. Identity comes to rely more heavily on our sense of dispositional traits from late childhood, in which we begin to see ourselves as comprising certain attributes and characteristics (McAdams & Cox, 2010). There are potholes on the road to identity formation that can veer us off into role confusion, where there is a lack of clarity about one's place in the world,

DOI: 10.4324/9781003468189-1

which can cause issues with other developmental tasks including occupational and relationship difficulties (Erikson, 1968).

Croce et al. (2024) noted that comparatively scant attention has been dedicated to the role of identity in AN, despite the seeming centrality of identity to the experience. In their review, individuals with AN frequently spoke of concerns relating to identity, including a fragmented sense of self which lacks coherence, characterised by highly critical self-evaluations. Broadly speaking, AN may be a mechanism by which some individuals attempt to arrive at a stronger sense of identity, offering a framework through which to experience control, competence, or belonging. Notably, identity formation is a key developmental task of adolescence – the typical period of AN onset (Campbell & Peebles, 2014; Erikson, 1968). Identity-challenging life transitions during this time, such as starting secondary school, increasing independence from one's family, and the onset of puberty, may heighten vulnerability for those already struggling to form a coherent sense of self.

AN can be valued by those who experience it (Schmidt & Treasure, 2006). Work by Serpell et al. (1999, 2004) described the perceived benefits of AN for bolstering identity: enhancing confidence and a sense of self-control. AN is also valued for its social effects, perceived or otherwise: enhancing attractiveness to others, providing a sense of uniqueness, a special skill that others do not possess, and a way of communicating distress (Serpell et al., 1999, 2004). While these outcomes come to be viewed with ambivalence over time as the many negative consequences of AN take hold, they may help explain its persistence, especially when it feels as though few other viable identities are available.

Structure and Themes

We have organised the book in three parts, each shedding light on AN and its interplay with identity. Beginning with Part I, the book presents recent theoretical developments regarding identity development as a vulnerability and maintenance factor in AN, charting how an already-faint identity may become fainter as AN takes over. Chapter 2 presents the theory of the 'lost emotional self' (Oldershaw et al., 2019), which examines in detail how early childhood relationship-based experiences can leave a diminished sense of self, inhibiting healthy identity development in adolescence in a way that increases vulnerability to AN. Chapter 3 delves into the emotional consequences of identity disturbance in AN by providing a theory on the role of self-conscious emotions, and self-disgust in particular. In Chapter 4 we turn to the phenomenon of the anorexic voice, which becomes more powerful as AN takes hold. A sizeable number of people with AN meet criteria for an autism diagnosis (Westwood et al., 2017), and Chapter 5 explores the implications that autism has for identity development in the context of AN, including how attempts to camouflage one's autistic behaviours could contribute to AN. Part I concludes with an examination of longstanding and severe AN in Chapter 6 – where it is posited that, over time, the 'self' gives way almost entirely to AN.

In Part II our focus shifts beyond the individual to the social aspects of identity, considering the interplay between AN and emotional expression, group membership, social roles, gender and gender identity, and culture. Chapter 7 begins with research on emotional regulation in AN, and how attempts to suppress emotions can interfere with identity development in social contexts. Chapter 8 explores the social identity approach (Tajfel & Turner, 1979), the role of loneliness and belonging, and how the ability to identify with social groups can shape the development and maintenance of AN, as well as how recovery can be aided by changes in social identification. Chapter 9 considers how the degree to which people identify with a feminine/masculine gender role impacts on AN. Chapter 10 presents a summary of research and theoretical developments in understanding the overlap between AN and gender identity (including trans and non-binary identities). Finally, Chapter 11 examines differences in AN prevalence and presentation across cultures and the interplay between AN and cultural ideals of body weight and shape.

Part III concludes the book with lived-experience reflections and an integrative synthesis of key themes. Chapter 12 presents two first-person narratives of living with and recovering from AN. Drawing on narrative identity theory, these accounts illustrate how AN can reshape memory, language, and the sense of self, underscoring the importance of grounding theory and practice in lived experience. Chapter 13 then draws the volume to a close, pulling together insights from across the preceding chapters. It highlights the theoretical implications of the work presented, identifies empirical gaps, and outlines priorities for future research and clinical practice, with particular emphasis on identity-focused approaches to treatment and recovery.

In exploring the role of identity in AN, this volume aims to answer an array of questions under the following themes:

Early Life Experiences: How might childhood and adolescence shape self-perception in a way that fosters vulnerability to developing AN?

Neurodivergence: How does autism influence identity and emotional experiences in AN?

Gender Diversity and AN: How do gender identity and the challenges faced by gender-diverse individuals relate to AN?

Women, Femininity, and AN: Why has AN been predominantly associated with women?

Cultural and Global Perspectives: How do cultural identities and experiences, such as those of South Africans, shape the presentation and prevalence of AN?

Severe and Enduring AN (SE-AN): How does long-term AN impact identity over time?

Emotions and Identity: How do emotions such as self-disgust, shame, guilt, and pride – and the strategies used to regulate them – shape identity in individuals with AN?

Social Identity and AN: How do group memberships and social identities influence the development, maintenance, and recovery from AN – and what role do belonging and loneliness play in this process?

Experts by Experience: What is the lived experience of identity in those with experience of AN and recovery from AN?

References

Campbell, K., & Peebles, R. (2014). Eating disorders in children and adolescents: State of the art review. Pediatrics, 134(3), 582–592. https://doi.org/10.1542/peds.2014-0194

Croce, S. R., Malcolm, A. C., Ralph-Nearman, C., & Phillipou, A. (2024). The role of identity in anorexia nervosa: A narrative review. *New Ideas in Psychology*, *72*, 101060.

Erikson, E. H. (1968). *Identity youth and crisis* (No. 7). WW Norton & company.

McAdams, D. P. (2008). Personal narratives and the life story. In O. P. John, R. W. Robins, & L. A. Pervin (Eds.), *Handbook of personality: Theory and research* (3rd ed., pp. 242–262). American Psychological Association Press.

McAdams, D. P., & Cox, K. S. (2010). Self and identity across the life span. In R. M. Lerner, M. E. Lamb, & A. M. Freund (Eds.), Handbook of life-span development, 2, 158–207. John Wiley & Sons.

Oldershaw, A., Startup, H., & Lavender, T. (2019). Anorexia nervosa and a lost emotional self: A psychological formulation of the development, maintenance, and treatment of anorexia nervosa. *Frontiers in psychology*, *10*, 219.

Schmidt, U., & Treasure, J. (2006). Anorexia nervosa: Valued and visible. A cognitive-interpersonal maintenance model and its implications for research and practice. *British Journal of Clinical Psychology*, *45*(3), 343–366.

Serpell, L., Teasdale, J. D., Troop, N. A., & Treasure, J. (2004). The development of the P-CAN, a measure to operationalize the pros and cons of anorexia nervosa. *International Journal of Eating Disorders*, *36*(4), 416–433.

Serpell, L., Treasure, J., Teasdale, J., & Sullivan, V. (1999). Anorexia nervosa: Friend or foe?. *International Journal of Eating Disorders*, *25*(2), 177–186.

Tajfel, H., & Turner, J. C. (1979). An integrative theory of intergroup conflict. In W. G. Austin, & S. Worchel (Eds.), The social psychology of intergroup relations, 33-37. Brooks/Cole.

Westwood, H., Mandy, W., & Tchanturia, K. (2017). Clinical evaluation of autistic symptoms in women with anorexia nervosa. *Molecular Autism*, *8*, 1–9.

Part I

The Inner Self

How Identity Shapes and Is Shaped by Anorexia Nervosa

Chapter 2

Identity Development and the 'Real Me'

Anna Oldershaw and Tony Lavender

Introduction

Anorexia nervosa (AN) is an eating disorder (ED) characterised by self-starvation driven by weight, shape, and eating concerns and extreme dread of food, eating, and normal body weight (Walsh et al., 2023). The treatment of choice for AN is talking therapy (NICE, 2017); however, outcomes from clinical trials remain limited (Monteleone et al., 2022). AN carries a high mortality risk (Van Eeden et al., 2021) and relapse rates are as high as 40% to 50% after treatment (Sala et al., 2023). Therefore, better understanding of key factors underpinning AN is urgently required to inform the development of more effective therapeutic approaches (Bulik, 2014; Croce et al., 2024a). AN has been associated with numerous, complex, and broad-ranging risk and maintenance factors across genetic, biological, psychological, and socio-environmental elements (Oldershaw et al., 2019). One proposed underpinning factor that is of promise for treatment development is that of 'identity' – one's sense of self and of who they are (Amianto et al., 2016; Bruch, 1982; Casper, 1983; Oldershaw et al., 2019). This chapter will review the evidence for identity disturbance as a factor in the development and maintenance of AN and the role of AN in creating a 'False Self'. It will propose and review outcomes from a new treatment approach (Specialist Psychotherapy with Emotion for Anorexia in Kent and Sussex; SPEAKS) which understands difficulties with emotion as underpinning identity difficulties and that this is at the heart of AN. This approach seeks to work with identity and guide clients towards the development of the 'Real Me'.

Identity Formation

Identity and its synonyms (e.g. self-concept, personal identity, self-identity, sense of self) can be understood as the conscious awareness of oneself as a person, including feelings of clarity, coherence, and continuity of the self across time and situations. It encompasses a relational understanding of one's sameness and uniqueness from others (Erikson, 1959). Adolescence and emerging adulthood is a distinct developmental phase, characterised by multiple physical and psychological changes and transitions, creating an increased vulnerability to mental health

DOI: 10.4324/9781003468189-3

difficulties. Identity exploration and development are key aspects of development during this adolescent period, and the creation of a stable identity is a major task. Erikson's (1968) seminal theory on identity formation describes how active identity exploration, formation, and navigation in adolescence enable disparate conceptions about oneself from childhood to be consolidated into a unified whole, stable, and cohesive identity, resulting in feelings of independence and control over one's life. 'Identity disturbance', where this process does not successfully occur during adolescence, is characterised by a markedly and persistently unstable sense of self, evident through inconsistent perceptions of who one is and unclear boundaries between oneself and others, and lack of narrative coherence around the self (Uliaszek et al., 2022). Disturbance of identity is linked to the development of psychopathology, such as personality disorders (Bogaerts et al., 2024; Meisner et al., 2021), Obsessive Compulsive Disorder (OCD), Body Dysmorphic Disorder (BDD) (Malcolm et al., 2021), depression and EDs (Bouguettaya et al., 2022). Adolescence is a known period of particular risk for AN (Halmi, 2009).

Identity and Anorexia Nervosa

Identity Disturbance in the Development of Anorexia Nervosa

For decades, the role of identity in AN illness development and progression has been emphasised in theoretical frameworks of AN. Bruch first described AN as a *disorder of the self*, positing that the illness reflects a deficiency in self-formation and self-structure and arises in an attempt to obtain a sense of identity by creating a '*false self*' (Bruch, 1982). This aligns with Winnicott's (1958/1965) construct of the 'false self' as a response to cope with environmental difficulties, particularly during early childhood where a child's emotional needs were not met consistently by their primary caregiver due to neglect or inconsistency (Cresci, 2019). Since then many have argued that difficulties with identity development arising in childhood, and especially adolescence, contribute to an impoverished sense of self that is evident in people with AN and leads to vulnerability to the disorder (Stein & Corte, 2007). Indeed, people with AN have described the disorder as an attempt to forge a new identity (Nordbø et al., 2006). AN participants demonstrate greater negative self-views and less complex identities relative to people without any history of mental health disorder (Stein & Corte, 2007). Further, AN participants have significantly more difficulty making identity-related choices (e.g. regarding their autonomy) compared with non-affected individuals (Verschueren et al., 2017).

A recent systematic narrative review of the literature (Corce et al., 2024) identified empirical evidence highlighting that anorexia develops in the context of a reduced sense of agency and a less coherent sense of self, coinciding with despair over defining who to be and distress associated with an intense and harsh self-criticism (Bers et al., 2004; Stein & Corte, 2007). Shape and weight concerns are thought to arise as the result of a disturbance in the experience of one's own body (embodiment) and are known to be influential in how personal identity is determined (Stanghellini et al., 2012). It is argued that interoceptive signals in people with EDs are insufficient to integrate emotional information and sensory experience (Nunn et al., 2008). Moreover emotion dysregulation has been shown to be related to identity confusion and contribute to the development of ED symptomatology in adolescence (Verschueren et al., 2021). A substitute identity centred on one's thinness or weight affording control of one's body as a way to alleviate the distress experienced is thus proposed to directly result in the development of AN (Amianto et al., 2016).

Identity Disturbance and Maintenance of AN

Once AN has developed, research describes how identity is further impaired as the AN becomes merged with an individual's identity (Bryant et al., 2022), resulting in them coming to identify as 'anorexic' above all else (Corce et al., 2024) until it becomes the sole source of identity (Weaver et al., 2005). People with AN have described a process where AN gradually 'took over' until the individual's identity became shared with AN (Williams et al., 2016) or even taken over entirely (Higbed & Fox, 2010). This leads to a significant identity conflict and an inability to determine separateness from AN and their own identity (Conti et al., 2020). People with AN may vary from those who experience AN as an internal part of self to those who see it as an external invading force (Voswinkel et al., 2021). The difficulty distinguishing identity from AN is argued to relate to the perceived 'specialness' that AN provides (Weaver et al., 2005).

The impacts of identity disturbance itself further feedback into and contribute to the maintenance of AN symptoms and are connected to illness progression (Amianto et al., 2016; Higbed & Fox, 2010). In particular, identity disturbance results in psychological discomfort related to lacking a sense of self, increased emotional dysregulation, inability to integrate body image and physiology, and unhelpful cognitive and interpersonal patterns (Amianto et al., 2016). The duration of one's illness may also contribute to the severity of one's identity disturbance as the longer the illness goes on, the more ingrained the *AN identity* may become. One such maintaining influence can be interventions inadvertently leading to an increased identification with the ill 'AN role' and a disconnection with regular life (e.g. during hospital and missions, an inability to work) which furthers identification with the AN role and a vicious cycle ensues (O'Connell, 2023). There can be an emerging sense of empowerment, belonging, and community experienced with other people with AN. Individuals may increasingly value AN when it has become a significant part of their identities, contributing to the ego-syntonic nature of the illness and its pervasiveness (Bryant et al., 2022; Gregertsen et al., 2017) and treatment becomes seen as a threat to the self (Bulik & Kendler, 2000). Indeed, a systematic review of qualitative data recently concluded that a 'global impoverishment of self' underpins severe and enduring AN (Kiely et al., 2023).

Identity and Recovery from Anorexia Nervosa

The empirical work relating to the role of identity disturbance in the development and maintenance of AN is further crystallised by both quantitative and qualitative research with people who have recovered, and who emphasise identity development as a 'cornerstone' in recovery from AN (Corce et al., 2024). Identity functioning has been directly shown to relate to a reduction in ED symptomatology, with decreases in ED symptoms associated with a decrease in identity confusion (Verschueren et al., 2024). It is proposed that only with a cohesive and stable sense of identity can people with AN successfully process and manage stressful tasks and situations inherent in recovery, such as gaining weight (Goodsitt, 1997). People recovered from AN describe how successful treatment facilitates the construction of an authentic identity, encompassing a more realistic and complex self through understanding and connection with emotional and physical needs (Cruzat-Mandich et al., 2017). Furthermore, identity functioning of fully recovered individuals is significantly better than for people currently ill or weight-restored only, and does not differ from those with no history of AN (Croce et al., 2024b). This highlights the crucial importance of identity in full recovery from AN that goes beyond weight restoration.

People who have recovered from AN highlight the importance of 'letting go' of the AN identity as a key stage (Williams et al., 2016). They describe that achieving this involves recognising the harmful consequences of the disorder in 'seeing through its façade' (Drinkwater et al., 2022) and making an active decision to begin moving away from AN (Conti et al., 2020). To let go of the AN, the non-AN-centric self must be reclaimed (Lamoureux & Bottorff, 2005). This requires the active exploration and rediscovery of one's authentic identity: the 'real me' (Drinkwater et al., 2022; Lamoureux & Bottorff, 2005). This process involves the creation, reformation, or reclaiming of an identity that is independent from AN (Dawson et al., 2014; Lamoureux & Bottorff, 2005; Williams et al., 2016) and an experience of that self as 'good enough' (Lamoureux & Bottorff, 2005). Not achieving this is a barrier to recovery; indeed, fears around feeling lost without the condition, and that their 'real self' would be left vulnerable without AN, have been reported by those currently ill as preventing them from moving on from AN (Williams et al., 2016). This aligns with other lived experience research reporting that recovery is dependent upon the development of insight into the ED alongside acceptance of the self, contingent upon finding meaning and purpose, whilst increasing empowerment and self-compassion (Bardone-Cone et al., 2018; Bardone-Cone et al., 2020).

It should be noted that recovery can also be experienced as a loss for individuals with AN due to this necessary aspect of 'letting go', which can be a highly distressing experience and result in profound feelings of incompleteness (Avery et al., 2017; Broomfield et al., 2017; Lamoureux & Bottorff, 2005; Williams et al., 2016). This reflects the depth of the relationship with AN – which, over time, can come to represent an introjected attachment figure meeting needs that early caregivers did not (Forsén Mantilla et al., 2019). This reflects the complexity of the task of identity development and further underscores the importance of this to the recovery process and future healthy functioning.

Identity Development as a Treatment Focus for Anorexia Nervosa

Bruch proposed that individuals with AN need to build an authentic identity to effectively tackle underlying problems and move on from the illness (Bruch, 1982). As described above, the evidence that has been gathered since then supports the role of poor identity development and a sense of identity confusion in the development and maintenance of AN, which must be worked with for recovery. Indeed, it is argued that therapeutic approaches developed for EDs to date may miss important factors in treatment because key difficulties are rarely ED-related themes, but rather identity-related and interpersonal difficulties, including fears of rejection and abandonment, negative self-perception, and experience of difficult or overwhelming emotion (Sternheim et al., 2012). Moreover, even therapies seeking to address identity prioritise refeeding and weight gain to such an extent that identity may not be addressed until too late in the stages of treatment (Croce et al., 2024a). This has led to proposals that facilitating the development of identity should be a key focus of treatment in order to achieve recovery, especially for severe and enduring AN (Amianto et al., 2016; Oldershaw et al., 2019). Accordingly contemporary theories have sought to develop theories of identity disturbance and change that may account for difficulties and provide a guide for therapy (Amianto et al., 2016). One particular approach is the 'Lost Emotional Self' theory (Oldershaw et al., 2019) which is of direct relevance to building an identity in treatment and is supported by empirical evidence (Croce et al., 2024a). A therapy built on this theory to facilitate identity development, specifically that pertaining to emotional experience (SPEAKS; (Oldershaw et al., 2025); Oldershaw, Startup & Lavender 2025; Oldershaw et al., 2024; Oldershaw & Startup, 2020 has been described as a potential first step toward understanding the role of these previously neglected aspects of treatment for AN, namely in a '*deepening* of clinical work to engage all aspects of being human' (Kiely et al., 2023).

The 'Lost Emotional Self' Theory

The 'lost emotional self' theory proposes that emotional processing difficulties underpin difficulties with identity formation and confusion and lead to a lost sense of 'emotional self' and that this plays a role in the development and maintenance of AN. Empirical evidence supports the notion that emotional difficulties are central issues in EDs and should be considered in treatment (Lavender et al., 2015; Oldershaw et al., 2015; Sala et al., 2016). Emotional avoidance and unhelpful overregulation strategies predict clinical outcomes following treatment (Oldershaw et al., 2015). This includes coping strategies connected to ED behaviours (Dolhanty & Greenberg, 2009; Schmidt & Treasure, 2014; Wildes & Marcus, 2011). Common emotion regulation methods (or ways of interrupting or blocking emotional experience) include avoiding emotion triggers in social interaction (e.g. using submissiveness or self-subjugation to manage social situations) or disproportionately relying on reassurance from others or social comparison with others (Oldershaw et al., 2015). Strategies to control emotion are perceived as useful in the first instance and initially decrease emotion. Ultimately, however, they are unhelpful and serve only to trigger further negative emotional experience and reinforce negative beliefs and schemata, thereby heightening reliance upon (maladaptive) emotion regulation strategies and generating a vicious cycle where emotions are increasingly feared and avoided (Oldershaw et al., 2015).

Emotions are seen as fundamentally important as they are core to human experience, understood as (instinctive or learnt) responses to external or internal stimuli that inform us about our immediate environments, relationships, and crucially our needs. They rapidly alert us to significant current and emerging information in an environment or relationship, preparing us for action in order to meet our associated needs, thereby enabling us to survive and thrive. We are born with the capacity to feel and express emotion and to learn how to productively respond to the inherent needs, but this is significantly affected by our experiences and relationships. External and internal (conscious and unconscious) reactions to our emotions become an integral part of our existence and the basis from which we learn about ourselves and the world, shaping our sense of self (Damasio, 2003). People do not simply have an emotion; they live in a constant process of making sense of their emotions to obtain personal meaning from their emotional experience and self-organisation (Greenberg, 2006). Difficulty connecting with emotion and missing associated needs can thus become so pervasive and damaging that they undermine our sense of self (Damasio, 2003). Indeed, difficulties with emotion and emotion regulation have been shown to directly relate to an identity disturbance across a range of mental health presentations (Neacsiu et al., 2015).

The 'lost self' theory suggests that an overreliance on emotion regulation strategies emerges from early life and/or developmental factors (e.g. interoceptive differences) that leave the person vulnerable to experiencing emotion as overwhelming and confusing and that is at the heart of identity disturbance. People with AN have been shown to have reductions in the bodily interoceptive perception and integration of internal bodily sensations that give rise to self-awareness and emotion perception (Gaudio et al., 2014; Stanghellini et al., 2018). Indeed, emotional experience emerges out of physical arousal, including interoceptive and proprioceptive experiences, alongside processes such as neural activation (Barrett et al., 2007) and emotional memory networks (Greenberg, 2004). Our interoceptive emotion signals are argued to afford us a mental representation of selfhood experienced within the body – 'a material me' (Seth, 2013). Interoceptive differences and difficulties may relate to sensory differences associated with neurodivergence and may be exacerbated by the physiological effects of low weight. People with AN report a lack of confidence in the body as a trustworthy source of information associated with low interoceptive awareness (Monteleone et al., 2021) and this may undermine a confident and grounded sense of self (Stanghellini et al., 2015). Thus without a clear emotional experience grounded in the body ('a material me'), our emotions can feel diffuse, overwhelming, unpredictable, and unhelpful, and we may lose important information and an opportunity for a known and integrated sense of self.

The 'lost emotional self' theory of AN (Oldershaw et al., 2019) suggests that due to emotion being unintegrated during adolescence, this impedes the development of a coherent sense of self and creates a context of vague and overwhelming emotional experience in which AN emerges. During adolescence, when moving into an adult developmental stage where the ability to deal with emotional experiences is exposed, AN emerges as an attempt both to regulate emotion (Oldershaw et al., 2015) and to regain a sense of bodily self, focused on tangible markers of identity (body, weight and shape) (Oldershaw et al., 2019), defined by the other's gaze and external appearance (Monteleone et al., 2017). AN becomes a 'blind search for identity' (Bruch, 1974) (i.e. the 'lost emotional self'), resulting in a false sense of self, including a false sense of needs, and offers concrete and certain means to meet those needs (e.g. weight and shape goals). This results in poor understanding or perceived value in the individual's emotions and 'true' needs, resulting in reliance upon external signalling and validation. Due to the 'lost emotional self', a person struggles to navigate the world, themselves and others, without an internal experiential guide.

This theory thus builds on work highlighting the role of identity in AN by specifically hypothesising that supporting the emergence and integration of an 'emotional self' should be a primary goal of therapy for adults, and especially those with established AN (Oldershaw et al., 2019). This self can experience emotions in their complexity and flexibly and adaptively direct an individual's needs and relationships, embedding healthy ways to get needs met and thereby reducing reliance on the AN to meet needs.

Facilitating Identity Development through Emergence of an 'Emotional Self'

The SPEAKS Approach

In order to begin to understand how to facilitate the emergence of the 'emotional self', and develop the related therapy (SPEAKS), a constructivist grounded theory analysis of qualitative interviews was employed to explore emotional change associated with recovery. Three super categories were produced, reflecting distinct but interrelated phases toward recovery: (1) *Coping in a world of uncertainty* (perceiving emotions negatively and using ways of coping, including AN, to avoid emotion and create predictability), (2) *Seeing through the façade of anorexia* (the realisation that, whilst drawing on strategies to cope, avoid, block, distract from, or displace emotions had felt helpful before, this had limits), and (3) *Recovery and growth* (seeing emotions as important and valuable; connecting self-self and self-others leading to knowing, liking, and accepting 'The Real Me') (Drinkwater et al., 2022). The concept of developing the 'Real Me' connected to core emotion and underpinning needs paralleled our proposed 'lost sense of emotional self' theory whilst outlining a clearer sense of important steps to reach that goal. Other development work of focus groups with people recovered from AN, carers and therapists found that accepting and validating emotion was described as a channel for change, alongside removing emotion blocks to support clients to acknowledge, identify, and express difficult feelings and appreciate them as meaningful with underlying reasons and needs that could inform about the self.

This aligns with clinical models of emotional processing (Pascual-Leone, 2018). Whilst several clinical models of *emotional processing and associated psychotherapeutic approaches* have been proposed with varying degrees of commonalities and differences in goals (Pascual-Leone, 2018), it is proposed that all psychotherapeutic approaches incorporate *subtypes* of 'emotional processing', including awareness, affective arousal, emotion regulation, and cognitive reflection on emotion (Pascual-Leone, 2018). For example, many clinical approaches recognise the importance of an ability to usefully regulate emotion (e.g. Dialectical Behaviour Therapy, CBT, and third wave approaches such as Acceptance and Commitment Therapy or Mindfulness-Based cognitive therapy, Emotion-Focused Therapy (EFT), Schema Therapy; Dadomo et al., 2016; Elliott & Greenberg, 2021; Hill & Updegraff, 2012; Neacsiu et al., 2015). Yet, our development work and the research reviewed above informed us that how emotion regulation is approached is important and also that an ability to connect with, tolerate, trust, and use embodied emotional information was required in order to facilitate development of the 'Real Me' (the lost emotional self). Highly relevant to this psychotherapeutic change process were the emotion change processes evidenced in the field of EFT (Greenberg, 2006; Greenberg & Pascual-Leone, 2024) and in Schema Therapy (ST) (Fassbinder & Arntz, 2021).

EFT distinguishes between emotional response types affording greater understanding of emotion processing difficulties and how to intervene in therapy. Our *primary emotion states* (emotions that come first in response to situations) can be adaptive (giving us good information about immediate needs and helpful action) or 'maladaptive'. The *maladaptive primary emotions* emerge in childhood as a response to unmet needs. They reflect over-learnt responses based on previous, often traumatic, experiences around unmet need. Unmet needs can broadly reflect (1) Unmet attachment needs – a need for love, connection, and closeness with loved ones associated with painful loneliness or sadness, (2) Unmet identity needs – for acceptance, respect, acknowledgement and understanding associated with shame-based feelings, (3) Unmet safety needs – for protection, control, and comfort, and which can include the safety to be myself (such as to express valid needs and emotions) associated with fear-based emotions.

These primary maladaptive emotions become stuck within adult life, with the most painful of these representing 'core pain', easily triggered even when not a good fit for current situations, adult needs, and appropriate adult actions. Often when people enter therapy, they are unaware of their primary emotions because they are automatically 'covered up' or hidden by *secondary emotion,* particularly as a reaction to underlying 'primary emotion' (such as expressing 'rejecting anger' in response to 'experiencing shame') or emerge as a broad undifferentiated feeling of global distress. EFT posits that alongside key emotional processing components of awareness, affective arousal, emotion regulation, and cognitive reflection on emotion, an important step in therapy is to 'change emotion with emotion' to transform core pain, leading to new adaptive emotional states and experience of the self (Greenberg & Pascual-Leone, 2024). This relies on a sequential emotional processing model for emotional change within therapy (Pascual-Leone, 2018) whereby people move from secondary emotions to locate primary maladaptive emotion, deepening to the core pain. Core pain is transformed when primary adaptive emotion is simultaneously evoked over time, generating a transformed state with self-efficacy and self-agency – a reconfigured, resilient, and integrated sense of self (Pos & Greenberg, 2007), the 'Real Me'.

Through our development work with focus groups and within the wider literature, we identified key emotions and emotional states of anxiety, shame, and abandonment (being left alone with emotion) as prevalent and recognised as important foci for therapy (Blythin et al., 2020; Davies et al.[1]; Oldershaw et al., 2025). People with AN highly endorse themes of *defectiveness and shame* ('I am unloveable and broken'), *social isolation* ('I am alone') and *subjugation* ('My feelings aren't important. It is not safe to be myself') (Oldershaw et al., 2015), alongside commonly expressed emotions of abandonment and worthlessness (Dolhanty & Greenberg, 2007). These prevalent, persistent emotions experienced by people with AN (Blythin et al., 2020; Oldershaw et al., 2015), indicated core pain encompassing themes of both chronically unmet identity needs (shame) and attachment needs (abandonment fears and sadness), with some unmet safety needs.

In SPEAKS, we therefore hypothesised the primary maladaptive emotion to be both shame-based linked to unmet identity needs, alongside the loneliness and sadness arising from unmet attachment needs. It is important to understand how this core pain may have developed in a connected pattern. Core pain of unmet attachment needs of emotional validation, closeness, connection, or caring internalised as 'I am alone; I have nobody to turn to; Nobody wants to hear or *can* hear me and my emotions' links to primary maladaptive emotion of sadness-loneliness. Yet there is also a pervasive sense of being undeserving of the closeness and connection craved which reflects unmet identity needs, and leads to the conclusion that 'I am unlovable, broken and defective' connected with shame. Thus shame is argued to be experienced in response to the lonely sadness/abandonment and sits over it, more prominent and visible in AN, but as a reaction to a deeper pain.

Shame is noted as a concept related to EDs (Blythin et al., 2020). CBT and other interventions for AN intervening with emotion primarily work with shame-based experiences and, as such, intervene to counter shame by targeting identity-related concepts such as self-esteem – which are conceptually related to identity, yet distinct (Croce et al., 2024a). AN is most evident as a means to meet identity-based needs of acceptance, respect, and acknowledgement. However, as noted above, AN can also meet attachment-based needs and can itself come to represent an introjected attachment figure (Forsén Mantilla et al., 2019). Now the possibility of AN recovery further triggers the experience of core pain of lonely abandonment/sadness, contributing to pervasiveness and stuckness, as highlighted by the deep sense of loss and experience of incompleteness by people with AN, noted as a barrier to change (Avery et al., 2017; Broomfield et al., 2017; Lamoureux & Bottorff, 2005; Williams et al., 2016). Thus interventions focusing on working primarily or exclusively with shame may miss important factors necessary for change, rendering them less helpful, particularly for those who have been unwell for longer periods and where identity confusion is more extreme. This is why the SPEAKS approach works with deepening emotion processing beyond shame to include processing of lonely abandonment/sadness (Figure 2.1).

This change process is supported by the analysis of data on emotional expression from the feasibility trial in two NHS Eating Disorder Services with people with established AN (Oldershaw et al., 2024). Emotional expression during therapy sessions was tracked across time, including emotion response types (secondary, primary maladaptive [core pain], primary adaptive), and temporal patterns for those with 'good' (fully recovered) or 'poor' (partially or not recovered) outcomes from SPEAKS therapy (Malik-Smith et al., submitted). The findings showed that the good outcome group expressed significantly more primary adaptive emotion than the poor outcome group, with this group difference becoming apparent mid-therapy. There was no significant difference between therapy phases for primary maladaptive shame; however, lonely abandonment/sadness significantly reduced for the 'good' outcome group during therapy, but not for the 'poor' outcome group. This highlights the emphasis on connecting with lonely abandonment (as opposed to just shame) in facilitating change, and the capacity of the SPEAKS therapy to facilitate this. Furthermore, qualitative interviews with clients and therapists who had completed SPEAKS, analysed by independent researchers, found two major themes of change: changing emotions and changing the self (Papastavrou Brooks et al., under review). The 'changing self' process was linked by participants to emotional change, and clients and therapists overwhelmingly expressed beliefs that SPEAKS was able to get to the heart of issues and that this facilitated understanding and development of the self.

In general, the SPEAKS psychotherapeutic approach was seen to have an impact on a range of clinical measures after therapy, with eating disorder symptomatology, anxiety, depression, stress, and quality of life all significantly improving after SPEAKS therapy (Oldershaw et al., 2024). Furthermore, the trial had no clients

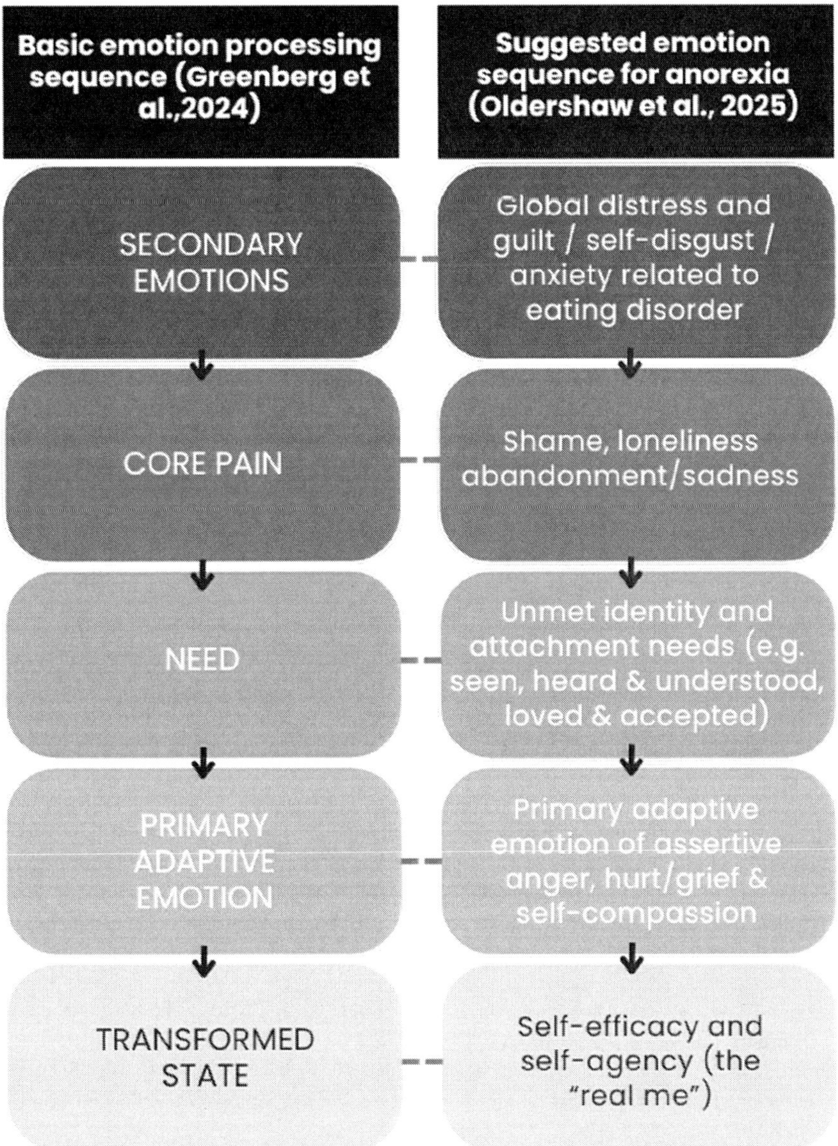

Figure 2.1 Emotion processing sequence proposed for AN (adapted from Greenberg et al., 2024, and Oldershaw et al., 2025).

(0%) who dropped out of therapy, which is striking for this population, particularly when working with emotion, and reflects the acceptability of the approach, which was also verified in qualitative interviews (Rennick et al., 2024).

Conclusion

Identity confusion is argued to be a factor in the development and maintenance of AN and identity formation to be crucial in recovery from AN. One prominent theory suggests that identity difficulties are intrinsically linked to underpinning emotional processing issues explained by 'a lost emotional self' (Oldershaw et al., 2019). This theory proposes that identity development in therapy requires connecting with and resolving emotional difficulties. A treatment approach (SPEAKS) based on the 'lost self' theory utilises and targets a sequential model of emotional change to build a stronger identity (the 'Real Me') through integrating emotional experiences with the self, thereby reducing emotional dysregulation and increasing feelings of autonomy. This approach to identity development and recovery from AN is supported by research that is consistent with emotion change process hypotheses, qualitative data on new experiences of self and emotion following SPEAKS therapy, and clinical findings indicating improvements across a range of clinical symptomatology.

Note

1 This refers to an unpublished study by Davies et al., currently in preparation.

References

Amianto, F., Northoff, G., Abbate Daga, G., Fassino, S., & Tasca, G. A. (2016). Is anorexia nervosa a disorder of the self? A psychological approach. *Frontiers in Psychology*, *7*, 849.

Avery, K. N., Williamson, P. R., Gamble, C., Francischetto, E. O. C., Metcalfe, C., Davidson, P., Williams, H., & Blazeby, J. M. (2017). Informing efficient randomised controlled trials: Exploration of challenges in developing progression criteria for internal pilot studies. *BMJ Open*, *7*(2), e013537.

Bardone-Cone, A. M., Hunt, R. A., & Watson, H. J. (2018). An overview of conceptualizations of eating disorder recovery, recent findings, and future directions. *Current Psychiatry Reports*, *20*, 1–18.

Bardone-Cone, A. M., Thompson, K. A., & Miller, A. J. (2020). The self and eating disorders. *Journal of Personality*, *88*(1), 59–75.

Barrett, L. F., Bliss-Moreau, E., Duncan, S. L., Rauch, S. L., & Wright, C. I. (2007). The amygdala and the experience of affect. *Social cognitive and affective neuroscience*, *2*(2), 73–83.

Bers, S. A., Blatt, S. J., & Dolinsky, A. (2004). The sense of self in anorexia-nervosa patients: A psychoanalytically informed method for studying self-representation. *The Psychoanalytic Study of the Child*, *59*(1), 294–315.

Blythin, S. P., Nicholson, H. L., Macintyre, V. G., Dickson, J. M., Fox, J. R., & Taylor, P. J. (2020). Experiences of shame and guilt in anorexia and bulimia nervosa: A systematic review. *Psychology and Psychotherapy: Theory, Research and Practice*, *93*(1), 134–159.

Bogaerts, A., de Moor, E. L., & Lind, M. (2024). Identity disturbance in dimensional and categorical models of personality disorder: The incremental value of self-rated identity and narrative identity. *Personality Disorders: Theory, Research, and Treatment,* 15(6), 479–491. https://doi.org/10.1037/per0000698

Bouguettaya, A., Jaeger, T., & Moulding, R. (2022). Yet you may see the meaning of within: The role of identity concerns and the self in psychopathology. In R. E. Menzies, R. G. Menzies, & Dinge, G. A. (Eds.), *Existential concerns and cognitive-behavioral procedures: An integrative approach to mental health* (pp. 167–183). Springer.

Broomfield, C., Stedal, K., Touyz, S., & Rhodes, P. (2017). Labeling and defining severe and enduring anorexia nervosa: A systematic review and critical analysis. *International Journal of Eating Disorders, 50*(6), 611–623.

Bruch, H. (1974). *Eating disorders. Obesity, anorexia nervosa, and the person within.* Routlege & Kegan, London.

Bruch, H. (1982). Treatment for anorexia nervosa. *Psychiatric Services, 33*(8), 618–618.

Bryant, E., Aouad, P., Hambleton, A., Touyz, S., & Maguire, S. (2022). "In an otherwise limitless world, I was sure of my limit." Experiencing anorexia nervosa: A phenomenological metasynthesis. *Frontiers in Psychiatry, 13*, 894178.

Bulik, C. M. (2014). The challenges of treating anorexia nervosa. *The Lancet, 383*(9912), 105–106.

Bulik, C. M., & Kendler, K. S. (2000). "I am what i (don't) eat": Establishing an identity independent of an eating disorder. *American Journal of Psychiatry, 157*(11), 1755–1760.

Casper, R. C. (1983). Some provisional Ideas concerning the psychologic structure in anorexia nervosa and. *Anorexia Nervosa: Recent Developments in Research* (pp. 387-392). Allan R. Liss: New York.

Conti, J. E., Joyce, C., Hay, P., & Meade, T. (2020). "Finding my own identity": A qualitative metasynthesis of adult anorexia nervosa treatment experiences. *BMC Psychology, 8*, 1–14.

Cresci, M. (2019). Winnicott's true self/false self concept: Using countertransference to uncover the true self. In *Psychoanalytic perspectives on knowing and being known* (pp. 101–109). Routledge.

Croce, S. R., Malcolm, A. C., Ralph-Nearman, C., & Phillipou, A. (2024a). The role of identity in anorexia nervosa: A narrative review. *New Ideas in Psychology, 72*, 10 1060.

Croce, S. R., Malcolm, A. C., Ralph-Nearman, C., & Phillipou, A. (2024b). Examining identity functioning in anorexia nervosa across illness and recovery stages. *International Journal of Eating Disorders, 57*(9), 1959-1968.

Cruzat-Mandich, C., Díaz-Castrillón, F., Escobar-Koch, T., & Simpson, S. (2017). From eating identity to authentic selfhood: Identity transformation in eating disorder sufferers following psychotherapy. *Clinical Psychologist, 21*(3), 227–235.

Dadomo, H., Grecucci, A., Giardini, I., Ugolini, E., Carmelita, A., & Panzeri, M. (2016). Schema therapy for emotional dysregulation: Theoretical implication and clinical applications. *Frontiers in psychology, 7*, 1987.

Damasio, A. (2003). Feelings of emotion and the self. *Annals of the New York Academy of Sciences, 1001*(1), 253–261.

Dawson, L., Rhodes, P., & Touyz, S. (2014). "Doing the impossible" the process of recovery from chronic anorexia nervosa. *Qualitative Health Research, 24*(4), 494–505.

Dolhanty, J., & Greenberg, L. S. (2007). Emotion-focused therapy in the treatment of eating disorders. *European Psychotherapy, 7*(1), 97-116.

Dolhanty, J., & Greenberg, L. S. (2009). Emotion-focused therapy in a case of anorexia nervosa. *Clinical Psychology & Psychotherapy: An International Journal of Theory & Practice*, *16*(4), 336–382.

Drinkwater, D., Holttum, S., Lavender, T., Startup, H., & Oldershaw, A. (2022). Seeing through the façade of anorexia: A grounded theory of emotional change processes associated with recovery from anorexia nervosa. *Frontiers in Psychiatry*, 1316.

Elliott, R., & Greenberg, L. (2021). Emotion-focused counselling in action. Sage Publishing.

Erikson, E. H. (1959). Identity and the life cycle. International Universities Press.

Erikson, E. H.(1968). *Identity youth and crisis* (No. 7). WW Norton & company.

Fassbinder, E., & Arntz, A. (2021). Schema therapy. In A. Wenzel (Ed.), Handbook of cognitive behavioral therapy: Overview and approaches (pp. 493–537). American Psychological Association. https://doi.org/10.1037/0000218-017

Forsén Mantilla, E., Clinton, D., & Birgegård, A. (2019). The unsafe haven: Eating disorders as attachment relationships. *Psychology and Psychotherapy: Theory, Research and Practice*, *92*(3), 379–393.

Gaudio, S., Brooks, S. J., & Riva, G. (2014). Nonvisual multisensory impairment of body perception in anorexia nervosa: a systematic review of neuropsychological studies. *PloS one*, *9*(10), e110087.

Goodsitt, A. (1997). Eating disorders: A self-psychological perspective. In D. M. Garner & P. E. Garfinkel (Eds.), Handbook of treatment for eating disorders (2nd ed., pp. 205–228). The Guilford Press.

Greenberg, L. S. (2004). Emotion–focused therapy. *Clinical Psychology & Psychotherapy: An International Journal of Theory & Practice*, *11*(1), 3–16.

Greenberg, L. (2006). Emotion-focused therapy: A synopsis. *Journal of Contemporary Psychotherapy*, *36*, 87–93.

Greenberg, L., Pascual-Leone, J., & Johnson, J. (2024). Schematic processing and emotional change: Implications for treatment. *New Ideas in Psychology*, *73*, 101075.

Greenberg, L. S., & Pascual-Leone, A. (2024). Changing emotion with emotion. In A. C. Samson, D. Sander, & U. Kramer (Eds.), *Change in emotion and mental health* (pp. 325–344). Elsevier.

Gregertsen, E. C., Mandy, W., & Serpell, L. (2017). The egosyntonic nature of anorexia: An impediment to recovery in anorexia nervosa treatment. *Frontiers in Psychology*, *8*, 2273.

Halmi, K. A. (2009). Anorexia nervosa: An increasing problem in children and adolescents. *Dialogues in Clinical Neuroscience*, *11*(1), 100–103.

Higbed, L., & Fox, J. R. (2010). Illness perceptions in anorexia nervosa: A qualitative investigation. *British Journal of Clinical Psychology*, *49*(3), 307–325.

Hill, C. L., & Updegraff, J. A. (2012). Mindfulness and its relationship to emotional regulation. *Emotion*, *12*(1), 81.

Kiely, L., Conti, J., & Hay, P. (2023). Conceptualisation of severe and enduring anorexia nervosa: A qualitative meta-synthesis. *BMC Psychiatry*, *23*(1), 606.

Lamoureux, M. M., & Bottorff, J. L. (2005). "Becoming the real me": Recovering from anorexia nervosa. *Health Care for Women International*, *26*(2), 170–188.

Lavender, J. M., Wonderlich, S. A., Engel, S. G., Gordon, K. H., Kaye, W. H., & Mitchell, J. E. (2015). Dimensions of emotion dysregulation in anorexia nervosa and bulimia nervosa: A conceptual review of the empirical literature. *Clinical Psychology Review*, *40*, 111–122.

Malcolm, A., Pikoos, T., Castle, D. J., Labuschagne, I., & Rossell, S. L. (2021). Identity and shame in body dysmorphic disorder as compared to obsessive-compulsive disorder. *Journal of Obsessive-Compulsive and Related Disorders*, *31*, 100686.

Meisner, M. W., Lenzenweger, M. F., Bach, B., Vestergaard, M., Petersen, L. S., Haahr, U. H., Kongerslev, M., & Simonsen, E. (2021). Exploring identity disturbance and psychotic spectrum symptoms as predictors of borderline and schizotypal personality disorders. *Psychopathology*, *54*(4), 193–202.

Monteleone, A. M., Cascino, G., Martini, M., Patriciello, G., Ruzzi, V., Delsedime, N., Abbate-Daga, G., & Marzola, E. (2021). Confidence in one-self and confidence in one's own body: The revival of an old paradigm for anorexia nervosa. *Clinical Psychology & Psychotherapy*, *28*(4), 818–827.

Monteleone, A. M., Monteleone, P., Esposito, F., Prinster, A., Volpe, U., Cantone, E., Pellegrino, F., Canna, A., Milano, W., & Aiello, M. (2017). Altered processing of rewarding and aversive basic taste stimuli in symptomatic women with anorexia nervosa and bulimia nervosa: An fMRI study. *Journal of Psychiatric Research*, *90*, 94–101.

Monteleone, A. M., Pellegrino, F., Croatto, G., Carfagno, M., Hilbert, A., Treasure, J., Wade, T., Bulik, C. M., Zipfel, S., & Hay, P. (2022). Treatment of eating disorders: A systematic meta-review of meta-analyses and network meta-analyses. *Neuroscience & Biobehavioral Reviews*, *142*, 104857.

Neacsiu, A. D., Herr, N. R., Fang, C. M., Rodriguez, M. A., & Rosenthal, M. Z. (2015). Identity disturbance and problems with emotion regulation are related constructs across diagnoses. *Journal of Clinical Psychology*, *71*(4), 346–361.

NICE. (2017). Eating disorders: Recognition and treatment (NICE Guideline No. 69). https://www.nice.org.uk/guidance/ng69

Nordbø, R. H., Espeset, E. M., Gulliksen, K. S., Skårderud, F., & Holte, A. (2006). The meaning of self-starvation: Qualitative study of patients' perception of anorexia nervosa. *International Journal of Eating Disorders*, *39*(7), 556–564.

Nunn, K., Frampton, I., Gordon, I., & Lask, B. (2008). The fault is not in her parents but in her insula—a neurobiological hypothesis of anorexia nervosa. *European Eating Disorders Review: The Professional Journal of the Eating Disorders Association*, *16*(5), 355–360.

O'Connell, L. (2023). Being and doing anorexia nervosa: An autoethnography of diagnostic identity and performance of illness. *Health*, *27*(2), 263–278.

Oldershaw, A., Basra, R. S., Lavender, T., & Startup, H. (2024). Specialist psychotherapy with emotion for anorexia in Kent and Sussex: An intervention development and non-randomised single arm feasibility trial. *European Eating Disorders Review*, *32*(2), 215–229.

Oldershaw, A., Lavender, T., Sallis, H., Stahl, D., & Schmidt, U. (2015). Emotion generation and regulation in anorexia nervosa: A systematic review and meta-analysis of self-report data. *Clinical Psychology Review*, *39*, 83–95.

Oldershaw, A., & Startup, H. (2020). Building the healthy adult in eating disorders: A schema mode and emotion-focused therapy approach for anorexia nervosa. In *Creative methods in schema therapy* (pp. 287–300). Routledge.

Oldershaw, A., Startup, H., & Lavender, T. (2019). Anorexia nervosa and a lost emotional self: A psychological formulation of the development, maintenance, and treatment of anorexia nervosa. *Frontiers in Psychology*, *10*, 219.

Oldershaw, A., Startup, H., & Lavender, T. (2025). *Transforming Emotional Pain and Rediscovering the Self in Anorexia Nervosa: A Clinical Guide*. Taylor & Francis.

Pascual-Leone, A. (2018). How clients "change emotion with emotion": A programme of research on emotional processing. *Psychotherapy Research*, *28*(2), 165–182.

Pos, A. E., & Greenberg, L. S. (2007). Emotion-focused therapy: The transforming power of affect. *Journal of Contemporary Psychotherapy*, *37*, 25–31.

Rennick, A., Papastavrou Brooks, C., Singh Basra, R., Startup, H., Lavender, T., & Oldershaw, A. (2024). Acceptability of Specialist Psychotherapy with Emotion for Anorexia in Kent and Sussex (SPEAKS): A novel intervention for anorexia nervosa. *International Journal of Eating Disorders*, *57*(3), 611–623.

Sala, M., Heard, A., & Black, E. A. (2016). Emotion-focused treatments for anorexia nervosa: A systematic review of the literature. *Eating and Weight Disorders-Studies on Anorexia, Bulimia and Obesity*, *21*, 147–164.

Sala, M., Keshishian, A., Song, S., Moskowitz, R., Bulik, C. M., Roos, C. R., & Levinson, C. A. (2023). Predictors of relapse in eating disorders: A meta-analysis. *Journal of Psychiatric Research*, *158*, 281–299.

Schmidt, U., & Treasure, J. (2014). The Maudsley Model of Anorexia Nervosa Treatment for Adults (MANTRA): Development, key features, and preliminary evidence. *Journal of Cognitive Psychotherapy*, *28*(1), 48.

Seth, A. K. (2013). Interoceptive inference, emotion, and the embodied self. *Trends in cognitive sciences*, *17*(11), 565–573.

Stanghellini, G., Castellini, G., Brogna, P., Faravelli, C., & Ricca, V. (2012). Identity and eating disorders (IDEA): A questionnaire evaluating identity and embodiment in eating disorder patients. *Psychopathology*, *45*(3), 147–158.

Stanghellini, G., Trisolini, F., Castellini, G., Ambrosini, A., Faravelli, C., & Ricca, V. (2015). Is feeling extraneous from one's own body a core vulnerability feature in eating disorders? *Psychopathology*, *48*(1), 18–24.

Stanghellini, G., Mancini, M., Castellini, G., & Ricca, V. (2018). Eating disorders as disorders of embodiment and identity: Theoretical and empirical perspectives. In *Embodiment and eating disorders* (pp. 127-141). Routledge.

Stein, K. F., & Corte, C. (2007). Identity impairment and the eating disorders: Content and organization of the self-concept in women with anorexia nervosa and bulimia nervosa. *European Eating Disorders Review: The Professional Journal of the Eating Disorders Association*, *15*(1), 58–69.

Sternheim, L., Startup, H., Saeidi, S., Morgan, J., Hugo, P., Russell, A., & Schmidt, U. (2012). Understanding catastrophic worry in eating disorders: Process and content characteristics. *Journal of Behavior Therapy and Experimental Psychiatry*, *43*(4), 1095–1103.

Uliaszek, A. A., Fournier, M. A., Southward, M. W., Al-Dajani, N., & Quitasol, M. (2022). Bridging development and disturbance: A translational approach to the study of identity. *Personality Disorders: Theory, Research, and Treatment*, *13*(5), 460.

Van Eeden, A. E., Van Hoeken, D., & Hoek, H. W. (2021). Incidence, prevalence and mortality of anorexia nervosa and bulimia nervosa. *Current Opinion in Psychiatry*, *34*(6), 515–524.

Verschueren, M., Claes, L., Palmeroni, N., Raemen, L., Buelens, T., Moons, P., & Luyckx, K. (2021). Identity functioning and eating disorder symptomatology: The role of cognitive emotion regulation strategies. *Frontiers in psychology*, *12*, 667235.

Verschueren, M., Claes, L., Palmeroni, N., Raemen, L., Moons, P., Bruckers, L., Molenberghs, G., Dierckx, E., Schoevaerts, K., & Luyckx, K. (2024). Identity functioning in patients with an eating disorder: Developmental trajectories throughout treatment. *Nutrients, 16*(5), 591.

Verschueren, M., Luyckx, K., Kaufman, E. A., Vansteenkiste, M., Moons, P., Sleuwaegen, E., Berens, A., Schoevaerts, K., & Claes, L. (2017). Identity processes and statuses in patients with and without eating disorders. *European Eating Disorders Review, 25*(1), 26–35.

Voswinkel, M. M., Rijkers, C., van Delden, J. J., & van Elburg, A. A. (2021). Externalizing your eating disorder: A qualitative interview study. *Journal of Eating Disorders, 9*, 1–12.

Walsh, B. T., Hagan, K. E., & Lockwood, C. (2023). A systematic review comparing atypical anorexia nervosa and anorexia nervosa. *International Journal of Eating Disorders, 56*(4), 798–820.

Weaver, K., Wuest, J., & Ciliska, D. (2005). Understanding women's journey of recovering from anorexia nervosa. *Qualitative Health Research, 15*(2), 188–206.

Wildes, J. E., & Marcus, M. D. (2011). Development of emotion acceptance behavior therapy for anorexia nervosa: A case series. *International Journal of Eating Disorders, 44*(5), 421–427.

Williams, K., King, J., & Fox, J. R. (2016). Sense of self and anorexia nervosa: A grounded theory. *Psychology and Psychotherapy: Theory, Research and Practice, 89*(2), 211–228.

Winnicott, D. W. (1965). *Ego distortion in terms of true and false self.* In D. W. Winnicott (), *The maturational processes and the facilitating environment* (pp. 140–152). Hogarth Press.

Chapter 3

Self-Conscious Emotions

Klaske A. Glashouwer and Peter J. de Jong

Introduction

The development of self and identity are central to adolescence. Adolescents seek autonomy and become more and more independent from their parents. At the same time, they become increasingly aware of their larger social context and the connection with their peers gains importance. Adolescents become more self-conscious, and they become concerned with and interested in others' perceptions of the self. Anorexia nervosa (AN) is a severe mental disorder that typically develops during adolescence. In this chapter, we will describe how self-identity development and related self-conscious emotions – with a specific focus on self-disgust – might be intertwined with the development and maintenance of AN.

Self-conscious emotions are emotions related to how we see ourselves and how we think others perceive us. Emotions such as shame, guilt, pride, or embarrassment typically come up when one's self-worth is at stake either in one's own or in others' eyes. Most of the time self-conscious emotions are adaptive and helpful for our social interactions, because they promote prosocial behaviors, and help to recognize and repair social errors (Parrott, 2014). A lack of self-conscious emotions might even cause problems in social functioning. However, a surplus of negative self-conscious emotions has been consistently linked to negative mental health outcomes such as (social) anxiety, depression, and eating disorders.

It seems plausible that negative self-conscious emotions contribute to the start of dieting as a way to "repair the self" and fulfill societal beauty ideals, especially when control over the own body and being someone who is slim (or not too fat) have become an important element of self-identity. However, it is difficult to understand how self-conscious emotions keep fueling food restriction outside of social situations meal after meal. Therefore, in this chapter, we will discuss another self-directed emotion, self-disgust, which so far is largely overlooked in theoretical models of AN. In the current chapter, we will describe a further developed, more elaborated version of the theoretical model that we published in 2021 (see Figure 3.1; adapted version of Glashouwer & de Jong, 2021). We will describe how self-disgust might play a central role in the onset and maintenance of AN and how other self-conscious emotions such as shame may be integrated into this model. At the

DOI: 10.4324/9781003468189-4

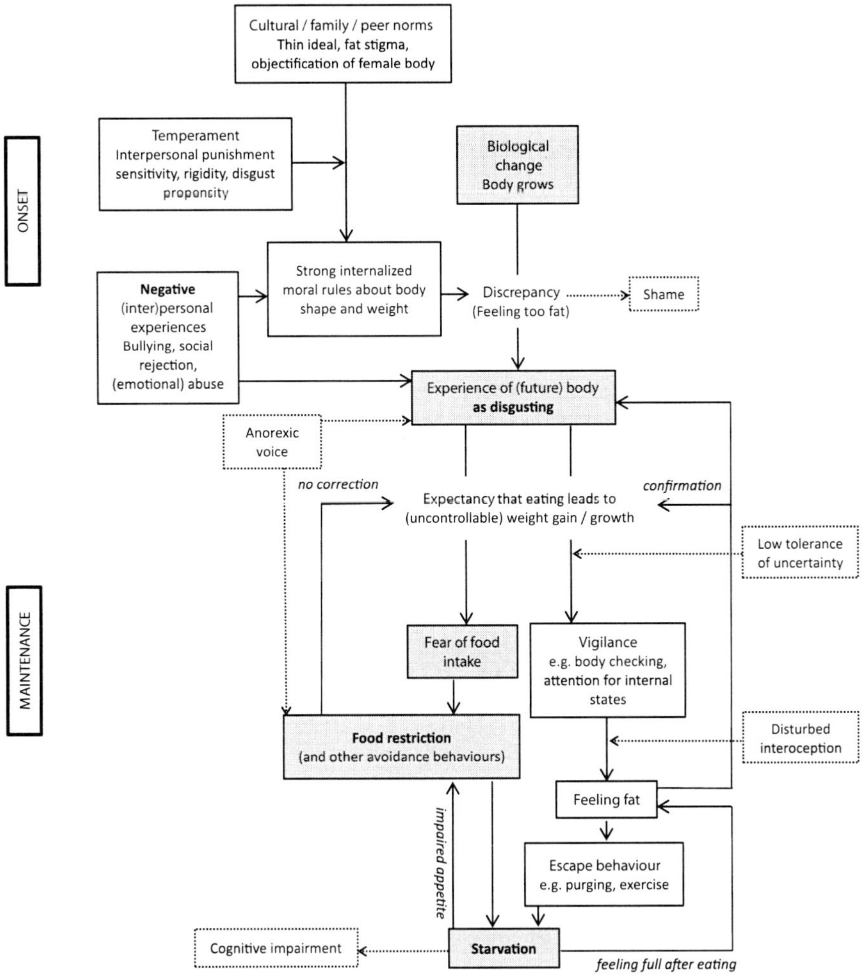

Figure 3.1 Theoretical model of (food restriction in) AN with experiencing self-disgust as a key factor (based on Glashouwer & de Jong, 2021). Licensed under CC BY 4.0 (https://creativecommons.org/licenses/by/4.0/).

end of the chapter, we will discuss future directions and potential implications for AN treatment.

The theoretical model that we propose is complex in nature with many hypothesized moderators and interactions. Yet, we believe it takes an exceptional combination of temperamental factors and external circumstances to explain the exceptional (and low prevalence) eating behaviors seen in AN. On the basis of the literature and clinical observations, we hypothesize which specific conditions are required for

AN to develop and persist. By explicitly presenting this theoretical model, our aim is to fuel future research that will help determine which of the proposed mechanisms are valid and which parts of the model need to be adapted. This way we hope to unravel the crucial factors in the onset and maintenance of AN, which then can guide the improvement of treatments for this severe mental disorder.

Onset of Anorexia Nervosa

Many existing models stress the role of negative self-conscious emotions (and related interpersonal difficulties) in the onset and maintenance of AN. There is a clear link between AN and an increased sensitivity to interpersonal rejection, social anxiety, and low self-esteem, as well as related self-conscious emotions, such as shame (e.g., Fairburn et al., 2003; Munro et al., 2017; Treasure et al., 2020). Rules about which physical characteristics are "good" and which are "bad" are omnipresent in our social environment. It is likely that low self-esteem and social anxiety increase the chance of perceiving one's own body as not fulfilling such societal ideals, leading to feelings of shame and embarrassment. Eating-disorder behaviors, such as dieting, might function as a way to cope with these negative emotions, prevent the rejection of others, and feel better about oneself (e.g., Goss & Allan, 2009). Moreover, having control over food intake and the own body, and being someone who is slim can become part of identity, which, in turn, might further fuel identity congruent (eating disorder) behaviors (e.g., Pfeifer & Berkman, 2018). On the one hand, food restriction is thought to be negatively reinforced by avoiding (uncontrollable) weight gain to prevent social judgments and rejection (cf. Murray et al., 2016). On the other hand, positive reinforcement such as receiving compliments and feelings of pride and personal accomplishment might also contribute to the continuation of food restriction (e.g., Goss & Allan, 2009; Murray et al., 2016; Walsh, 2013).

Although the internalized importance of being slim for one's self-identity and the reinforcing impact of self-conscious emotions seem closely linked to eating disorder pathology, it is unclear how they can explain the puzzling presence of food restriction in the face of starvation, when the focus on food and the drive to eat become exceptionally strong (e.g., Keys et al., 1950). In an attempt to solve this puzzle, we propose that (self-)disgust in the prospect of food intake might play a crucial role in food restriction. The power of disgust might have the potential to overrule the biological urge to eat and to drive the avoidance of food (Rozin et al., 1987).

Disgust and Self-Disgust

Several researchers already linked disgust and disgust-related mechanisms to AN (Davey et al., 1998; Fox et al., 2013; Hildebrandt et al., 2015; Moncrieff-Boyd et al., 2013; Troop & Baker, 2009). Disgust is such an intense aversive feeling that it not only results in a strong urge to escape situations that elicit disgust, but also drives the avoidance of potential disgust elicitors in order to prevent future negative experiences (Rozin & Fallon, 1987). Both escape and avoidance behaviors are negatively reinforced by the direct decrease or prevention of disgust. Moreover, once something has acquired disgusting properties, it becomes intrinsically revolting and difficult to change with rational arguments ("cognitively impenetrable"). Disgust has also been described as an "essentialising emotion" meaning that disgust becomes part of the essence of the entity that is deemed disgusting (e.g., Katzir et al., 2019). These features render disgust highly robust to corrective information (Olatunji et al., 2007). This "stickiness" of disgust makes sense considering its evolutionary role in preventing infection from pathogens that are omnipresent but invisible to the naked eye (Oaten et al., 2009; Tybur et al., 2013). When it comes to life or death, it is "better to be safe than sorry". However, in the context of AN, this inherent power of disgust might have a paradoxical effect: when eating, or even the prospect of eating, elicits overwhelming feelings of disgust in individuals with AN, this could explain why food restriction persists even when someone is in a state of starvation. Although the idea that avoidance is an important factor in the maintenance of AN is not new, zooming into disgust as a driving force behind these behaviors could add to our understanding of the persistence of food restriction and provide fresh starting points for treatment.

The critical source of disgust might not be the food *per se*, but the implied impact of food on the own body (i.e., "becoming fat"). Disgust can be elicited by external objects, but can also become directed to stable features of the self (Powell et al., 2015; Clarke et al., 2018). The source of self-disgust may lie in the transgression of moral rules. Disgust not only has an important function in avoiding potential contaminants (pathogen disgust) to safeguard the physical integrity of the individual but also in avoiding socio-moral transgressions (moral disgust) as a means to maintain the integrity of the social group (Rozin et al., 2008). Moral transgressions elicit disgust (Chapman & Anderson, 2013) and even when individuals were asked to transgress their own internalized socio-moral rules, they were shown to experience feelings of disgust (Rachman et al., 2012). Such instances of moral disgust are thought to help individuals stay on the right track and prevent exclusion from the social group (Tybur et al., 2013).

Societal rules about which physical characteristics are "good" and which are "bad" are omnipresent in our social environment. From an early age, children internalize societal norms regarding body ideals and report dissatisfaction with their bodies (Möllmann et al., 2024). Adolescents might be extra sensitive to such social rules due to their increased self-awareness together with the increased importance of social aspects of identity and their need to connect with peers. When moral rules regarding body shape and weight are strongly endorsed, the transgression of these rules by others or by oneself ("I am too fat") can result in disgust (cf. Borg et al., 2011). So, when one's appearance does not match one's self-identity and related internalized moral rules regarding shape and weight, confrontation with the own body can elicit self-disgust (Masselman et al., 2023). In line with this, it has been argued / theorized that "ugliness is in the gut of the beholder" suggesting that more generally disgust lies at the basis of aesthetic judgments (Doran, 2022, p. 88).

Apart from processes related to the developmental phase, certain personality characteristics may strengthen the internalization of societal norms regarding thinness and fatness. Punishment sensitivity could enhance the sensitivity to pick up socio-moral rules to prevent punishment such as interpersonal rejection (Treasure et al., 2020) and has been consistently linked to AN (e.g., Harrison et al., 2010; Jonker et al., 2025). Other personality characteristics that are associated with AN are rigidity and high disgust propensity (Aharoni & Hertz, 2012). Also these characteristics might facilitate the detection and internalization of moral rules (e.g., Inbar, Pizarro, Iyer & Haidt, 2012). In addition, negative life events can contribute to the internalization of moral rules about weight and shape and may also more directly give rise to self-disgust. In particular, negative interpersonal experiences like bullying, social rejection, emotional neglect, or sexual abuse could turn the own body into a disgust elicitor (cf. Rachman, 2010; Lenk et al., 2019).

The onset of AN during adolescence (Javaras et al., 2015), might also be explained by the rapid changes in body morphology and bodily growth in this developmental phase, which requires major adaptations in existing body representations (Möllmann et al., 2024). Because of these changes, adolescents might have an increased chance of developing dysfunctional body representations, including body image problems. We propose that, in particular, the physical changes can magnify the perceived discrepancy between internalized moral rules regarding shape and weight and the own current body, or even the own expected future body when it keeps growing. This discrepancy can lead to disgust towards the own body, which in turn may lead to behaviors to minimize and/or avoid self-disgust.

As mentioned, the development of self-identity can be seen as a catalyst that can both fuel the search for and the internalization of societal rules regarding the own body. Then, in interaction with certain interpersonal experiences, an identity can be formed that centers around the value of controlling weight and being slim. Over time, "being someone who is slim", or even "being someone with an eating disorder" become more and more connected to someone's sense of self-worth and meaning in life (Croce et al., 2024), and not meeting this ideal results in judging oneself as an unworthy person and feelings of shame and disgust. Such aspects of identity can even become so prominent that other life domains are overshadowed and that the regular developmental tasks are hampered (e.g., van Doornik et al., 2022).

Shame Vs. Self-Disgust

As mentioned, perceiving one's own body as not fulfilling societal body ideals can lead to feelings of both disgust and shame; and self-disgust and shame often co-occur. However, there are important distinctions between disgust and shame that might be relevant to the understanding of AN. Both emotions originate from a different source and have different characteristics. Shame is conceptualized as an evolutionary adaptive mechanism for damage control in interpersonal contact and social competition (Parrott, 2014), characterized by a painful sense of the self as being flawed or bad (Lewis, 1971). For example, shame can motivate behaviors to restore someone's self after committing a social transgression. Just as other self-conscious emotions, shame is defined as a complex emotion, because it requires a certain level of self-awareness to be able to "see oneself through the eyes of others". Disgust, on the other hand, is defined as a basic emotion (just like fear, anger, or joy) and conceptualized as a disease avoidance mechanism. It is characterized by intense feelings of revulsion and a strong urge to distance oneself from the disgust elicitor. While shame is typically linked to conscious propositions ("they found my presentation awful"), disgust elicitors are often experienced as inherently disgusting, meaning that no propositional knowledge is necessary for disgust to arise, which might make disgust an even more overwhelming experience than shame.

Although shame can lead to the avoidance of specific situations that are expected to activate feelings of shame, such as eye contact, it cannot readily explain feelings of disgust towards the own body that have been found in AN (e.g., Kot et al., 2021; Bektas et al., 2022). In addition, it is difficult to see how shame can explain the strong urge to avoid confrontation with the own body when nobody else is present (i.e., in the absence of observing others), considering the interpersonal nature of shame (e.g., Smith et al., 2002). Nevertheless, it has been suggested that shame can also be experienced outside of social contexts, when someone takes a negative observer's perspective towards oneself. Individuals with AN who are often high in punishment sensitivity might have internalized such a (critical) observer perspective towards the self, and it has even been suggested that individuals with AN are literally "locked" into an allocentric representation of their own body (e.g., Riva, 2012). Yet, it is not directly clear how the body shame that might result from such a strongly internalized negative observer can, meal after meal, concur with the strong biological urge to eat and lead to continuous food restriction. Whether someone experiences disgust or shame after a perceived discrepancy between moral rules regarding body weight and shape and the current body might be dependent on the extent to which these moral rules are internalized. The stronger someone endorses these rules, the more likely that a perceived discrepancy will result in self-disgust. Under these conditions, the body may become inherently disgusting. However, we propose that when cued in an interpersonal context, an experienced discrepancy can also be a source of shame next to (self-)disgust.

Both disgust and shame can fuel body-related avoidance behaviors which are typically seen in individuals with AN (Nikodijevic et al., 2018). Disgust-induced avoidance serves the prevention of experiencing aversive feelings towards a potential disgust-elicitor (e.g., not touching their body or taking a shower with the lights turned off). Shame-induced avoidance is typically focused on the prevention of the discomfort when the self would be exposed to the expected negative judgments of others (e.g. avoiding that others can see the own body by wearing baggy clothes or avoiding going to the pool). Both disgust- and shame-driven avoidance behaviors could contribute to the persistence of a negative body image by preventing (1) attention towards and appreciation of attractive aspects of one's body, and (2) habituation to and re-evaluation of "aversive" (disgust eliciting) body parts (cf. Engelhard et al., 2011). As a result, access to critical information that could counteract pre-existing negative body-related associations or help to develop positive body-related associations might become blocked. Over time, avoidance behaviors might contribute to the aggravation of negative body-related emotions, behaviors, and cognitions (i.e., negative body image).

Self-Disgust as the Motor of Food Restriction

We propose that disgust towards the own current body and/or the expected own future body could play a central role in the persistence of food restriction in AN. As just described, body-related avoidance behaviors in which individuals with AN engage might serve to decrease or prevent intense and overwhelming feelings of revulsion that are automatically elicited by the confrontation with their body. Similarly, food restriction might also serve the avoidance of self-directed disgust by preventing (anticipated) appalling changes in body size. When individuals with AN feel forced to eat, they typically display an intense fear of food intake. This makes sense considering that the intake of food implicates a disgusting outcome ("food makes me fat"; Milos et al., 2017; Waller & Mountford, 2015). Via evaluative learning, food can even acquire disgust-eliciting properties itself and become intrinsically revolting (e.g., De Houwer et al., 2001). This process might be comparable to the fear of spiders, which has been shown to be determined by the product of the level of disgust towards the spider and the subjective probability of involuntary physical contact with the spider (de Jong et al., 2002). Similarly, the fear of food intake might be determined by the product of the level of disgust towards the own (future) body and the subjective probability (i.e., the expectancy) that eating leads to weight gain. Thus, according to this model, self-disgust is the source of fear of food intake, which in turn is the proximal factor that directly fuels the restriction/avoidance of food.

Over time, food avoidance can result in starvation, and biological processes develop that further contribute towards a vicious circle (Keys et al., 1950). First of all, a decrease in appetite can directly strengthen food restriction. Second, feelings of fullness after eating are often experienced as "feeling fat" which can be interpreted as evidence that one's body is actually too fat. Such "evidence" can again strengthen body-related self-disgust via the perceived discrepancy between the current body and internalized norms. In addition, feeling fat can confirm the expectation that eating indeed leads to weight gain. Third, starvation can also lead to general cognitive impairment, such as slowed thinking, impaired short-term memory, decreased cognitive flexibility, and concentration problems (e.g., Hatch et al., 2010). As a result, reasoning becomes more difficult and rigid black-and-white thinking increases.

Paradoxically, the experience of the own (future) body as disgusting might not only give rise to avoidance behaviors, it simultaneously could also fuel vigilance towards potential rule violation in order to prevent (worsening) of self-disgust. Individuals with AN indeed reported repeated checking of their body after food intake, and focusing on internal bodily states that could indicate being or becoming fat (Nikodijevic et al., 2018). These monitoring behaviors likely lower the threshold for someone to "feel fat", in particular, considering that some individuals with AN seem to show decreased/disturbed interoceptive capacities (e.g., Jacquemot & Park, 2020). Feeling fat could then again fuel feelings of self-disgust and can also lead to attempts to escape this unpleasant state, for instance by purging or compulsive exercise. Such escape behaviors again prevent the occurrence of expectancy violating experiences and could prevent the correction of the expectation that eating leads to weight gain ("I did not gain weight, because I compensated after eating"). There is some empirical evidence that checking behaviors indeed are followed by an increase in negative emotions (e.g., Kraus et al., 2015).

Finally, we incorporated two additional phenomena in the model that are often linked to AN. The first phenomenon is low tolerance of uncertainty (Brown et al., 2017). Individuals who have difficulty tolerating uncertainty are expected to show a stronger urge to check their body to detect potential signals of rule violation. The second phenomenon is the so-called anorexic voice (see Chapter 4 of this book) referring to critical self-talk in the form of negative comments on their own eating, weight and shape, and instructions to restrict or compensate (e.g., Pugh & Waller, 2017). We propose that the anorexic voice might lead to an increase in self-disgust and might promote food restriction.

Empirical Evidence

Despite some theoretical attention to disgust in AN, empirical evidence regarding self-disgust in individuals with AN is still scarce. Individuals with AN reported repulsive intrusive imagery of their own body (Kadriu et al., 2019) and higher self-disgust on questionnaires than individuals without an eating disorder (Bell et al., 2017; Kot et al., 2021). Qualitative findings indicate that self-disgust is linked to avoidance behaviors in AN (Cardi et al., 2018; Espeset et al., 2012). Individuals with AN reported that they try to avoid feelings of disgust by avoiding food- and body-related situations (Espeset et al., 2012), and that they are afraid of feeling disgusted or being perceived as disgusting by others when eating (Cardi et al., 2018).

More research is available regarding the relationship between shame and AN. Higher self-reported shame was found in individuals with (a history of) AN than in individuals without AN (Oldershaw et al., 2015) and shame levels were positively related to symptom severity (Blythin et al., 2020). Body shame and shame around eating showed the strongest relationships with eating disorder symptoms (Nechita et al., 2021). A longitudinal study indicated that body shame (but not internal or external shame) predicted AN symptoms following a 2.5-year period in women with a past or current eating disorder (Troop & Redshaw, 2012). In addition, another longitudinal study in individuals with an eating disorder showed a bidirectional relationship between shame and eating disorder symptoms during a 12-week period: decreases in shame predicted decreases in ED symptoms and decreases in ED predicted decreases in shame (Kelly & Tasca, 2016).

Self-Hate

In some cases, eating disorder behaviors can also stem from self-hate resulting from extremely low self-esteem and intense self-disgust. Someone might then restrict their food intake, because they find that they do not deserve to eat, or they have to punish themselves by not eating. The food avoidance serves a different function here: whereas disgust-induced avoidance is a way to distance oneself from the disgust elicitor (e.g., certain bodily features or foods), self-hate-induced food avoidance has the function of active demolition and punishment of the self.

Implications for Future Research and Clinical Practice

Investigating the Role of Self-Disgust in Anorexia Nervosa

The investigation of the proposed model starts with systematically testing the core assumption that body-related self-disgust leads to food restriction. The existing literature suggests that self-disgust levels indeed are heightened in individuals with AN. However, research so far was all retrospective in nature using self-report or interviews. Therefore, it remains unclear what exactly elicits disgust in individuals with AN. An important next step would be to study disgust towards the own body in real-time not only using self-report measures, but also physiological/behavioral indices to gauge difficulties that participants may have in distinguishing between emotions and to avoid demand characteristics (Nabi, 2002). Facial electromyography (fEMG) of the levator muscle along the nose may be helpful in this regard as a validated and specific index of psychophysiological disgust responses (e.g., Masselman et al., 2023).

However, when food restriction in AN is driven by the anticipated appalling consequences of food ingestion on weight and shape, exposure to the current body might not elicit disgust. To get a clear view of the role of body-related self-disgust in AN, it would be important not only to investigate the response of individuals with AN to their current body size but also to their healthy or even overweight body sizes. Recent developments point to virtual reality (VR) as a potentially effective tool for this challenging research design. VR could be used to study the effects of exposing patients with AN to healthy or even overweight versions of their body and compare their disgust responses to individuals without AN. As a next step, it is important to establish whether self-disgust prospectively predicts food restriction in AN, for instance, by testing whether self-disgust levels after treatment predict relapse. To investigate whether self-disgust is indeed a critical causal factor in the persistence of food restriction in AN, it would be important to test whether the modification of self-disgust leads to a decrease in food restriction.

Targeting Self-Disgust (and Shame)

Prior interventions targeting food restriction in AN have focused on the reduction of fear of food intake via exposure to feared eating situations without the use of anxiety-reducing rituals (Cardi et al., 2018; Steinglass et al., 2014), and via the violation of fear-eliciting expectancies (e.g., "if I eat, then I will lose control"; Cardi et al., 2018). In addition, exposure to feared situations is an important intervention to reduce shame, for example in the context of the treatment of social anxiety (e.g., Clark & Wells, 1995). In this case, the aim is both violation of expectancies regarding the overestimation of negative outcomes ("If I ask my colleague to drink coffee with me, she will reject me") as well as the underestimation of own resilience if rejection indeed would take place ("If she does not want to drink coffee with me, I would feel ashamed for weeks"). However, if food restriction originates from the anticipated effect of food intake on the body in an attempt to prevent self-disgust, these applications of exposure are likely to be ineffective in the long term, because self-disgust remains unaffected.

There might be different routes to changing body-related self-disgust. A first strategy to reduce disgust is prolonged exposure based on the notion that, in contrast to anxiety and fear (e.g., Craske et al., 2014), expectancies are not considered to play a prominent role in eliciting disgust. To effectively reduce disgust, not the violation of expectancies, but habituation via prolonged exposure is considered critical to weaken the intrinsically revolting nature of disgust-eliciting objects (de Jong, 2013; Rozin & Fallon, 1987). Prolonged exposure involves someone being confronted repeatedly and for a long time with the disgust-eliciting stimulus. For instance, individuals whose work forces them into close contact with disgust elicitors (e.g., cleaning toilets or dissecting dead bodies) tend to become neutral towards those stimuli after frequent exposure (Rozin, 2008). If in individuals with AN, the impact of food intake on the own body is the source of fear of eating, prolonged exposure to the own disgusting "future fat body" seems a promising approach to stop food restriction. The decrease in body-related self-disgust should then lead to a decrease in fear of food intake, resulting in a decrease in food restriction/avoidance. Again, VR could be applied to expose patients with AN for a prolonged period of time to healthy or even overweight versions of their body. Although the actual impact of body exposure on self-disgust is still unknown, several studies have demonstrated positive effects of body exposure on body dissatisfaction in individuals with eating disorders (e.g., Griffen et al., 2018). In addition, a recent study in which a small sample of individuals with AN was confronted with healthy weight avatars in VR showed a decrease in fear of gaining weight compared to a control group (Porras-Garcia et al., 2021). These findings provide a first indication that exposure to the own body in VR may be effective in decreasing self-disgust.

Another application of prolonged exposure could be to expose individuals to disgust-related autobiographical memories. Our self-images are thought to influence how we remember past events and how we derive self-defining information from these memories (Conway et al., 2004). In line with this idea, it was found that a more negative/disgust-related body image was associated with a higher endorsement of dissatisfaction and disgust-related body image in participants' memories (von Spreckelsen et al., 2022b) and increased disgust responses to body-related memories (von Spreckelsen et al., 2022a). In addition, body-related self-disgust was associated with stronger attempts to escape from the recalled memories (von Spreckelsen et al., 2022a). This relationship was mediated by an increased disgust response to these memories. Such reactive avoidance would likely obstruct habituation to the feeling of disgust (cf. Bosman et al., 2016; Lader & Wing, 1966) and decrease the opportunity to process corrective information. Because autobiographical memories serve as a crucial source of self-defining information (Conway, 2005), such an avoidance bias at the level of autobiographical memory would likely diminish the opportunity to challenge a negative/repulsive body image and thus contribute to the persistence of the aversive self-/body image (von Spreckelsen & de Jong, 2023). Consequently, prolonged exposure to such memories may help break avoidance and promote the habituation of disgust, thereby lowering body concerns. A first study in women with high body-related self-disgust showed that repeated exposure to disgust-focused body memories may help reduce disgust elicited by these memories and promote body acceptance (von Spreckelsen et al., 2024). Yet, the effect of the exposure did not extend to changing state disgust towards the body, possibly due to reactive avoidance.

The second strategy to reduce self-disgust is conceptual reorientation. An anecdote about someone who thinks they are drinking milk illustrates this well (cf. Rozin et al., 1987). When they unexpectedly taste a sour flavor, it elicits disgust. However, the disgust disappears instantaneously when they realize it is yogurt and not milk that they are drinking. The crux is to change the interpretation of the stimulus (reorientation) such that disgust no longer arises. When self-disgust results from strong internalized moral rules regarding overweight, it seems important to change or at least relativize these rules ("fat is bad"). One way to change internalized rules regarding body ideals towards healthier standards would be to change the distribution of body sizes to which individuals are being exposed in their everyday lives, for example, by making sure that body sizes presented on (social) media are representative of the actual variety in society. However, this is a rather challenging endeavor.

An alternative could be to more directly target appearance-related size judgments. The dissonance-based therapy seems a good starting point for such a reorientation (e.g., Stice et al., 2019). In this treatment, individuals learn to change their attitudes towards the "thin-ideal" by changing their behaviors (e.g., writing a counter-attitudinal letter). Since individuals like to be consistent in their behaviors and attitudes, counter-attitudinal behaviors are thought to lead to the adjustment of attitudes. Research has shown that this intervention effectively reduces body dissatisfaction (Stice et al., 2019). A different approach could be to change individuals' perspective on body size in a perceptual body image training (Gledhill et al., 2017; Irivine et al., 2020). In this computerized training program, participants have to decide repeatedly whether they judge the body size of a presented 3D image of a female model as either "fat" or "thin". By providing feedback, they are trained to slowly shift their categorical boundary upwards towards a healthier standard (i.e., heighten the threshold for classifying a body as "fat"). Compared to an active control condition, a decrease in eating disorder symptoms following the perceptual body image training was found in women with high body concerns (Gledhill et al., 2017, study 1; Irvine et al., 2020) and in individuals with AN (Gledhill et al., 2017, study 2).

A third strategy to reduce self-disgust as well as shame is by strengthening positive self-emotions such as empathy for the self/body and fostering self-pride, for example with compassion-focused therapy (CFT; Gilbert, 2014). CFT is a psychotherapeutic approach developed by clinical psychologist Paul Gilbert which integrates principles from cognitive behaviour therapy with elements of compassion training and mindfulness practices. The primary focus of CFT is to cultivate self-compassion, which involves treating oneself with kindness, understanding, and acceptance, particularly during times of distress or difficulty. By fostering self-compassion, individuals can develop greater emotional resilience, self-worth, and overall well-being, which may undermine critical self-talk and work as a buffer against the negative effects of self-disgust and shame. There is evidence showing that CFT helps to improve self-compassion and eating disorder symptoms in individuals with different eating disorders (Millard et al., 2023). Another approach to more directly strengthen positive emotions regarding the own body is by focusing on increasing functionality appreciation. Functionality appreciation is considered a core component of positive body image and can be defined as "appreciating, respecting, and honoring the body for what it is capable of doing, extending beyond mere awareness of body functionality" (Alleva et al., 2017, p. 29). For example, a functionality-based writing exercise (named "Expand your horizon") in which individuals are instructed to describe their body's functions and why they are important and meaningful to them was effective in enhancing positive body image in different samples with negative body image (Guest et al., 2019; Linardon et al., 2023). Enhancing functionality appreciation might be a way to decrease feelings of disgust and shame towards the own body shape and weight.

A final strategy could be to change the importance of the body and bodily features for defining the self (self-identity) and to redirect the focus to intrinsically valued goals that may have been overshadowed by extrinsic values and goals (e.g., internalization of societal norms / peer reinforced importance of being slim). Meaning-centered psychotherapy (MCP-ED) for eating disorders might be a suitable intervention in this regard (van Doornik et al., 2024). MCP-ED is a manualized 6-week intervention that makes use of theory, discussions, exercises, and homework assignments that focus on themes related to life meaning and eating disorders with the aim to increase engagement with intrinsically valued life goals. During each session, one of four sources of meaning is discussed: (1) your personal life story, (2) dealing with life's limitations, (3) creating your own life, and (4) meaningful experiences. The efficacy of the intervention was investigated in a randomized controlled trial in female students (N = 134) high in weight and shape concerns (van Doornik et al., 2024). Findings were promising with participants in the experimental condition showing a stronger increase in meaning than participants in the waiting-list condition after the intervention and at follow-up. The intervention also resulted in lower eating disorder symptoms and general distress, and higher psychological well-being and satisfaction with meaningful life domains. If indeed such an intervention would be effective in rewriting a person's narrative about themselves (about what they should value and how they need to be to be worthy) and reduce the importance of the body for defining the self/one's identity, this might potentially also take the edge off the body as a source of self-disgust.

Conclusion

Current treatments for AN already address many relevant factors incorporated in the current model, which might explain their partial effectiveness. However, when self-disgust indeed is a key factor in the maintenance of food restriction, residual levels of self-disgust after treatment could make individuals vulnerable to relapse. Treatments currently do not specifically address self-disgust, which can potentially explain why the effectiveness is often limited in the long term. Therefore, it seems worthwhile to investigate whether body-related self-disgust is indeed a crucial treatment target for AN. Interventions that help to decrease self-disgust and that break through disgust- (and shame-)induced avoidance behaviors regarding the own body and eating might be an important key to improving the effectiveness of existing AN treatments.

References

Aharoni, R., & Hertz, M. M. (2012). Disgust sensitivity and anorexia nervosa. *European Eating Disorders Review, 20*(2), 106–110. http://dx.doi.org/10.1002/erv.1124

Alleva, J. M., Tylka, T. L., & Van Diest, A. M. K. (2017). The Functionality Appreciation Scale (FAS): Development and psychometric evaluation in US community women and men. *Body Image, 23,* 28–44. https://doi.org/10.1016/j.bodyim.2017.07.008

Bell, K., Coulthard, H., & Wildbur, D. (2017). Self-disgust within eating disordered groups: Associations with anxiety, disgust sensitivity and sensory processing. *European Eating Disorders Review, 25,* 373–380. https://doi.org/10.1002/erv.2529

Bektas, S., Keeler, J. L., Anderson, L. M., Mutwalli, H., Himmerich, H., & Treasure, J. (2022). Disgust and self-disgust in eating disorders: A systematic review and meta-analysis. *Nutrients, 14*(9), 1728. https://doi.org/10.3390/nu14091728

Blythin, S. P. M., Nicholson, H. L., Macintyre, V. G., Dickson, J. M., Fox, J. R. E., & Taylor, P. J. (2020). Experiences of shame and guilt in anorexia and bulimia nervosa: A systematic review. *Psychology and Psychotherapy, 93*(1), 134–159. https://doi.org/10.1111/papt.12198

Borg, C., de Jong, P. J., & Weijmar Schultz, W. (2011). Vaginismus and dyspareunia: Relationship with general and sex-related moral standards. *Journal of Sexual Medicine, 8*, 223–231. https://doi.org/10.1111/j.1743-6109.2010.02080.x

Bosman, R. C., Borg, C., & de Jong, P. J. (2016). Optimising extinction of conditioned disgust. *PLoS One, 11*(2), e0148626. https://doi.org/10.1371/journal.pone.0148626

Brown, M., Robinson, L., Campione, G. C., Wuensch, K., Hildebrandt, T., & Micali, N. (2017). Intolerance of uncertainty in eating disorders: A systematic review and meta-analysis. *European Eating Disorders Review, 25,* 329–343. https://doi.org/10.1002/erv.2523

Cardi, V., Leppanen, J., Mataix-Cols, D., Campbell, I. C., & Treasure, J. (2018). A case series to investigate food-related fear learning and extinction using in vivo food exposure in anorexia nervosa: A clinical application of the inhibitory learning framework. *European Eating Disorders Review, 27,* 173–181. https://doi.org/10.1002/erv.2639

Chapman, H. A., & Anderson, A. K. (2013). Things rank and gross in nature: A review and synthesis of moral disgust. *Psychological Bulletin, 139*(2), 300–327. doi.org/10.1037/a0030964

Clark, D. M., & Wells, A. A. (1995). *Cognitive model of social phobia.* In R. G. Heimberg, M. Liebowitz, D. A. Hope, & F. R. Schneier (Eds.), Social phobia: Diagnosis, assessment, and treatment (pp. 69–93). Guilford Press.

Clarke, A., Simpson, J., & Varese, F. (2018). A systematic review of the clinical utility of the concept of self-disgust. *Clinical Psychology and Psychotherapy, 26,* 110–134. doi.org/10.1002/cpp.2335

Conway, M. A. (2005). Memory and the self. *Journal of Memory and Language, 53*(4), 594–628. https://doi.org/10.1016/j.jml.2005.08.005

Conway, M. A., Singer, J. A., & Tagini, A. (2004). The self and autobiographical memory: Correspondence and coherence. *Social Cognition, 22*(5), 491–529. https://doi.org/10.1521/soco.22.5.491.50768

Craske, M. G., Treanor, M., Conway, C. C., Zbozinek, T., & Vervliet, B. (2014). Maximizing exposure therapy: An inhibitory learning approach. *Behaviour Research and Therapy, 58,* 10–23. https://doi.org/10.1016/j.brat.2014.04.006

Croce, S. R., Malcolm, A. C., Ralph-Nearman, C., & Phillipou, A. (2024). The role of identity in anorexia nervosa: A narrative review. *New Ideas in Psychology, 72,* 101060. https://doi.org/10.1016/j.newideapsych.2023.101060

Davey, G. C. L., Buckland, G., Tantow, B., &, Dallos, R. (1998). Disgust and eating disorders. *European Eating Disorder Review, 6,* 201–211. https://doi.org/10.1002/erv.2373

De Houwer, J., Thomas, S., & Baeyens, F. (2001). Association learning of likes and dislikes: A review of 25 years of research on human evaluative conditioning. *Psychological Bulletin, 127*(6), 853–869. https://doi.org/10.1037//0033-2909.127.6.853

de Jong, P. J. (2013). Learning mechanisms in the acquisition of disgust. In D. Hermans, B. Rimé, & B. Mesquita (Eds.), *Changing emotions* (pp. 74–80). Psychology Press.

de Jong, P. J., & Muris, P. (2002). Spider phobia: Interaction of disgust and perceived likelihood of involuntary physical contact. *Journal of Anxiety Disorders, 16*, 51–65.

Doran, R. P. (2022). Ugliness is in the gut of the beholder. *Ergo an Open Access Journal of Philosophy, 9*, 5. https://doi.org/10.3998/ergo.2261

Engelhard, I. M., Olatunji, B. O., & de Jong, P. J. (2011). Disgust and the development of posttraumatic stress among soldiers deployed to Afghanistan. *Journal of Anxiety Disorders*, *25*(1), 58–63. https://doi.org/10.1016/j.janxdis.2010.08.003

Espeset, E. M. S., Gulliksen, K. S., Nordbø, R. H. S., Skårderud, F., & Holte, A. (2012). The link between negative emotions and eating disorder behaviour in patients with anorexia nervosa. *European Eating Disorders Review, 20,* 451–460. https://doi.org/10.1002/erv.2183

Fairburn, C. G., Cooper, Z., & Shafran, R. (2003). Cognitive behaviour therapy for eating disorders: A transdiagnostic theory and treatment. *Behaviour Research and Therapy, 41*, 509–528.

Fox, J. R. E., Smithson, E., Baillie, S., Ferreira, N., Mayr, I., & Power, M. J. (2013). Emotion coupling and regulation in anorexia nervosa. *Clinical Psychology and Psychotherapy, 20,* 319–333. https://doi.org/10.1002/cpp.1823

Gilbert, P. (2014). The origins and nature of compassion focused therapy. *British Journal of Clinical Psychology*, *53*, 6–41. https://doi.org/10.1111/bjc.12043

Glashouwer, K. A., & de Jong, P. J. (2021). The revolting body: Self-disgust as a key factor in anorexia nervosa. *Current Opinion in Psychology*, *41*, 78–83. https://doi.org/(...) j.copsyc.2021.03.008

Gledhill, L. J., Cornelissen, K. K., Cornelissen, P. L., Penton-Voak, I. S., Munafò, M. R., & Tovée, M. J. (2017). An interactive training programme to treat body image disturbance. *British Journal of Health Psychology, 22,* 60–76. http://dx.doi.org/10.1111/bjhp.12217

Goss, K., & Allan, S. (2009). Shame, pride and eating disorders. *Clinical Psychology & Psychotherapy*, *16*(4), 303–316. https://doi.org/10.1002/cpp.627

Griffen, T. C., Naumann, E., & Hildebrandt, T. (2018). Mirror exposure therapy for body image disturbances and eating disorders: A review. *Clinical Psychology Review*, *65*, 163–174.

Guest, E., Costa, B., Williamson, H., Meyrick, J., Halliwell, E., & Harcourt, D. (2019). The effectiveness of interventions aiming to promote positive body image in adults: A systematic review. *Body Image*, *30*, 10–25. https://doi.org/10.1016/j.bodyim.2019.04.002

Harrison, A., O'Brien, N., Lopez, C., & Treasure, J. (2010). Sensitivity to reward and punishment in eating disorders. *Psychiatry Research, 177,* 1–11.

Hatch, A., Madden, S., Kohn, M., Clarke, S., Touyz, S., & Williams, L. M. (2010). Anorexia nervosa: Towards an integrative neuroscience model. *European Eating Disorders Review, 18,* 165–179.

Hildebrandt, T., Grotzinger, A., Reddan, M., Greif, R., Levy, I., Goodman, W., & Schiller, D. (2015). Testing the disgust conditioning theory of food-avoidance in adolescents with recent onset anorexia nervosa. *Behaviour Research and Therapy, 71,* 131–138. doi.org/10.1016/j.brat.2015.06.008

Inbar, Y., Pizarro, D., Iyer, R., & Haidt, J. (2012). Disgust sensitivity, political conservatism, and voting. *Social Psychological and Personality Science, 3,* 537–544.

Irvine, K. R., Irvine, A. R., Maalin, N., McCarty, K., Cornelissen, K. K., Tovée, M. J., & Cornelissen P. L. (2020). Using immersive virtual reality to modify body image. *Body Image, 33,* 232–243. https://doi.org/10.1016/j.bodyim.2020.03.007

Jacquemot, A. M. M., & Park, R. (2020). The role of interoception in the pathogenesis and treatment of anorexia nervosa: A narrative review. *Frontiers in Psychology, 11,* 281. https://doi.org/10.3389/fpsyt.2020.00281

Javaras, K. N., Runfola, C. D., Thornton, L. M., Agerbo, E., Birgegard, A., Norring, C, Yao, S., Råstam, M., Larsson, H., Lichtenstein, P., & Bulik, C. M. (2015). Sex- and age-specific incidence of healthcare-register-recorded eating disorders in the complete swedish 1979–2001 birth cohort. *International Journal of Eating Disorders, 48,* 1070–1081. https://doi.org/10.1002/eat.22467

Jonker, N. C., Glashouwer, K. A., & de Jong, P. J. (2025). Delving into the role of reward and punishment sensitivity in anorexia nervosa. *European Eating Disorder Review* https://doi.org/10.1002/erv.3138

Kadriu, F., Claes, L., Witteman, C., Norré, J., Vrieze, E., & Krans, J. (2019). Characteristics and content of intrusive images in patients with eating disorders. *European Eating Disorders Review, 27,* 495–506. doi.org/10.1002/erv.2671

Katzir, M., Hoffmann, M., & Liberman, N. (2019). Disgust as an essentialist emotion that signals nonviolent outgrouping with potentially low social costs. *Emotion, 19*(5), 841–862. https://doi.org/10.1037/emo0000480

Kelly, A. C., & Tasca, G. A. (2016). Within-persons predictors of change during eating disorders treatment: An examination of self-compassion, self-criticism, shame, and eating disorder symptoms. *International Journal of Eating Disorders, 49,* 716–722. https://doi.org/10.1002/eat.22527

Keys, A., Brozek, J., Henschel, A., Mickelsen, O., & Taylor, H. L. (1950). *The biology of human starvation.* University of Minnesota Press.

Kot, E., Grzegorzewski, P., Kostecka, B., & Kucharska, K. (2021). Self-disgust and disgust sensitivity are increased in anorexia nervosa inpatients, but only self-disgust mediates between comorbid and core psychopathology. *European Eating Disorders Review, 29*(6), 879–892. doi.org/10.1002/erv.2862

Kraus, N., Lindenberg, J., Zeeck, A., Kosfelder, J., & Vocks, S. (2015). Immediate effects of body checking behaviour on negative and positive emotions in women with eating disorders: An ecological momentary assessment approach. *European Eating Disorders Review, 23*(5), 399–407. doi.org/10.1002/erv.2380

Lader, M. H., & Wing, L. (1966). *Physiological measures, sedative drugs and morbid anxiety.* Oxford University Press.

Lenk, M., Ritschel, G., Abele, M., Roever, P., Schellong, J., Joraschky, P., … Croy, I. (2019). The source effect as a natural function of disgust in interpersonal context and its impairment in mental disorders. *Scientific Reports, 9,* 4239. doi.org/10.1038/s41598-019-40802-4

Lewis, H. B. (1971). *Shame and guilt in neurosis*. International Universities Press.

Linardon, J., Messer, M., & Tylka, T. L. (2023). Functionality appreciation and its correlates: Systematic review and meta-analysis. *Body Image, 45,* 65–72. https://doi.org/10.1016/j.bodyim.2023.02.002

Masselman, I., de Jong, P. J., & Glashouwer, K. A. (2023). Subjective disgust and facial EMG responses towards unedited and morphed overweight self-pictures in women with varying levels of eating disorder symptomatology. *European Eating Disorders Review, 31,* 98–109. https://doi.org/10.1002/erv.2940

Millard, L. A., Wan, M. W., Smith, D. M., & Wittkowski, A. (2023). The effectiveness of compassion focused therapy with clinical populations: A systematic review and meta-analysis. *Journal of Affective Disorders, 326,* 168–192. https://doi.org/10.1016/j.jad.2023.01.010

Milos, G., Baur, V., Schumacher, S., Kuenzli, C., Schnyder, U., Mueller-Pfeiffer, C., & Martin-Soelch, C. (2017). How fat will it make me? Estimation of weight gain in anorexia nervosa. *Appetite, 114,* 368–373. doi:10.1016/j.appet.2017.04.002

Möllmann, A., Heinrichs, N., & Herwig, A. (2024). A conceptual framework on body representations and their relevance for mental disorders. *Frontiers in Psychology, 14,* 1231640. https://doi.org/10.3389/fpsyg.2023.1231640

Moncrieff-Boyd, J., Byrne, S., & Nunn, K. (2013). Disgust and anorexia nervosa: Confusion between self and non-self. *Advances in Eating Disorders: Theory, Research and Practice, 2,* 4–18. doi.org/10.1080/21662630.2013.820376

Munro, C., Randell, L., & Lawrie, S. M. (2017). An integrative bio-psycho-social theory of anorexia nervosa. *Clinical Psychology & Psychotherapy, 24*(1), 1–21. doi.org/10.1002/cpp.2047

Murray, S. B., Treanor, M., Liao, B., Loeb, K. L., Griffiths, S., & Le Grange, D. (2016). Extinction theory & anorexia nervosa: Deepening therapeutic mechanisms. *Behaviour Research and Therapy, 87,* 1–10. https://doi.org/10.1016/j.brat.2016.08.017

Nabi, R. L. (2002). The theoretical versus the lay meaning of disgust: Implications for emotion research. *Cognition and Emotion, 16*(5), 695–703. https://doi.org/10.1080/02699930143000437

Nechita, D. M., Bud, S., & David, D. (2021). Shame and eating disorders symptoms: A meta-analysis. *International Journal of Eating Disorders, 54*(11), 1899–1945. https://doi.org/10.1002/eat.23583

Nikodijevic, A., Buck, K., Fuller-Tyszkiewicz, M., de Paoli, T., & Krug, I. (2018). Body checking and body avoidance in eating disorders: Systematic review and meta-analysis. *European Eating Disorders Review, 26*(3), 159–185. doi.org/10.1002/erv.2585

Oaten, M., Stevenson, R. J., & Case, T. I. (2009). Disgust as a disease-avoidance mechanism. *Psychological Bulletin, 135,* 303–321. https://doi.org/10.1037/a0014823

Olatunji, B. O., Forsyth, J. P., & Cherian, A. (2007). Evaluative differential conditioning of disgust: A sticky form of relational learning that is resistant to extinction. *Journal of Anxiety Disorders, 21,* 820–834. doi.org/10.1016/j.janxdis.2006.11.004

Oldershaw, A., Lavender, T., Sallis, H., Stahl, D., & Schmidt, U. (2015). Emotion generation and regulation in anorexia nervosa: A systematic review and meta-analysis of self-report data. *Clinical Psychology Review, 39,* 83–95. https://doi.org/10.1016/j.cpr.2015.04.005

Parrott, W. G. (Ed.). (2014). *The positive side of negative emotions.* The Guilford Press.

Pfeifer, J. H., & Berkman, E. T. (2018). The development of self and identity in adolescence: Neural evidence and implications for a value-based choice perspective on motivated behavior. *Child Development Perspectives, 12*(3), 158–164. https://doi.org/10.1111/cdep.12279

Porras-Garcia, B., Ferrer-Garcia, M., Serrano-Troncoso, E., Carulla-Roig, M., Soto-Usera, P., Miquel-Nabau, H., Olivares, L., Marnet-Fiol, R., Santos-Carrasco, I. M., Borszewski, B., Díaz-Marsá, M., Sánchez-Díaz, I., Fernández-Aranda, F., & Gutiérrez-Maldonado, J. (2021). AN-VR-BE. A randomized controlled trial for reducing fear of gaining weight and other eating disorder symptoms in anorexia nervosa through virtual reality-based body exposure. *Journal of Clinical Medicine, 10*(4), 682. https://doi.org/10.3390/jcm10040682

Powell, P. A., Simpson, J., & Overton, P. G. (2015). An introduction to the revolting self: Self-disgust as an emotion schema. In P. A. Powell, J. Simpson, & P. G. Overton (Eds.),

The revolting self: Perspectives on the psychological, social, and clinical implications of self-directed disgust (pp. 1–24). Karnac.
Pugh, M., & Waller, G. (2017). Understanding the "anorexic voice" in anorexia nervosa. *Clinical Psychology and Psychotherapy, 24,* 670–676. https://doi.org/10.1002/cpp.2034
Rachman, S. (2010). Betrayal: A psychological analysis. *Behaviour Research and Therapy, 48,* 304–311.
Rachman, S., Radomsky, A. S., Elliott, C. M., & Zysk, E. (2012). Mental contamination: The perpetrator effect. *Journal of Behavior Therapy and Experimental Psychiatry, 43,* 587–593.
Riva, G. (2012). Neuroscience and eating disorders: The allocentric lock hypothesis. *Medical Hypotheses, 78,* 254–257. https://doi.org/10.1016/j.mehy.2011.10.039
Rozin, P. (2008). Hedonic "adaptation": Specific habituation to disgust/death elicitors as a result of dissecting a cadaver. *Judgment and Decision Making, 3,* 191–194.
Rozin, P., & Fallon, A. E. (1987). A perspective on disgust. *Psychological Review, 94,* 23–41. https://doi.org/10.1037/0033-295X.94.1.23
Rozin, P., Haidt, J., & McCauley, C. R. (2008). Disgust: The body and soul emotion in the 21st century. In B. O. Olatunji & D. McKay (Eds.), *Disgust and its disorders* (pp. 9–29). American Psychological Association.
Smith, R. H., Webster, J. M., Parrott, W. G., & Eyre, H. L. (2002). The role of public exposure in moral and nonmoral shame and guilt. *Journal of Personality and Social Psychology, 83*(1), 138–159. https://doi.org/10.1037/0022-3514.83.1.138
Steinglass, J. E., Albano, A. M., Simpson, H. B., Wang, Y., Zou, J., Attia, E., & Walsh, B. T. (2014). Confronting fear using exposure and response prevention for anorexia nervosa: A randomized controlled pilot study. *International Journal of Eating Disorders, 47*(2), 174–180. doi.org/10.1002/eat.22214
Stice, E., Rohde, P., Shaw, H., & Gau, J. M. (2019). Randomized trial of a dissonance-based group treatment for eating disorders versus a supportive mindfulness group treatment. *Journal of Consulting and Clinical Psychology, 87,* 79–90. dx.doi.org/10.1037/ccp0000365
Treasure, J., Willmott, D., Ambwani, S., Cardi, V., Bryan, D. C., Rowlands, K., & Schmidt, U. (2020). Cognitive interpersonal model for anorexia nervosa revisited: The perpetuating factors that contribute to the development of the severe and enduring illness. *Journal of Clinical Medicine, 9,* 630. doi.org/10.3390/jcm9030630
Troop, N., & Baker, A. (2009). Food, body, and soul: The role of disgust in eating disorders. In B. Olatunji, & D. McKay (Eds.), *Disgust and its disorders: Theory, assessment, and treatment implications* (pp. 229–251). American Psychological Association. doi.org/10.1037/11856-011
Troop, N. A., & Redshaw, C. (2012). General shame and bodily shame in eating disorders: A 2.5-year longitudinal study. *European Eating Disorders Review, 20*(5), 373–378.
Tybur, J. M., Lieberman, D., Kurzban, R., & DeScioli, P. (2013). Disgust: Evolved function and structure. *Psychological Review, 120,* 65–84. https://doi.org/10.1037/a0030778
van Doornik, Glashouwer, K. A., Ostafin, B. D., & de Jong, P. J. (2024). The effects of a meaning-centered intervention on meaning in life and eating disorder symptoms in undergraduate women with high weight and shape concerns: A randomized controlled trial. *Behavior Therapy, 55*(1), 177–190. https://doi.org/10.1016/j.beth.2023.05.012
van Doornik, S. W. F., Ostafin, B. D., Jonker, N. C., Glashouwer, K. A., & de Jong, P. J. (2022). Satisfaction with normative life domains and the course of anorexia nervosa.

International Journal of Eating Disorders, 55(4), 553–563. https://doi.org/10.1002/eat.23691

von Spreckelsen, P., & de Jong, P. J. (2023). Disgust-induced avoidant processing of autobiographical memories as a transdiagnostic mechanism in the persistence of psychopathology. *Bulletin of the Menninger Clinic, 87*(Suppl. A), 31–52. https://doi.org/10.1521/bumc.2023.87.suppA.113

von Spreckelsen, P., Wessel, I., Glashouwer, K. A., & de Jong, P. J. (2022a). Escaping from revulsion - disgust and escape in response to body-relevant autobiographical memories. *Memory, 30*, 104–116. https://doi.org/10.1080/09658211.2021.1993923

von Spreckelsen, P., Wessel, I., Glashouwer, K. A., & de Jong, P. J. (2022b). Averting repulsion? The role of body-directed self-disgust in autobiographical memory retrieval. *Journal of Experimental Psychopathology, 13.* https://doi.org/10.1177/20438087211073244

von Spreckelsen, P., Wessel, I., Glashouwer, K. A., & de Jong, P. J. (2024). Repeated exposure to body-related memories in women with high body-related self-disgust: Impact on disgust, avoidance, and acceptance. *Behaviour Research and Therapy, 175*, 104496. https://doi.org/10.1016/j.brat.2024.104496

Waller, G., & Mountford, V. A. (2015). Weighing patients within cognitive-behavioural therapy for eating disorders: How, when and why. *Behaviour Research and Therapy, 70,* 1–10. https://dx.doi.org/10.1016/j.brat.2015.04.004

Walsh B. T. (2013). The enigmatic persistence of anorexia nervosa. *American Journal of Psychiatry, 170*(5), 477–484. https:/ss1/doi.org/10.1176/appi.ajp.2012.12081074

Chapter 4

The Anorexic Voice

John R.E. Fox and Marc O. Williams

Introduction

Anorexia nervosa (AN) remains one of the most serious mental health conditions, with mortality rates higher than any other psychiatric condition (Arcelus et al., 2011; Klump et al., 2009). Treatment outcomes remain modest and relapse rates remain worryingly high (e.g. Dobrescu et al., 2019; Zipfel et al., 2015). It is clear that there is a need to improve our theoretical understanding of AN so that we develop better, more person-centred treatments for individuals with AN. There has been a trend in the research literature to consider the meaning of AN for the sufferer, as a number of authors have discussed that AN is an ego-syntonic condition that has a profound impact upon the self and identity (e.g. Higbed & Fox, 2010; Geller et al., 2001), but the precise processes that link AN, identity and severity remain unclear.

Phenomenological Aspects of the Anorexic Voice

For those living with AN – whether personally or as a family member – it can feel both confusing and frightening. Perhaps most confusing is how someone with AN courts something that is visibly harming them. Families and professionals often ask why someone would be determined to starve themselves, especially when the consequences are so stark. This paradox was summed up by an AN pioneer, Hilde Bruch, who was one of the first people to study AN. While some of her ideas have since been challenged, her writing in *The Golden Cage* (Bruch, 1978) remains an insightful reflection on the lived experience of AN. In the opening chapter, she shares a letter from the mother of a 20-year-old who had been unwell with AN for five years. 'You watch your child deliberately hurting herself and obviously suffering and yet, you are unable to help her' (Bruch, 1978, p. 1). Even in these early accounts, AN was recognised as involving a harsh internal world, dominated by extremely punitive and critical thoughts about body image, eating, as well as other aspects of life such as schoolwork and relationships. Bruch discussed how these heavily distorted and critical thoughts drive the restriction of food and create the sense that nothing is ever good enough. By noting the presence of these punitive

DOI: 10.4324/9781003468189-5

thoughts, Bruch (1978) was one of the first authors to recognise these internal conflicts within AN and it is these extremely critical dialogues between parts of the self that fuel AN. In many ways, Bruch's writings foreshadowed what would come to be referred to as the first accounts of the AV – though the concept would not be formally explored until the 21st century.

Since 2010, there has been a growth of interest in the AV with a number of authors working on its phenomenological and relational aspects (e.g. Tierney & Fox, 2010; Pugh, 2016). These authors found that people with anorexic presentations often reported hearing a 'voice' which was highly distressing and often extremely critical to the self (in keeping with Bruch's observations). The AV can be characterised as 'a hostile and abusive presence', which undermines the individual's self-esteem and encourages destructive patterns of eating (Pugh, 2016, p. 76). Many individuals with eating disorders – including those with AN – report experiencing an internal 'voice' relating to eating, weight, and shape (e.g. Tierney & Fox, 2010; Pugh, 2016). Although the precise prevalence of the AV *per se* is not clearly quantified, broader studies suggest that a large majority of those with eating disorders more broadly have had the experience of a critical inner 'voice' (95%; Noordenbos et al., 2014). Crucially, the AV does not appear to be a psychotic voice as most individuals recognise that the AV is internally generated and, as such, is not perceived to originate from external sources or entities (e.g. God or some mythical being) (Pugh et al., 2016). Although it is not perceived as being generated by an external agent, reports do highlight how it can still be perceived as being both ego-syntonic and ego-dystonic, as some people with AN describe it as being 'alien to the self', manifesting as second- or third-person commentary on weight, shape, and eating (Pugh et al., 2016).

Pugh et al. (2016) also discussed that the AV is not a static phenomenon, as it can change over time, both in terms of its nature and intensity. In the early stages of the eating disorder, it appears that the AV is perceived as being both functional/adaptive as it gives the impression of providing comfort and security. However, as time passes, the AV changes as it becomes critical and hostile (Tierney & Fox, 2010). Some of these temporal shifts may well be due to the biological difficulty in maintaining a severely restrictive diet, but these biological factors are further compounded by the relational aspects of living with the AV. This interaction was discussed by Tierney and Fox (2011) where they highlighted that the AV has an insidious relationship with the self, as it will gradually enter the person's consciousness by being a comfort and support for the person, but this changes over time as the AV becomes very critical and forces the person to push their bodies and self-control to marked extremes. This conflict between the AV's relentless drive to push the person to go further and resist the biological needs of their bodies creates a situation where some are no longer able to meet these demands while others adopt an unquestioning obedience. Over time, the AV starts to strip the person's sense of autonomy and efficacy, as it is constantly commenting upon the person's perceived failures which reduces self-reliance and trust in their own abilities. This process of how the AV leaves the sufferer feeling incompetent and without a defined sense of themself as a separate/autonomous individual will be picked up later in the chapter. Tierney and Fox (2011) reported on how their participants shared that this relational tension between their AV and the self led them to withdraw into their AN by giving up their previous life, such as socialising, enjoying hobbies, etc. In other words, the AV starts to become increasingly dominant and unforgiving, which then reinforces the gradual loss of the person's previous life. Tierney and Fox (2011) discussed how the dynamic with the AV echoes that of relationships where there is domestic violence. For example, as the AV becomes increasingly dominant, the relationship becomes increasingly one-sided with the person living in fear and intimidation from the AV. People start to respond to the voice in a submissive way or perceiving the AV as being powerful (e.g. Hormoz et al., 2019). In a rather worrying twist for the treating clinician, the dialogical aspect of the relationship is highlighted by how the AV will try and seduce the person back into AN if they try to start eating normally (Duncan et al., 2015; Fox et al., 2012). Thus the AV is not just a set of critical thoughts but – phenomenologically – one side of an abusive and controlling relationship with the self.

However, questions remain about the AV. For example, how does it account for the fact that the vast majority of AN sufferers are female? Are there specific, gendered factors that start to explain why women and girls are not only more susceptible to AN, but also to some of the internal mechanisms, such as the AV? Across this chapter, it will be argued that this is in part due to the way that Western society objectifies female bodies. Furthermore, women and girls are significantly more likely to experience childhood and adult interpersonal trauma, such as childhood sexual abuse. It will be argued that these societal factors interact with early trauma to play a significant role in the development of AN.

The Objectification of the Female Body: Impact on Body Shame and Self-Perception

It is well-established that AN affects vastly more women and girls, whose lifetime prevalence of AN stands at 4%, whereas for boys and men this figure is far lower at 0.3% (van Eeden et al., 2021). Any discussion of what leads to and maintains AN needs to consider these gender differences in prevalence. Not only does this disparity suggest a role for differences in the challenges of living for different genders, but it also raises the question of how the world views the female body and more traditionally 'female' roles in society. Fox et al. (2015) discussed how feminist theory proposes that society objectifies female bodies as sexual objects which become introjected over time, in which girls and women may adopt this way of looking at themselves, leading to self-objectification (Fredrickson & Roberts, 1997). Furthermore, and rather worryingly, these levels of objectification of the female body are potentially increasing with the prevalence of social media (see Vandenbosch et al., 2022). Fredrickson and Roberts (1997) found that women were much more likely to self-objectify than men and this was related to higher levels of shame, body disgust, and self-criticism in women than men. Importantly, shame has continually been shown to be higher within eating disorder populations even when compared to other psychiatric conditions (e.g. Nechita et al., 2021). Fox et al. (2015) argue that these gendered high levels of shame are linked to not just the objectification of the female body, but the near impossible positions that women often inhabit within modern society. For example, women often work within demanding jobs, but are still the main providers of care at home, while also being 'expected' to be slim and attractive. There is a paradox in which cosmetic surgery is normalised and encouraged, but women who undergo these procedures attract condemnation (Bonell et al., 2021). Fox et al. (2015) argue that these social processes have a profound impact upon women and girls as these interactions give rise to an 'emotional tone of contempt and criticism' that is internalised, leading to the development of an 'internal critical voice' which reinforces the sense of failure, self-criticism, and shame (p. 175, 179). These internal 'voices' can potentially exert high levels of shame, especially upon the body and it is, perhaps, not hard to see that, with a few extra ingredients, this can then lead to the development of AN with a hostile AV. One of these crucial ingredients may be trauma and this is where we turn our attention to next in this chapter.

Trauma and Anorexia Nervosa

At the end of the previous section, it was proposed that trauma may make a significant contribution to the understanding of the origins of the AV. Before discussing the specifics of the relation between trauma and AN, it is important to point out that women and girls experience significantly more abuse (with the exception of physical abuse) than men and boys (see Moody et al., 2018). Given that women are likely to have significantly higher levels of self-objectification (as discussed in the previous section) than men, the higher prevalence of trauma is another potentially important factor in understanding the gender split in eating disorders and AN. Within broader mental health, trauma theory and the development of the complex PTSD concept have been hugely influential (see Herman, 1992). This has led to the development of trauma-informed practices that see a clear aetiological role for trauma in mental health difficulties. For example, up to 85% of people with a diagnosis of psychosis report a history of trauma (e.g. sexual or physical abuse, witnessing or being involved in domestic abuse, emotional neglect, and bullying) (Larkin & Morrison, 2006; Read et al., 2005; Read & Bentall, 2012). Porter et al. (2020) reported that around 70% of individuals with a diagnosis of borderline personality disorder reported one adverse childhood experience at least. In depression, research has shown a clear dose effect of childhood trauma with more severe trauma having a stronger link with depression (e.g. Nelson et al. 2017). Despite the fact that childhood trauma is a significant risk factor for general poor mental health, the question remains whether it can be considered a specific risk factor for eating disorders and, if so, which trauma typology is specific to AN? This will be considered now.

Sexual Abuse

Across a number of recent reviews (e.g. Molendijk et al., 2017), individuals with eating disorders were significantly more likely to report a history of adversity than psychiatric controls. When different subgroups of eating disorders were considered, people with bulimia nervosa (BN) reported higher childhood sexual abuse (CSA) and childhood emotional abuse (CEA), while those with binge eating disorder (BED) were more likely to report all forms of abuse compared to healthy controls (i.e. CSA, childhood physical abuse [CPA], and CEA). However, there was an important nuance within this literature as it is not necessarily specific diagnoses that are linked to specific trauma histories; rather, it is certain ED symptom clusters, such as bingeing and vomiting. Within the review of Molendijk et al. (2017), those with AN binge-purge subtype were more likely to report CSA than those with the restrictive subtype. In keeping with Holman (2012), these findings suggest that people with histories of sexual abuse may develop an array of maladaptive coping strategies to manage the emotional consequences of the abuse and trauma that they have suffered.

Abuse and Neglect

Specific patterns of CPA and neglect are associated with a significant increase in risk for developing an eating disorder, especially BN where a dose-response effect was observed (e.g. Norman et al., 2012). The findings from the research literature are more mixed for the linkage between CEA and eating disorders, as Kimber at al. (2017) highlighted a range of weak to strong associations between CEA and eating disorders (including childhood neglect). There are real issues in defining emotional abuse and neglect, due to the very subjective way they are experienced by the person concerned, and this is likely to be influencing the patterns of research findings in this area. However, it is noteworthy to see that for more objective forms of CSA, neglect, and childhood trauma (e.g. witnessing domestic violence), there are much stronger associations with eating disorders. When AN is considered specifically, there are some interesting nuances in the findings within the research literature, including that individuals with AN are more likely to report CPA and CEA than controls (e.g. Molendijk et al, 2017). Pike et al. (2008) undertook a case-control study looking at risk factors for AN where 50 people with AN were compared to 50 psychiatric controls and 50 non-psychiatric controls. They found evidence that perfectionism, family discord, and high levels of parental demands were specifically linked to AN even when compared to other psychiatric groups. Interestingly, the pattern of experiencing emotional abuse, living with high levels of family disagreement and high parental demands appear to be potentially exacerbated by bullying at school. Research indicates that people with eating disorders are two to three times more likely to have experienced bullying and appearance-related teasing in childhood before their eating disorder has started (Sweetingham & Waller, 2007).

Childhood Trauma: Problems with Self-Development, Dissociation, and the Anorexic Voice

As detailed in the previous section, there is evidence linking emotional abuse/neglect with AN, although this research requires further replication. Furthermore, as yet it is not well understood what processes might link early trauma with the development of AN. Understanding these processes is crucial in developing a coherent theoretical account of both AN and AV. As discussed by Briere (1996) and Herman (1992), it is likely that early trauma leads to problems with self-identity and interpersonal functioning but, via introjection, these experiences are also more likely to lead to the AV. However, in order to develop a theoretical understanding of trauma, AV and the self, it is important to briefly discuss what the key ingredients are for the normal development of the self across childhood. The 'self' (operationalised as self-concept) has been described as knowledge individuals gain by paying close attention to their internal world and their responses to it (Baumeister, 2011). It is this knowledge about the self, including both emotional and cognitive responses to events, situations, and relationships, that ultimately forms the foundation of personal identity. While a full account of childhood self-development is beyond the scope of this chapter, it is worth noting that children develop their own sense of self through their experiences with their families, especially their parents and their peers (Erickson, 1959). Furthermore, these experiences are dynamic, shaped by ongoing changes and tensions, especially during adolescence (Erikson, 1959). As discussed above, these experiences are internalised over time, shaping not only how individuals relate to themselves and others, but also their expectations of how others will relate to them.

Trauma, Dissociation, and Personality Development

Herman (1992) and Briere (1996) have argued that the most damaging impacts of childhood trauma on self-development arise from disturbed attachment relationships and emotional dysregulation. Forming secure attachments is an innate need, and these early relationships provide the foundation for learning to regulate emotions. Through attunement and 'mirroring', caregivers help the child build a coherent sense of emotional self. Within this relational dialogue, the child begins to experience themselves as an autonomous being, capable of influencing their environment (Fonagy et al., 2004). Over time, these experiences form the building blocks of a personal narrative (for example, 'I like to play the piano and I know I'm good at it') which, with 'good enough parenting' (Winnicott, 1964), helps shape a stable identity and emotional repertoire.

Trauma profoundly disrupts these processes. Children exposed to abuse or neglect may internalise harmful messages about their worth, develop insecure or disorganised attachments, and struggle to identify or regulate their emotions. As Holman (2012) notes, it is often the internalised narrative – 'I am bad' or 'I am unlovable' – that leaves the deepest scars. Emotional responses become confusing or overwhelming rather than informative. Given that so much of our self-understanding comes from how we feel and what we enjoy, such emotional disconnection can impair identity development. It is this profound disruption to the child's developing narrative about the self that is so damaging to the sense of self. This leads to problems with trust, difficulties in learning how to navigate relationships safely, and feeling overwhelmed by one's emotions. As we have already seen, there is a relationship between the more emotional types of abuse (e.g. family discord, high demand, criticism) and AN. Theoretically, it is likely that these early histories play a significant role in some of the common features of AN, such as alexithymia, perfectionism/self-criticism, and the AV.

Over the last few years, several studies have explored the relationship between early childhood trauma and the AV. Tierney and Fox (2011), using thematic analysis of interviews with 21 individuals diagnosed with AN, highlighted how the AV was often rooted in earlier relational experiences. More recently, Morrison et al. (2022) developed a grounded theory examining this link in women with histories of childhood trauma. Initially, the AV offered a sense of comfort and containment (echoing the earlier findings of Tierney & Fox, 2011), but it gradually became toxic, punitive, and controlling. Participants described how the AV mirrored the harmful relational dynamics they had experienced in childhood. It also began to shape their self-identity, offering a distorted sense of purpose and competence – something they could excel at. Over time, this contributed to increasing disconnection from others, further entrenching both the AV and the anorexia.

Pugh et al. (2018) explored the relationship between the AV, dissociation, and early trauma. Drawing on research into psychosis, they considered how dissociation may play a key role in the experience of voice hearing. The trauma-dissociation model (TDM) of voice hearing (e.g. Longden et al., 2012) suggests that internal voices may represent decontextualised thoughts and feelings rooted in early trauma, which, through dissociative processes, become intrusive and take on the quality of external voices. In this way, voices can become embodied representations of traumatic experiences – a finding that closely aligns with the work of Morrison et al. (2022). In their study, Pugh et al. found that the perceived power of the AV was associated with experiences of CEA, and that this relationship was partially mediated by dissociation. These findings build on earlier research linking heightened AV criticism to more negative eating attitudes (Pugh & Waller, 2017), and highlight dissociation as a potential mechanism through which early trauma becomes embedded in the lived experience of AN.

Summary

Over this section, it has been argued that women and girls experience a world fraught with significant gendered challenges. The work of Fredrickson and Roberts (1997) highlights how female bodies are objectified, leading women and girls to absorb and internalise this message. This internalisation exacerbates a propensity toward self-criticism, in which one judges oneself by society's harsh standards.

This, we propose, is a vulnerability factor for developing AN. The AV reflects AN-related concerns, such as eating, weight, and shape, but is a compelling relational experience in its own right. There is evidence that additional experiences, including early trauma, are compounding factors that may increase the likelihood of experiencing the AV. As pointed out by Kent and Waller (2000) and Holman (2012), particular types of abuse are particularly challenging for the developing child, as they leave the child with a sense that they are 'bad', 'flawed', or 'worthless' as they often internalise these experiences as being justified or right due to them often coming from significant attachment figures. Furthermore, these experiences are often reinforced by childhood bullying at school (see Sweetingham & Waller, 2007), which 'confirm' these profoundly negative core beliefs. These experiences are deeply distressing to the child and they often adopt basic/primitive ways to cope such as dissociation and emotional suppression.

Theoretical Understanding of the Anorexic Voice

The AV has been conceptualised as closely linked to the development of the self and its emotional foundations. Fox et al. (2012) developed the SPAARS-ED model, integrating Power and Dalgleish's (2008) SPAARS framework with Deci and Ryan's (2002) Self-Determination Theory. Within this framework, the AV is viewed as a phenomenological representation of distorted emotional processes rooted in early life experience – particularly in relation to unmet core psychological needs.

SPAARS-ED presents emotions as rapid appraisal systems that help the self-monitor progress toward broad life goals – such as success, connection, and autonomy – across domains of self, others, and the world. These needs are typically nurtured through secure early attachments, allowing extrinsic motivations (e.g. learning from guidance) to be internalised into intrinsic motivations over time. Disruptions in early attachment may interfere with this internalisation process. Instead of developing a stable internal guide grounded in emotional understanding, the person may develop alternative strategies to cope with unmet needs – such as through the AV. In this way, the AV can be seen as a rigid, critical internal voice that mimics unmet relational needs, offering a distorted form of competence, control, or belonging.

As Fox et al. (2012) highlight, much of the research on childhood trauma in AN is retrospective, and causality is likely to be complex and multifactorial. However, at a minimum, these studies suggest a 'poor fit' between child and caregiver – meaning the environment fails to meet the child's core psychological needs. Through the lens of Self-Determination Theory (Deci & Ryan, 2002), this poor fit may disrupt the development of autonomy and competence.

Empirical studies offer some support for this hypothesis. For example, individuals with AN have been found to share dismissive attachment styles with their mothers (Ward et al., 2000, 2001), and Cooper (2005) reported widespread parent-child attunement difficulties. While not all individuals with AN report overt trauma, many describe early experiences of emotional neglect or relational dysfunction, which are theoretically and clinically important.

According to Self-Determination Theory, children develop healthy motivation through the internalisation of values and behaviours initially shaped by caregivers. However, when caregiving is inconsistent, critical, or neglectful, children may instead introject these expectations – feeling compelled to meet them without fully integrating them into the self. These introjected demands are often ego-dystonic and can become internalised as critical self-talk or voices, which, according to Fox et al. (2012), may develop into the AV. This voice reinforces perfectionism and conditional self-worth, leaving individuals preoccupied with meeting others' standards for fear of abandonment or rejection.

The SPAARS-ED model also emphasises the role of maladaptive emotional processing. It proposes that emotional conflicts outside conscious awareness may fuel AV activity. For example, situations that elicit vulnerable emotions like sadness or anger may trigger heightened AV criticism – especially if accompanied by somatic discomfort such as feeling 'fat' or bloated (Fox et al., 2013). In cases of severe trauma, such as CSA, emotion regulation is further disrupted. Victims may dissociate from their bodies and emotions to cope, but unprocessed affect often becomes displaced onto the body – fuelling a punitive AV and intensifying eating disorder behaviours.

Clinical Implications/Recovery

The SPAARS-ED model of eating disorders has some clear treatment implications, some of which are clear general treatment factors when it comes to working with people with eating disorders. All good treatment plans for eating disorders, especially AN, emphasise that recovery needs to be based on solid nutrition and medical risk management. Once someone has reached some physical stabilisation, the SPAARS-ED model has two approaches, namely working directly with the AV and helping someone to develop their self-identity. A key feature of this work has been described by Fox et al. (2012) where emotions that have been avoided and/or suppressed need to be expressed as they are linked to unmet need. Authors, such as Pugh (2019), Fox et al. (2012), Dolhanty and Greenberg (2009), and Hibbs et al. (2021), describe the use of chair work (where a client is faced with an empty chair) where different parts of the self are 'placed in the chair' to process through dialogue. The use of an empty chair to place the AV is a powerful way of highlighting the function or the role that it has played in the individual's life. As we have discussed throughout this chapter, the AV represents a core unprocessed pain in a person's life and it has often developed as a powerful way to cope with significant challenges. It is the experience of the authors that the use of chairs to start a dialogue between the self and the AV is a powerful process that allows unvoiced emotions and beliefs to be expressed (see Hibbs et al., 2021). It may be helpful within this stage of treatment to provide some specific trauma work if warranted. Crucially, this use of chairs will also allow the therapist to incorporate a level of compassion and to help the person develop a response to the voice to allow the self to develop.

This final area of work is about providing an alternative to the anorexic identity that the AV has been cultivating via a process of internalising and withdrawing from the external world. Within the work of Geller et al. (2012) on severe and enduring eating disorders, there are helpful pointers in promoting self-development away from the eating disorder. These authors argue about the importance of clinicians needing to 'wear many hats', as they must keep strict boundaries, especially around physical health while cheering on interests and hobbies that help take the individual away from their eating disorder. In many ways, the SPAARS-ED model highlights how it is vitally important for someone to start to feel competent but, most importantly, autonomous. This area of therapeutic work is important for helping the person to move on from their AN, but they may not be able to do this easily without addressing the suppressing/bullying AV.

Conclusion

As we have seen throughout this chapter, the AV is a critical internal dialogue often experienced by people with AN. Although it initially appears supportive, it becomes increasingly hostile and controlling, similar to an abusive relationship. It has been argued that the AV develops through the interaction of societal objectification of female bodies, childhood trauma, and disrupted attachment patterns. These experiences become introjected rather than properly internalised, creating an ego-dystonic voice that drives perfectionism and social withdrawal. By keeping the person internally focused, the AV starts to limit their social interactions and, thus, prevent the development of external interests. One of the most problematic aspects of this withdrawal from the world is that it encourages further reliance upon the AV for both company and guidance (see Higbed & Fox, 2010 and Williams et al., 2016). While treatment first requires physical stabilisation, two key approaches may be beneficial for psychological recovery: direct work with the AV (e.g., using chair work techniques to create dialogue between self and voice), and developing autonomous self-identity through encouraging interests and hobbies outside the eating disorder. Therapists must balance strict health boundaries with compassionate support for non-eating disorder activities and competencies.

References

Arcelus, J., Mitchell, A. J., Wales, J., & Nielsen, S. (2011). Mortality rates in patients with anorexia nervosa and other eating disorders. A meta-analysis of 36 studies. *Archives of General Psychiatry*, *68*(7), 724–731.

Baumeister, R. F. (2011). Self and identity: A brief overview of what they are, what they do, and how they work. *Annals of the New York Academy of Sciences*, *1234*(1), 48–55. https://doi.org/10.1111/j.1749-6632.2011.06224.x

Bonell, S., Barlow, F. K., & Griffiths, S. (2021). The cosmetic surgery paradox: Toward a contemporary understanding of cosmetic surgery popularisation and attitudes. *Body Image*, 38, 230–240. https://doi.org/10.1016/j.bodyim.2021.04.008

Briere, J. (1996). *Therapy for adults molested as children: Beyond survival*. Springer Publishing Company.

Bruch, H. (1978). *The golden cage: The enigma of anorexia nervosa*. Harvard University Press.

Cooper, M. (2005). Cognitive theory in anorexia nervosa and bulimia nervosa: Progress, development and future directions. *Clinical Psychology Review*, *25*(4), 511–531. https://doi.org/10.1016/j.cpr.2005.01.003

Deci, E. L., & Ryan, R. M. (2002). *Handbook of self-determination research*. University of Rochester Press.

Dobrescu, S. R., Dinkler, L., Gillberg, C., Råstam, M., Gillberg, C., & Wentz, E. (2019). Anorexia nervosa: 30-year outcome. *British Journal of Psychiatry*, *216*(2), 97–104. https://doi.org/10.1192/bjp.2019.113

Dolhanty, J., & Greenberg, L. S. (2009). Emotion-focused therapy in a case of anorexia nervosa. *Clinical Psychology and Psychotherapy*, *16*(4), 366–82. https://doi.org/10.1002/cpp.624

Duncan, T. K., Sebar, B., & Lee, J. (2015). Reconstruing anorexia: An analysis of pro-anorexia websites. *Advances in Eating Disorders*, *3*(1), 5–16. https://doi.org/10.1080/21662630.2014.912018

Erikson, E. H. (1959). *Identity and the life cycle*. International Universities Press.

Fonagy, P., Gergely, G., Jurist, E., & Target, M. (2004). *Affect regulation, mentalization, and the development of the self*. Karnac Books.

Fox, J. R. E., Federici, A., & Power, M. J. (2012). Emotions and eating disorders. In J. R. E. Fox & K. P. Goss (Eds.), *Eating and its disorders* (Chapter 12). Wiley-Blackwell. https://doi.org/10.1002/9781118328910.ch12

Fox, J. R., Grange, N., & Power, M. J. (2015). Self-disgust in eating disorders: A review of the literature and clinical implications. In P. A. Powell, P. G. Overton, & J. Simpson (Eds.), *The revolting self* (pp. 167–186). Routledge. https://doi.org/10.4324/9780429483042-9

Fox, J. R., Smithson, E., Baillie, S., Ferreira, N., Mayr, I., & Power, M. J. (2013). Emotion coupling and regulation in anorexia nervosa. *Clinical Psychology and Psychotherapy*, *20*(4), 319–333. https://doi.org/10.1002/cpp.1823

Fredrickson, B. L., & Roberts, T. A. (1997). Objectification theory: Toward understanding women's lived experiences and mental health risks. *Psychology of Women Quarterly*, *21*(2), 173–206. https://doi.org/10.1111/j.1471-6402.1997.tb00108.x

Geller, J., Cockell, S. J., & Drab, D. L. (2001). Assessing readiness for change in the eating disorders: The psychometric properties of the readiness and motivation interview. *Psychological Assessment*, *13*(2), 189–198. https://doi.org/10.1037/1040-3590.13.2.189

Geller, J., Srikameswaran, S., Zelichowska, J. and Williams, K.D. (2012). Working with Severe and Enduring Eating Disorders: Enhancing Engagement and Matching Treatment to Client Readiness. In Fox, J. and Goss, K. Eating and its Disorders. Wiley Series in Clinical Psychology. Wiley-Blackwell: Chichester.

Herman, J. L. (1992). *Trauma and recovery: The aftermath of violence–from domestic abuse to political terror*. Basic Books.

Hibbs, R., Pugh, M., & Fox, J. R. E. (2021). Applying emotion-focused therapy to work with the "anorexic voice" within anorexia nervosa: A brief intervention. *Journal of Psychotherapy Integration, 31*(4), 327–347. https://doi.org/10.1037/int0000252

Higbed, L., & Fox, J. R. (2010). Illness perceptions in anorexia nervosa: A qualitative investigation. *British Journal of Clinical Psychology, 49*(3), 307–325. https://doi.org/10.1348/014466509X454598

Holman, C. (2012). Trauma and eating disorders. In J. R. E. Fox & K. P. Goss (Eds.), Eating and its disorders. https://doi.org/10.1002/9781118328910.ch10

Hormoz, E., Pugh, M., & Waller, G. (2019). Do eating disorder voice characteristics predict treatment outcomes in anorexia nervosa? A pilot study. *Cognitive Behaviour Therapy, 48*(2), 137–145. https://doi.org/10.1080/16506073.2018.1476581

Kent, A., & Waller, G. (2000). Childhood emotional abuse and eating psychopathology. *Clinical Psychology Review, 20*(7), 887–903. https://doi.org/10.1016/S0272-7358(99)00018-5

Kimber, M., McTavish, J. R., Couturier, J., Boven, A., Gill, S., Dimitropoulos, G., & MacMillan, H. L. (2017). Consequences of child emotional abuse, emotional neglect and exposure to intimate partner violence for eating disorders: A systematic critical review. *BMC Psychology, 5*(1), 33. https://doi.org/10.1186/s40359-017-0202-3

Klump, K. L., Bulik, C. M., Kaye, W. H., Treasure, J., & Tyson, E. (2009). Academy for eating disorders position paper: Eating disorders are serious mental illnesses. *International Journal of Eating Disorders, 42*(2), 97–103. https://doi.org/10.1002/eat.20589

Larkin, W., & Morrison, A. P. (2006). *Trauma and psychosis: New directions for theory and therapy*. Routledge.

Longden, E., Madill, A., & Waterman, M. G. (2012). Dissociation, trauma, and the role of lived experience: Toward a new conceptualization of voice hearing. *Psychological Bulletin, 138*(1), 28–76. https://doi.org/10.1037/a0025995

Molendijk, M. L., Hoek, H. W., Brewerton, T. D., & Elzinga, B. M. (2017). Childhood maltreatment and eating disorder pathology: A systematic review and dose-response meta-analysis. *Psychological Medicine, 47*(8), 1402–1416. https://doi.org/10.1017/S0033291716003561

Moody, G., Cannings-John, R., Hood, K., Kemp, A., & Robling, M. (2018). Establishing the international prevalence of self-reported child maltreatment: A systematic review by maltreatment type and gender. *BMC Public Health, 18*(1), 1164. https://doi.org/10.1186/s12889-018-6044-y

Morrison, J., Williams, M. O., & Fox, J. R. E. (2022). Negative childhood events and the development of the anorexic voice: A grounded theory. *Psychology and Psychotherapy: Theory, Research and Practice, 95*, 1018–1035. https://doi.org/10.1111/papt.12416

Nechita, D. M., Bud, S., & David, D. (2021). Shame and eating disorders symptoms: A meta-analysis. *International Journal of Eating Disorders, 54*(11), 1899–1945.

Nelson, J., Klumparendt, A., Doebler, P., & Ehring, T. (2017). Childhood maltreatment and characteristics of adult depression: Meta-analysis. *British Journal of Psychiatry, 210*(2), 96–104. https://doi.org/10.1192/bjp.bp.115.180752

Noordenbos, G., Aliakbari, N., & Campbell, R. (2014). The relationship among critical inner voices, low self-esteem, and self-criticism in eating disorders. *Eating Disorders, 22*(4), 337–351.

Norman, R. E., Byambaa, M., De, R., Butchart, A., Scott, J., & Vos, T. (2012). The long-term health consequences of child physical abuse, emotional abuse, and neglect: A systematic review and meta-analysis. *PLoS Medicine*, *9*(11), e1001349. https://doi.org/10.1371/journal.pmed.1001349

Pike, K. M., Hilbert, A., Wilfley, D. E., Fairburn, C. G., Dohm, F. A., Walsh, B. T., & Striegel-Moore, R. (2008). Toward an understanding of risk factors for anorexia nervosa: A case-control study. *Psychological Medicine*, *38*(10), 1443–1453. https://doi.org/10.1017/S0033291707002310

Porter, C., Palmier-Claus, J., Branitsky, A., Mansell, W., Warwick, H., & Varese, F. (2020). Childhood adversity and borderline personality disorder: A meta-analysis. *Acta Psychiatrica Scandinavica*, *141*(1), 6–20. https://doi.org/10.1111/acps.13118

Power, M. J., & Dalgleish, T. (2008). *Cognition and emotion: From order to disorder*. Psychology Press.

Pugh, M., & Waller, G. (2016). The anorexic voice and severity of eating pathology in anorexia nervosa. *International Journal of Eating Disorders*, *49*, 622–625. https://doi.org/10.1002/eat.22499

Pugh, M., & Waller, G. (2017). Understanding the "anorexic voice" in anorexia nervosa. *Clinical Psychology and Psychotherapy*, *24*, 670–676. https://doi.org/10.1002/cpp.2034

Pugh, M., Waller, G., & Esposito, M. (2018). Childhood trauma, dissociation, and the internal eating disorder "voice". *Child Abuse & Neglect*, *86*, 197–205. https://doi.org/10.1016/j.chiabu.2018.10.005

Read, J., & Bentall, R. P. (2012). Negative childhood experiences and mental health: Theoretical, clinical and primary prevention implications. *British Journal of Psychiatry*, *200*(2), 89–91. https://doi.org/10.1192/bjp.bp.111.096727

Read, J., van Os, J., Morrison, A. P., & Ross, C. A. (2005). Childhood trauma, psychosis and schizophrenia: A literature review with theoretical and clinical implications. *Acta Psychiatrica Scandinavica*, *112*(5), 330–350. https://doi.org/10.1111/j.1600-0447.2005.00634.x

Sweetingham, R., & Waller, G. (2007). Childhood experiences of being bullied and teased in the eating disorders. *European Eating Disorders Review*, *16*(5), 401–407. https://doi.org/10.1002/erv.839

Tierney, S., & Fox, J. R. (2010). Living with the anorexic voice: A thematic analysis. *Psychology and Psychotherapy*, *83*(3), 243–254. https://doi.org/10.1348/147608309X480172

Tierney S & Fox JRE (2011) Trapped in a toxic relationship: comparing the views of women living with anorexia nervosa to those experiencing domestic violence. *Journal of Gender Studies*, *20*(1), 31–41.

van Eeden, A. E., van Hoeken, D., & Hoek, H. W. (2021). Incidence, prevalence and mortality of anorexia nervosa and bulimia nervosa. *Current Opinion in Psychiatry*, *34*(6), 515–524. https://doi.org/10.1097/YCO.0000000000000739

Vandenbosch, L., Fardouly, J., & Tiggemann, M. (2022). Social media and body image: Recent trends and future directions. *Current Opinion in Psychology*, *45*, 101289. https://doi.org/10.1016/j.copsyc.2021.12.002

Ward, A., Ramsay, R., & Treasure, J. (2000). Attachment research in eating disorders. *British Journal of Medical Psychology*, *73*(1), 35–51. https://doi.org/10.1348/000711200160282

Ward, A., Ramsay, R., Turnbull, S., Steele, M., Steele, H., & Treasure, J. (2001). Attachment in anorexia nervosa: A transgenerational perspective. *British Journal of Medical Psychology*, *74*, 497–505. https://doi.org/10.1348/000711201161145

Williams, K., King, J., & Fox, J. R. (2016). Sense of self and anorexia nervosa: A grounded theory. *Psychology and Psychotherapy: Theory, Research and Practice*, *89*(2), 211–228. https://doi.org/10.1111/papt.12068

Winnicott, D. W. (1964). *The child, the family and the outside world.* Penguin Books.

Zipfel, S., Giel, K. E., Bulik, C. M., Hay, P., & Schmidt, U. (2015). Anorexia nervosa: Aetiology, assessment, and treatment. *The Lancet Psychiatry*, *2*(12), 1099–1111. https://doi.org/10.1016/S2215-0366(15)00356-9

Chapter 5

Autism and Identity

Sarah L. Field, Marc O. Williams, and Will Mandy

Introduction

Autism is a term describing a spectrum of neurodevelopmental differences encompassing differences in social communication, repetitive interests and behaviours, and sensory experience (American Psychiatric Association, 2013). Theoretical perspectives on autism have shifted over the past decade (Pellicano & den Houting, 2022), although autistic academics and self-advocates have proposed a change in perspective for significantly longer (Sinclair, 1993; Singer, 1998).

Until recently, a 'pathology model' predominated professional and public understandings of autism (Mandy, 2023). This held that autism should be understood as a collection of deficits relative to non-autistic people, and that the ultimate goal of interventions should be the reduction of autistic symptoms and behaviour (Fletcher-Watson & Happé, 2019; Pellicano & den Houting, 2022). Recently, a contrasting 'neurodiversity paradigm' has grown in influence. This posits that there is a broad spectrum of cognitive development encompassing both typical neurotypes and those tending to attract diagnoses such as autism and attention deficit/hyperactivity disorder (ADHD). Within this neurodiversity framework, autism (and other neurodevelopmental conditions) are seen as states of neurodivergence that should be understood as difference not disorder (Bagatell, 2010; Pellicano & den Houting, 2022; Singer, 1998). Consequences of the neurodiversity paradigm include shifts in the language used to describe autism towards that preferred by autistic people (Bury et al., 2022; Kenny et al., 2016; Sinclair, 2012), an increase in the meaningful participation of autistic people in research (Fletcher-Watson et al., 2018; Poulsen et al., 2022) and a move towards a view of autism as an immutable part of a person's identity (Bagatell, 2010; Botha et al., 2022; Cooper et al., 2017). Crucially, within the neurodiversity paradigm, the aim of treatment is not to make a person less autistic, but rather to promote outcomes (e.g., wellbeing, quality of life) that they value (Mandy, 2023).

It is important to recognise autistic people as a group who may have different experiences of health conditions, including anorexia nervosa (AN) and other eating disorders (EDs), because of their autistic experiences and identity. This chapter will explore the prevalence and treatment of AN in autistic people, consider

DOI: 10.4324/9781003468189-6

research into identity and body image in autistic people, the relationship between 'camouflaging' and mental health, and how these different factors might affect autistic people with AN.

Prevalence and Treatment Outcomes of Anorexia Nervosa in Autistic People

Gillberg (1983) initially observed similarities in the social and cognitive flexibility difficulties between autism and AN and hypothesised that there might be a relationship between the two presentations. Critiques of this theoretical overlap have suggested this may be due to the cognitive effects of starvation in acute AN (Katzman et al., 2001) and that social and cognitive difficulties in AN may superficially resemble, but not truly reflect, underlying autism (Hiller & Pellicano, 2013; Treasure, 2013). However, subsequent research has indicated that autistic traits and social difficulties in people with EDs are relatively stable over time (Boltri & Sapuppo, 2021; Nazar et al., 2018) and a higher than expected number of people with AN who have restored their weight continue to meet criteria for autism (Bentz et al., 2017). This suggests a relationship between autistic traits and AN beyond the acute effects of starvation alone.

Concerns have been raised about the generalisability of results from the extensively studied Swedish community-based sample of participants (Gillberg & Råstam, 1992; Nilsson et al., 1999). Additionally, much of the early research assesses autistic traits instead of using modern clinical diagnostic measures (Baron-Cohen et al., 2013; Hambrook et al., 2008; Tchanturia et al., 2013). These factors have cast doubt on the validity of the relationship between autism and AN. However, more recent studies using 'gold standard' autism diagnostic assessments also suggest an overrepresentation of autistic people amongst those diagnosed with AN (Kerr-Gaffney et al., 2020; Mandy & Tchanturia, 2015; Westwood et al., 2017); it is estimated that 20–37% of people with AN are autistic (Adamson et al., 2022; Huke et al., 2013; Westwood & Tchanturia, 2017). There is also a higher prevalence of AN and ED symptoms in the autistic population (Margari et al., 2019; Sedgewick et al., 2021). Overall, evidence suggests an increased prevalence of autism in people with AN.

In addition to the increased prevalence of AN in autistic people, the literature suggests autistic people with AN have higher levels of ED symptoms and poorer responses to ED treatment. People with higher levels of autistic traits appear to have longer illness durations (Babb et al., 2022; Saure et al., 2020), higher levels of ED psychopathology when admitted for treatment (Tchanturia et al., 2019), require more intensive treatment (Nazar et al., 2018), and have poorer psychological outcomes (Leppanen et al., 2022). After a 30-year follow-up, autistic adolescents with AN had worse outcomes than their non-autistic peers in terms of their mental health, independence from their families, social contact, and employment (Nielsen et al., 2022).

Poorer treatment outcomes could be due, in part, to conventional ED treatments not being adapted to autistic people's needs. Autistic people describe having unique needs relating to their autism which are not met by standard ED treatment (Brede et al., 2020; Kinnaird et al., 2019). Compared to non-autistic people, autistic people rated treatment as less beneficial and were particularly dissatisfied with inpatient care, dietetic input, and CBT (Babb et al., 2022). During treatment, autistic people felt their autistic behaviours were attributed to the ED and they were labelled as 'resistant' as a result (Babb et al., 2021). Autistic people also called for adaptations to interventions, communication, and service environments for ED care (Babb et al., 2021). The following sections consider the research on identity, body image, and camouflaging in autistic people and the implications of these insights for understanding and treating AN in this population.

Autism and Identity

Historically, research has not focused on autistic people's identity and sense of self. Researchers have typically posited that autistic people have deficits in their sense of self and self-awareness (Frith & Happé, 1999; Hobson, 2010; Williams, 2010), linked with difficulties in attributing mental states to themselves and others (theory of mind) (Baron-Cohen et al., 1985). It has been noted that the nature of this proposed deficit is somewhat contradictory (Zahavi, 2010), with researchers concluding that autistic children are both unaware of their own mental states (Baron-Cohen, 1989) and have a total focus on themselves (Baron-Cohen, 2005). Historically there has been a lack of qualitative research involving the self-reflections of autistic people (Botha, 2021; Jaswal & Akhtar, 2019; Milton & Bracher, 2013), possibly related to this assumed deficit. However, the theory that autistic individuals have an impaired sense of self conflicts with the wide body of autistic autobiographical work (Lilley et al., 2021; May, 2018; Page, 2009; Robison, 2008; Schneider, 1999). Qualitative research on the experiences of autistic people has increased in recent years (Bölte, 2014; van Schalkwyk & Dewinter, 2020), including research on the self and identity.

Predominantly, research has focussed on how people without EDs integrate autism into their wider identity. This has the potential to be particularly relevant to autistic people with EDs, as the majority do not have an autism diagnosis prior to presenting to ED services (Adamson et al., 2022; Babb et al., 2021; Brede et al., 2020; Kinnaird et al., 2019). Leedham et al. (2019) explored the experiences of women who received a diagnosis of autism in adulthood and noted the varying impact this had on identity. Autistic women described diagnosis as changing their perspectives on their lives and contextualising their previous difficulties. The women described this as allowing them to reduce the pressure on themselves to 'assimilate' or be an idealised version of themselves. Leedham et al. (2019) noted that many of the women appeared to become less self-critical and more self-compassionate. It is possible people with AN may find receiving an autism diagnosis helpful in understanding themselves and their difficulties with eating, and qualitative research corroborates this (Kinnaird et al., 2019). However, it is important to note that the impact of receiving an autism diagnosis on identity varies between individuals. Some noted little impact on their lives or described frustration about their difficulties being similar to prior to diagnosis (Corden et al., 2021; Leedham et al., 2019; Lilley et al., 2021).

Studies provide varying perspectives on how different autistic people view autism and being autistic. Qualitative research suggests many autistic adults view autism as central to their identity (Botha et al., 2022). Most participants viewed autism as inherently value-neutral in the same way as height or right/left-handedness, but described an awareness that society views autism negatively (Botha et al., 2022). Quantitative research suggests variation in how autistic people view autism, with individuals generating positive, neutral, and negative attributes when asked to describe autism (Cooper et al., 2021). Autistic individuals who described autism more positively were more likely to view autism as part of their identity and have positive collective self-esteem relating to this (Cooper et al., 2021). Autistic people on average have lower self-esteem than non-autistic people; however, those who identify more with autism as a social identity may have higher self-esteem (Cooper et al., 2017). Lower dissatisfaction with being autistic and higher pride in autism predicts higher self-esteem in autistic people (Corden et al., 2021) and positive autism identity is associated with higher wellbeing and lower anxiety, depression and stress (Davies et al., 2024). A higher number of years since diagnosis was associated with lower dissatisfaction with autism, suggesting that coming to terms with one's autistic identity may be a process which occurs over time (Corden et al., 2021).

Autistic people's views of autism and integration of this into identity may also vary depending on their age. Although research suggests many adults perceive diagnosis as central to their identity and contextualising their difficulties (Botha et al., 2022; Leedham et al., 2019), research involving adolescents suggests a more complex relationship. Although parents describe autism diagnosis as useful and improving understanding of their child, few adolescents describe the diagnosis as useful themselves (Ruiz Calzada et al., 2012). Autistic adolescents describe an awareness of being different from their peers (Mesa & Hamilton, 2022). While some adolescents identify positively with their diagnosis, others describe not wanting the 'label' or finding it 'oppressive' (Davies et al., 2024; Mesa & Hamilton, 2022). Adolescents describe wishing to be treated the same as their peers and wanting to hide their diagnosis from others (Mesa & Hamilton, 2022). Autistic adolescents often preferentially align with non-autistic culture and less than half mention autism when describing themselves (Cresswell & Cage, 2019). The difference between adults' and adolescents' relationship with autism could relate to several factors. Autistic adolescents' desire for similarity to their peers may reflect typical developmental pressures (Newman et al., 2006), but may also be affected by the age at which they learn about their diagnosis (Davies et al., 2024; Oredipe et al., 2022) and adjustment to it over time (Corden et al., 2021). It is important to consider the difference in how autistic adolescents may feel about diagnosis when working with adolescents with ED. As recognition of autism improves and reduces late diagnosis, it is possible this will change how people with AN feel about their autism as they are more likely to have been aware of it from adolescence. It is unclear how this may affect individuals' autistic identity or ED due to the lack of longitudinal research into how autistic identity changes over time.

Overall, the research suggests that receiving a diagnosis of autism can impact an individual's identity, with many adults describing diagnosis as significantly changing their understanding of themselves and their difficulties (Cooper et al., 2021; Corden et al., 2021; Leedham et al., 2019; Lilley et al., 2021) and this allowing more self-compassion (Leedham et al., 2019). Many adults feel that autism is central to their identity (Botha et al., 2022) although there is variation in how individuals view their autism, attaching positive, negative, and neutral labels to it (Cooper et al., 2021). Adolescents may experience autism diagnosis differently and may wish to conceal a 'label' which makes them different to their peers (Davies et al., 2024; Mesa & Hamilton, 2022). Where individuals positively identify with being autistic this appears to have a positive relationship with self-esteem (Cooper et al., 2017; Cooper et al., 2021; Corden et al., 2021). These factors may have a complex impact on autistic people with AN, who often have not received an autism diagnosis prior to presenting to ED services (Adamson et al., 2022; Babb et al., 2021; Brede et al., 2020; Kinnaird et al., 2019). If autistic people with AN can develop a positive autistic identity this may have a positive impact on their overall wellbeing. Weaknesses in the current literature include a lack of research into how autistic identity changes over time or how it differs across cultural contexts. Much of the existing research either does not ask participants if they have a co-occurring learning disability or actively excludes those with learning disabilities. Finally, there is a relative dearth of research into other aspects of identity which have been studied in non-autistic populations, such as occupational/professional identity (Skorikov & Vondracek, 2011) and ethnic/racial identity (Williams et al., 2020).

Autism and Body Image

An emerging area of identity research is that of body image in autism. The majority of research has explored the relationship between autistic traits and body image dissatisfaction in neurotypical populations, or body image in autistic people with EDs (Longhurst, 2023). People with higher levels of autistic traits appear to experience higher levels of body-image related difficulties (Galvin et al., 2022; Krumm et al., 2017; Mansour et al., 2016) although the evidence for this is preliminary and does not explore this in representative samples of autistic individuals (Longhurst, 2023). Early qualitative research suggests many autistic people without EDs experience body dissatisfaction similarly to non-autistic people in the form of negative thoughts and feelings about their appearance and a desire to change this (Healy et al., 2021; Jachyra et al., 2018). Quantitative research also suggests the prevalence of weight and shape concerns is similar between autistic and non-autistic people with restrictive EDs (Brede et al., 2024). Despite this, autistic individuals often describe body image concerns as a less significant feature of their ED (Babb et al., 2021; Brede et al., 2020). It has been suggested that this apparent inconsistency may represent a subset of autistic people with AN without weight and shape concerns or a qualitative difference in how autistic people with ED experience body image concerns (Brede et al., 2024).

Longhurst (2023) proposes three ways in which autistic people's experiences of negative body image may differ from non-autistic people. First, autistic people may consider their sensory experiences such as internal feelings of digestion as part of their body image (Longhurst, 2023; Longhurst et al., 2024). Autistic people describe a sense of separation between their mind and body and difficulties identifying with their external appearance (Longhurst et al., 2024). A further challenge is the unpredictability and uncontrollability of internal bodily sensations (Longhurst, 2023; Longhurst et al., 2024).

Second, Longhurst (2023) proposes that the relationship between low self-esteem and poor body image in autistic people may be particularly driven by social isolation. Autistic people link body image difficulties with their experiences of receiving stigmatising comments regarding their autism (Longhurst et al., 2024). Some autistic people may engage in negative appearance-related behaviours as a way to fit in or 'mask' (Healy et al., 2021).

Finally, Longhurst (2023) suggests autistic people might be affected by societal messages about appearance, but these messages might be processed differently, e.g., internalised as an inflexible rule. Although autistic people with ED appear to experience body image concerns to a similar extent as non-autistic people with ED, the lived experience of this may differ in important ways. This hypothesis warrants further empirical investigation.

It is also important to consider how positive body image might differ in autistic people, as this might affect our understanding of recovery from AN for this group. This may include autistic people needing to connect with their body in alternative ways such as through physical experience and embodying movement (Longhurst et al., 2024). Similarly to non-autistic people, autistic people describe having a positive body image via appreciation for the functionality of the body (Longhurst et al., 2024). Appreciating neurodivergent strengths such as intellect was also considered an important part of positive autistic body image (Longhurst et al., 2024). Some people described being able to be more distant or critical of societal norms about appearance and attributed this to their autism (Longhurst et al., 2024). This may partially explain why autistic people with AN describe appearance-related concerns less frequently than non-autistic people with AN (Brede et al., 2020). Many autistic people described striving for neutrality and willing acceptance of transient negative internal experiences such as overstimulation and considered this part of positive body image (Longhurst et al., 2024). Autistic people's experiences of positive body image are an important area for future research.

Autistic Identity, Camouflaging, and Mental Health

Although many people describe receiving an autism diagnosis as useful and helping them have a better understanding of themselves (Cooper et al., 2021; Corden et al., 2021; Leedham et al., 2019; Lilley et al., 2021), autistic people experience higher levels of many mental health difficulties than the general population (Lai et al., 2019). This suggests that after diagnosis many autistic people continue to experience challenges to their wellbeing. Many autistic people describe desiring but struggling to fit in with neurotypical social contexts (Bradley et al., 2021; Cage & Troxell-Whitman, 2019; Cook, Crane, Bourne et al., 2021; Hull et al., 2017; Livingston et al., 2019). Autistic people are more likely to experience bullying and rejection than neurotypical people (Wainscot et al., 2008). Some describe attempting to 'mask' or 'camouflage' by using strategies to attempt to hide autistic traits and appear more neurotypical or socially able (Field et al., 2024; Hull et al., 2019; Hull et al., 2017; Livingston et al., 2019). Camouflaging strategies are varied and highly individual but can include deliberately maintaining the appearance of eye contact, using pre-planned 'scripts' for conversation, and suppressing 'autistic' body language such as stimming (Cook, Crane, Hull et al., 2021).

Camouflaging has been linked with poor mental health (Cook, Hull et al., 2021), with some autistic people describing it leading to 'burn out' (Bradley et al., 2021; Livingston et al., 2019). Higher levels of self-reported camouflaging have been linked with higher levels of depression, anxiety, stress, and suicidal thoughts and behaviours (Beck et al., 2020; Bernardin et al., 2021; Cassidy et al., 2020). Recent research has also begun to link camouflaging with symptoms of disordered eating. Higher levels of self-reported camouflaging were found to predict higher levels of ED symptoms in a sample of autistic adults with and without diagnoses of a variety of EDs (Bradley et al., 2024). There was also a positive relationship between sensory sensitivities and ED symptomatology, but this explained only a small amount of variance compared to camouflaging (Bradley et al., 2024). It is important to understand how camouflaging may have a potential role in the development or maintenance of ED for autistic people with AN.

There are multiple possible theoretical explanations which may underlie the relationship between camouflaging and poor mental health. The Social Identity Approach (SIA), which combines social identity and self-categorisation theory (Tajfel & Turner, 1979), provides a framework for understanding both the relationship between positive autistic identity and higher self-esteem (Cooper et al., 2017; Cooper et al., 2021; Corden et al., 2021) and the context in which camouflaging may arise. The SIA posits that our sense of self and self-esteem is comprised of the interplay of multiple personal and group identities (Tajfel & Turner, 1979). We may emphasise or minimise different aspects of our identity depending on the context. It may be particularly necessary to minimise a group identity in contexts where this group is undesirable or stigmatised (Perry et al., 2022; Tajfel & Turner, 1979). Non-autistic people often associate autism with negative traits (Butler & Gillis, 2011; Wood & Freeth, 2016) and autistic people experience enacted social stigma such as others being less likely to want to share time and space with them (Botha et al., 2022; Turnock et al., 2022). As such, autistic people can be considered part of a stigmatised identity-based minority group (Botha & Frost, 2018). In this context, camouflaging can be understood through an SIA lens as an attempt to disassociate from the stigmatised group and 'pass' as non-autistic to avoid stigmatisation (Pearson & Rose, 2021; Perry et al., 2022). Greater perception of autism-related stigma is associated with higher levels of camouflaging in autistic adults (Perry et al., 2022). For a fuller discussion of stigma as understood by the SIA, see Chapter 8.

The experience of stigma itself is associated with poorer wellbeing and mental health. According to the Minority Stress Model (Meyer, 2003), stigmatised minority groups experience greater health disparities due to being both more likely to experience stressful life events and less likely to have access to resources to manage these events. Autistic people who experience higher levels of victimisation, rejection, and discrimination have lower psychological wellbeing and higher levels of distress (Botha & Frost, 2018). Stereotypes of autism have the potential to perpetuate the social isolation of autistic people, with loneliness linked to depression and anxiety in autistic people (Turnock et al., 2022). As a result, the relationship between camouflaging and mental health difficulties in autism could be partially understood as relating to the independent effect of stigma on both camouflaging and mental health.

Camouflaging may also have its own impact on mental health. Qualitative research into autistic people's experiences of camouflaging has been synthesised to generate a model of potential relationships between camouflaging and mental health (Field et al., 2024). Autistic people link camouflaging itself with poor mental health in a variety of ways (Field et al., 2024). When camouflaging is superficially 'successful', autistic people describe this leading to a lack of accommodation and support (Bradley et al., 2021; Hull et al., 2017; Livingston et al., 2019). For some autistic people, camouflaging involves high levels of vigilance to their social performance, which increases anxiety (Cook et al., 2021; Hull et al., 2017; Ryan & Räisänen, 2008). Autistic people describe camouflaging as 'draining' (Bernardin et al., 2021; Hull et al., 2017; Ryan & Räisänen, 2008; Schneid & Raz, 2020) and link it with feeling burnt out and struggling with daily tasks (Bradley et al., 2021). Finally, some autistic people describe feelings of inauthenticity and uncertainty about their 'true' identity due to camouflaging (Bernardin et al., 2021; Bradley et al., 2021; Hull et al., 2017; Miller et al., 2021; Tierney et al., 2016). It is important to consider how these experiences affect autistic people's ability to integrate their neurotype into their identity and develop a positive autistic identity. Field et al. (2024) formulates camouflaging as an understandable attempt to cope with a stressful social context whereby neurotypical behaviour is expected and autistic people experience bullying and isolation. Although some autistic people find camouflaging helpful and do not feel it has drawbacks, many others experience unintended negative consequences which make the social context increasingly stressful and impact mental health. Overall, autistic people find they are negatively affected by the social context or the effects of the camouflaging that they use to attempt to cope with it. This is similar to the 'double bind' discussed by Botha et al. (2022) whereby autistic people are faced with the choice to disclose their diagnosis and experience stigma, or not disclose and be judged for their behaviour.

It is important to consider how camouflaging and experiences of stigma might affect autistic people with AN given the relationship between camouflaging and higher levels of ED symptomatology in autistic adults (Bradley et al., 2024). A Minority Stress (Meyer, 2003) perspective suggests autistic people may find it more difficult to access ED treatment due to experiences of and concerns about stigma toward their autistic behaviour or diagnosis. This could theoretically reduce the likelihood of autistic people accessing early intervention, an important factor in prognosis for non-autistic people with AN (Andrés-Pepiñá et al., 2019; Austin et al., 2021; Fernández-Aranda et al., 2021; Treasure et al., 2021). This could also contribute to autistic people having longer ED durations compared to non-autistic people (Babb et al., 2022; Saure et al., 2020). Stigma toward autistic behaviour may affect autistic people's experiences of ED treatment. Some autistic people describe being labelled as 'resistant', 'naughty', or 'rude' during treatment due to their autistic behaviours (Babb et al., 2021). This could be considered an example of autistic people experiencing felt stigma during ED treatment, with poorer professional knowledge about autism being linked with less positive attitudes (Turnock et al., 2022). Experiences of stigma are suggested to decrease wellbeing and increase camouflaging (Turnock et al., 2022).

Camouflaging could also play a role in the development of disordered eating. Some autistic people describe efforts to lose weight or cultivate an interest in dieting as an attempt to 'fit in' (Brede et al., 2020; Healy et al., 2021). As previously discussed, camouflaging is an attempt to manage a stressful social environment which can unintentionally lead to further distress due to associated feelings of exhaustion, anxiety, and inauthenticity (Field et al., 2024). Brede et al.'s (2020) model of restrictive eating in autism suggests two pathways through which autism-related difficulties may lead to restricted eating as a way to cope. They propose a direct pathway where the autism-related difficulty itself is coped with by restricting eating, i.e., a sensory sensitivity which is managed by avoiding foods, and an indirect pathway where the autism-related difficulty leads to negative emotions which are coped with by restricting eating, i.e., restricting eating to numb overwhelm due to difficulties with uncertainty.

Camouflaging and distress due to stigma could be considered an indirect route to disordered eating as part of this model. For example, attempting to camouflage by losing weight or cultivating an interest in dieting could directly affect restricted eating. Experiences of stigma and unintended negative consequences of camouflaging could indirectly increase restricted eating as a way of trying to cope. This could be through trying to numb overwhelm and burnout by restricting eating, or by seeking an identity within AN in response to feelings of lack of identity from camouflaging. This may also partially explain the relationship between higher levels of camouflaging and higher levels of ED symptoms (Bradley et al., 2024). It is important for future research to investigate these relationships further.

Autism and Identity: Relevance for Anorexia Nervosa

Many autistic people, especially women, have historically experienced their autistic traits being overshadowed by other diagnoses (Bargiela et al., 2016; Leedham et al., 2020). Autistic individuals with AN have reported that behaviours employed to cope with sensory sensitivities are misconstrued as AN-related (e.g., fidgeting), and communication difficulties and a lack of flexibility are misinterpreted as treatment non-compliance (Babb et al., 2021). Even after receiving an autism diagnosis, autistic individuals with AN have found services to dismiss the role of autism (Babb et al., 2021).

Nonetheless, receiving a diagnosis of autism may be pivotal in helping individuals understand their AN, given that research has shown the benefits that receiving a diagnosis of autism can bring to an individual in terms of helping to contextualise their difficulties and life experiences (Leedham et al., 2019). Thinking styles and behaviours, previously attributed to AN, can be reconceptualised as due, in part, to autism: Brede et al. (2020) illustrate this with a quote from an autistic individual with experience of AN: 'For me, the anorexia is just a symptom, and the cause is autism' (p. 4288).

Autistic individuals with AN have described how lacking understanding of their own autistic traits affected the development of their sense of self. For many, this led them to feel different from others, which can be associated with a sense of failure or fault (Brede et al., 2020), which echoes findings that a diagnosis can help build understanding and self-compassion (Leedham et al., 2019). Brede et al. (2020) proposed that autism can have a direct impact on the development of eating difficulties, such as the consequences of sensory sensitivities on eating, and more indirect impacts, in which restrictive eating becomes a coping mechanism for negative experiences associated with living as an autistic person, impacting individuals' sense of self and mental health. Whereas some individuals felt that difficulties with their sense of self resulted in them focusing on their weight and shape, for others, AN and its values provided an opportunity to develop a sense of self, and copying others' anorexic values was a way of camouflaging (Brede et al., 2020).

Another point of relevance for identity in autistic individuals with AN is the role of stigma. Autistic individuals have recounted experiences of stigmatising comments and harassment about their autism that can undermine a positive body image (Longhurst et al., 2024). Body acceptance can come, in part, from finding a community where neurodivergence can be accepted and individuals can accept themselves as they are (Longhurst et al., 2024).

There are parallels between the findings from research on AN in autistic people and the 'lost emotional self' model of Oldershaw et al. (2019; see Chapter 2), in which an underdeveloped identity leaves an individual more dependent on external sources of validation, such as the thin ideal. It is possible that the lack of opportunity to develop an understanding of oneself as an autistic person contributes to reliance on a sense of self that is externally defined, which dovetails with some statements made by autistic individuals with AN in previous research (Brede et al., 2020). Whereas Oldershaw et al. (2019) consider life experiences such as early childhood attachment, peer interactions, and the role of parents in identity development, it would be useful to develop such conceptualisations of AN development to include the role of autism, e.g., how identity formation in autism is impacted by the experiences of autistic individuals in a social context, and the role of neurodevelopment. Indeed, considering the historical under-recognition of the potential impacts of autism in previous research, it is likely that models are omitting some of its important influences on AN. Nimbley et al. (2023) found that social identity or social sense of self is important to the development and maintenance of AN for both autistic and non-autistic people. Whereas non-autistic people with AN described a sense of inadequacy based on their comparisons of themselves to others, autistic people described a core sense of social difference and 'defectiveness', which was a factor in the development of their AN. For autistic people, this was accompanied by confusion about why they were different, which some described improving when they received their autism diagnosis. Both autistic and non-autistic people with AN described the protectiveness of belonging and social connectedness (Nimbley et al., 2023).

Treatment Implications

Evidence-based treatments for AN include interventions to develop a new identity that does not include the ED. In cognitive behaviour therapy for EDs (Fairburn et al., 2008), individuals with AN are explicitly advised to broaden their 'domains for self-evaluation' (p. 96) beyond weight, shape, and their control, thereby exploring new and under-examined facets of their identity. The Maudsley model of AN treatment for adults (Schmidt et al., 2014) incorporates a module on identity exploration, and there is preliminary evidence that this facet can be especially beneficial in helping individuals to envision a future beyond AN (Koskina & Schmidt, 2019).

Developing a positive identity as an autistic person could be crucial to recovery from AN. The PEACE (Pathway for Eating disorders and Autism developed from Clinical Experience) centres the autistic experience in treatment for AN, homing in on features of autism to understand their relevance to the individual's presentation, including sensory sensitivities (Tchanturia et al., 2020). Further research, including the voices of clinicians, individuals with AN, autistic individuals, and autistic individuals with AN, has proposed that autistic individuals with AN could be supported to explore their special interests outside the ED (Field et al., 2023), which could be a route towards developing one's sense of self as an autistic person beyond AN. Indeed, it is known that developing a positive autistic identity is associated with better mental health (Davies et al., 2024), and interventions designed to strengthen a positive autistic identity are currently in development (Davies et al.,

2025); we might expect these interventions to reduce the risk of developing AN and other EDs.

This chapter has also explored the social identity aspects of autism, and these also have implications for treatment. For autistic individuals with AN who may have internalised negative stereotypes and social stigma in relation to their autistic behaviours, approaches such as compassion-focused therapy (CFT; Gilbert, 2009) could be beneficial. Studies have begun to show that CFT can reduce self-stigma and shame in autism (Riebel et al., 2024). CFT is also receiving increasing support for its potential to reduce body image and eating concerns (Turk & Waller, 2020), although it has not been extensively researched as an approach for autistic people with AN. CFT conceptualises the unintended consequences of understandable attempts to cope with adverse internal and external experiences (Irons & Beaumont, 2017), and as such could be a framework for building understanding in therapy about what some of the negative consequences of camouflaging might be for an autistic individual with AN, as found in previous studies (Field et al., 2024), including where camouflaging might entail disordered eating or ascribing to unhelpful attitudes about (Healy et al., 2021).

References

Adamson, J., Brede, J., Babb, C., Serpell, L., Jones, C. R. G., Fox, J., & Mandy, W. (2022). Towards identifying a method of screening for autism amongst women with restrictive eating disorders. *European Eating Disorders Review*, *30*(5), 592–603. https://doi.org/https://doi.org/10.1002/erv.2918

American Psychiatric Association. (2013). *Diagnostic and statistical manual of mental disorders* (5th ed.). American Psychiatric Association.

Andrés-Pepiñá, S., Plana, M. T., Flamarique, I., Romero, S., Borràs, R., Julià, L., Gárriz, M., & Castro-Fornieles, J. (2019). Long-term outcome and psychiatric comorbidity of adolescent-onset anorexia nervosa. *Clinical Child Psychology and Psychiatry*, *25*(1), 33–44. https://doi.org/10.1177/1359104519827629

Austin, A., Flynn, M., Richards, K., Hodsoll, J., Duarte, T. A., Robinson, P., . . . Schmidt, U. (2021). Duration of untreated eating disorder and relationship to outcomes: A systematic review of the literature. *European Eating Disorders Review*, *29*(3), 329–345. https://doi.org/https://doi.org/10.1002/erv.2745

Babb, C., Brede, J., Jones, C. R. G., Elliott, M., Zanker, C., Tchanturia, K., . . . Fox, J. R. E. (2021). "It's not that they don't want to access the support . . . it's the impact of the autism": The experience of eating disorder services from the perspective of autistic women, parents and healthcare professionals. *Autism*, *25*(5), 1409–1421. https://doi.org/10.1177/1362361321991257

Babb, C., Brede, J., Jones, C. R. G., Serpell, L., Mandy, W., & Fox, J. (2022). A comparison of the eating disorder service experiences of autistic and non-autistic women in the UK. *European Eating Disorders Review*, *30*(5), 616–627. https://doi.org/https://doi.org/10.1002/erv.2930

Bagatell, N. (2010). From cure to community: Transforming notions of autism. *Ethos*, *38*(1), 33–55. https://doi.org/https://doi.org/10.1111/j.1548-1352.2009.01080.x

Bargiela, S., Steward, R., & Mandy, W. (2016). The experiences of late-diagnosed women with autism spectrum conditions: An investigation of the female autism phenotype. *Journal of Autism and Developmental Disorders*, *46*(10), 3281–3294.

Baron-Cohen, S. (1989). Are autistic children "Behaviorists"? An examination of their mental-physical and appearance-reality distinctions. *Journal of Autism and Developmental Disorders*, *19*(4), 579–600. https://doi.org/10.1007/BF02212859

Baron-Cohen, S. (2005). Autism «Autos»: Literally. In *The lost self: Pathologies of the brain and identity: Pathologies of the brain and identity* (pp. 166–180). Oxford University Press.

Baron-Cohen, S., Jaffa, T., Davies, S., Auyeung, B., Allison, C., & Wheelwright, S. (2013). Do girls with anorexia nervosa have elevated autistic traits? *Molecular Autism*, *4*, 1–8.

Baron-Cohen, S., Leslie, A. M., & Frith, U. (1985). Does the autistic child have a "theory of mind" ? *Cognition*, *21*(1), 37–46. https://doi.org/https://doi.org/10.1016/0010-0277(85)90022-8

Beck, J. S., Lundwall, R. A., Gabrielsen, T., Cox, J. C., & South, M. (2020). Looking good but feeling bad: "Camouflaging" behaviors and mental health in women with autistic traits. *Autism*, *24*(4), 809–821. https://doi.org/10.1177/1362361320912147

Bentz, M., Jepsen, J. R. M., Pedersen, T., Bulik, C. M., Pedersen, L., Pagsberg, A. K., & Plessen, K. J. (2017). Impairment of social function in young females with recent-onset anorexia nervosa and recovered individuals. *Journal of Adolescent Health*, *60*(1), 23–32. https://doi.org/https://doi.org/10.1016/j.jadohealth.2016.08.011

Bernardin, C. J., Mason, E., Lewis, T., & Kanne, S. (2021). "You must become a chameleon to survive": Adolescent experiences of camouflaging. *Journal of Autism and Developmental Disorders*, *51*(12), 4422–4435. https://doi.org/10.1007/s10803-021-04912-1

Bölte, S. (2014). The power of words: Is qualitative research as important as quantitative research in the study of autism? *Autism*, *18*(2), 67–68. https://doi.org/10.1177/1362361313517367

Boltri, M., & Sapuppo, W. (2021). Anorexia nervosa and autism spectrum disorder: A systematic review. *Psychiatry Research*, *306*, 114271. https://doi.org/https://doi.org/10.1016/j.psychres.2021.114271

Botha, M. (2021). Academic, activist, or advocate? Angry, entangled, and emerging: A critical reflection on autism knowledge production [Conceptual Analysis]. *Frontiers in Psychology*, *12*. https://doi.org/10.3389/fpsyg.2021.727542

Botha, M., Dibb, B., & Frost, D. M. (2022). "Autism is me": An investigation of how autistic individuals make sense of autism and stigma. *Disability & Society*, *37*(3), 427–453. https://doi.org/10.1080/09687599.2020.1822782

Botha, M., & Frost, D. M. (2018). Extending the minority stress model to understand mental health problems experienced by the autistic population. *Society and Mental Health*, *10*(1), 20–34. https://doi.org/10.1177/2156869318804297

Bradley, L., Shaw, R., Baron-Cohen, S., & Cassidy, S. (2021). Autistic adults' experiences of camouflaging and its perceived impact on mental health. *Autism in Adulthood*, *3*(4), 320–329. https://doi.org/10.1089/aut.2020.0071

Bradley, S., Moore, F., Duffy, F., Clark, L., Suratwala, T., Knightsmith, P., & Gillespie-Smith, K. (2024). Camouflaging, not sensory processing or autistic identity, predicts eating disorder symptoms in autistic adults. *Autism*, 13623613241245749. https://doi.org/10.1177/13623613241245749

Brede, J., Babb, C., Jones, C., Elliott, M., Zanker, C., Tchanturia, K., Serpell, L., Fox, J., & Mandy, W. (2020). "For me, the anorexia is just a symptom, and the cause is the autism": Investigating restrictive eating disorders in autistic women. *Journal of Autism and Developmental Disorders*, *50*(12), 4280–4296. https://doi.org/10.1007/s10803-020-04479-3

Brede, J., Babb, C., Jones, C. R., Serpell, L., Hull, L., Adamson, J., Baker, H., Fox, J. R., & Mandy, W. (2024). The clinical characteristics of autistic women with restrictive eating disorders. *BJPsych Open*, *10*(4), e131.

Bury, S. M., Jellett, R., Haschek, A., Wenzel, M., Hedley, D., & Spoor, J. R. (2022). Understanding language preference: Autism knowledge, experience of stigma and autism identity. *Autism*, *27*(6), 1588–1600. https://doi.org/10.1177/13623613221142383

Butler, R. C., & Gillis, J. M. (2011). The impact of labels and behaviors on the stigmatization of adults with asperger's disorder. *Journal of Autism and Developmental Disorders*, *41*(6), 741–749. https://doi.org/10.1007/s10803-010-1093-9

Cage, E., & Troxell-Whitman, Z. (2019). Understanding the reasons, contexts and costs of camouflaging for autistic adults. *Journal of Autism and Developmental Disorders*, *49*(5), 1899–1911. https://doi.org/10.1007/s10803-018-03878-x

Cassidy, S. A., Gould, K., Townsend, E., Pelton, M., Robertson, A. E., & Rodgers, J. (2020). Is camouflaging autistic traits associated with suicidal thoughts and behaviours? Expanding the interpersonal psychological theory of suicide in an undergraduate student sample. *Journal of Autism and Developmental Disorders*, *50*(10), 3638–3648. https://doi.org/10.1007/s10803-019-04323-3

Cook, J., Crane, L., Bourne, L., Hull, L., & Mandy, W. (2021). Camouflaging in an everyday social context: An interpersonal recall study. *Autism*, *25*(5), 1444–1456. https://doi.org/10.1177/1362361321992641

Cook, J., Crane, L., Hull, L., Bourne, L., & Mandy, W. (2021). Self-reported camouflaging behaviours used by autistic adults during everyday social interactions. *Autism*, *26*(2), 406–421. https://doi.org/10.1177/13623613211026754

Cook, J., Hull, L., Crane, L., & Mandy, W. (2021). Camouflaging in autism: A systematic review. *Clinical Psychology Review*, *89*, 102080. https://doi.org/https://doi.org/10.1016/j.cpr.2021.102080

Cooper, K., Smith, L. G. E., & Russell, A. (2017). Social identity, self-esteem, and mental health in autism. *European Journal of Social Psychology*, *47*(7), 844–854. https://doi.org/https://doi.org/10.1002/ejsp.2297

Cooper, R., Cooper, K., Russell, A. J., & Smith, L. G. E. (2021). "I'm proud to be a little bit different": The effects of autistic individuals' perceptions of autism and autism social identity on their collective self-esteem. *Journal of Autism and Developmental Disorders*, *51*(2), 704–714. https://doi.org/10.1007/s10803-020-04575-4

Corden, K., Brewer, R., & Cage, E. (2021). Personal identity after an autism diagnosis: Relationships with self-esteem, mental wellbeing, and diagnostic timing [Original Research]. *Frontiers in Psychology*, *12*. https://doi.org/10.3389/fpsyg.2021.699335

Cresswell, L., & Cage, E. (2019). "Who am i?": An exploratory study of the relationships between identity, acculturation and mental health in autistic adolescents. *Journal of Autism and Developmental Disorders*, *49*(7), 2901–2912. https://doi.org/10.1007/s10803-019-04016-x

Davies, J., Cooper, K., Killick, E., Sam, E., Healy, M., Thompson, G., Mandy, W., Redmayne, B., & Crane, L. (2024). Autistic identity: A systematic review of quantitative research. *Autism Research*, *17*(5), 874-897.

Davies, J., Redmayne, B., Allain, L., Portway, L., Mandy, W., Cooper, K., & Crane, L. (2025). The codesign and initial evaluation of a peer support program for autistic young adults. *Autism in Adulthood*, *7*(5), 650–662.

Fernández-Aranda, F., Treasure, J., Paslakis, G., Agüera, Z., Giménez, M., Granero, R., Jiménez-Murcia, S. (2021). The impact of duration of illness on treatment nonresponse and drop-out: Exploring the relevance of enduring eating disorder concept. *European Eating Disorders Review*, *29*(3), 499–513. https://doi.org/https://doi.org/10.1002/erv.2822

Fairburn, C. G. (2008). *Cognitive behavior therapy and eating disorders*. Guilford Press.

Field, S. L., Fox, J. R. E., Jones, C. R. G., & Williams, M. O. (2023). "Work WITH us": A Delphi study about improving eating disorder treatment for autistic women with anorexia nervosa. *Journal of Eating Disorders*, *11*(1), 17. https://doi.org/10.1186/s40337-023-00740-z

Field, S. L., Williams, M. O., Jones, C. R. G., & Fox, J. R. E. (2024). A meta-ethnography of autistic people's experiences of social camouflaging and its relationship with mental health. *Autism*, 13623613231223036. https://doi.org/10.1177/13623613231223036

Fletcher-Watson, S., Adams, J., Brook, K., Charman, T., Crane, L., Cusack, J., . . . Pellicano, E. (2018). Making the future together: Shaping autism research through meaningful participation. *Autism*, *23*(4), 943–953. https://doi.org/10.1177/1362361318786721

Fletcher-Watson, S., & Happé, F. (2019). *Autism: A new introduction to psychological theory and current debate*. Routledge.

Frith, U., & Happé, F. (1999). Theory of mind and self-consciousness: What it like to be autistic? *Mind & Language*, *14*(1), 82–89. https://doi.org/https://doi.org/10.1111/1468-0017.00100

Galvin, J., Evans, E. H., Talbot, C. V., Wilson, C., & Richards, G. (2022). The associations between autistic traits and disordered eating/drive for muscularity are independent of anxiety and depression in females but not males. *PLOS ONE*, *17*(10), e0276249. https://doi.org/10.1371/journal.pone.0276249

Gillberg, C. (1983). Are autism and anorexia nervosa related? *British Journal of Psychiatry*, *142*(4), 428. https://doi.org/10.1192/bjp.142.4.428b

Gillberg, C., & Råstam, M. (1992). Do some cases of anorexia nervosa reflect underlying autistic-like conditions? *Behavioural Neurology*, *5*, 259318. https://doi.org/10.3233/BEN-1992-5105

Gilbert, P. (2009). Introducing compassion-focused therapy. *Advances in Psychiatric Treatment*, *15*(3), 199–208. https://doi.org/10.1192/apt.bp.107.005264

Hambrook, D., Tchanturia, K., Schmidt, U., Russell, T., & Treasure, J. (2008). Empathy, systemizing, and autistic traits in anorexia nervosa: A pilot study. *British Journal of Clinical Psychology*, *47*(3), 335–339.

Healy, S., Pacanowski, C., Kennedy, L., & Obrusnikova, I. (2021). "This cage that I'm stuck inside": Autistic adults' perceptions of weight management, body weight, and body image. *Autism*, *25*(7), 1985–1998. https://doi.org/10.1177/13623613211006989

Hiller, R., & Pellicano, L. (2013). Anorexia and autism – A cautionary note. *Psychologist*, *26*(11), 780.

Hobson, R. P. (2010). Explaining autism: Ten reasons to focus on the developing self. *Autism*, *14*(5), 391–407. https://doi.org/10.1177/1362361310364142

Huke, V., Turk, J., Saeidi, S., Kent, A., & Morgan, J. F. (2013). Autism spectrum disorders in eating disorder populations: A systematic review. *European Eating Disorders Review*, *21*(5), 345–351. https://doi.org/https://doi.org/10.1002/erv.2244

Hull, L., Mandy, W., Lai, M.-C., Baron-Cohen, S., Allison, C., Smith, P., & Petrides, K. V. (2019). Development and validation of the Camouflaging Autistic Traits Questionnaire (CAT-Q). *Journal of Autism and Developmental Disorders*, *49*(3), 819–833. https://doi.org/10.1007/s10803-018-3792-6

Hull, L., Petrides, K. V., Allison, C., Smith, P., Baron-Cohen, S., Lai, M.-C., & Mandy, W. (2017). "Putting on my best normal": Social camouflaging in adults with autism spectrum conditions. *Journal of Autism and Developmental Disorders*, *47*(8), 2519–2534. https://doi.org/10.1007/s10803-017-3166-5

Irons, C., & Beaumont, E. (2017). *The compassionate mind workbook: A step-by-step guide to developing your compassionate self.* Robinson.

Jachyra, P., Anagnostou, E., Knibbe, T. J., Petta, C., Cosgrove, S., Chen, L., . . . McPherson, A. C. (2018). "Girls don't have big tummies": The experiences of weight-related discussions for children with autism spectrum disorders. *Autism*, *23*(5), 1096–1105. https://doi.org/10.1177/1362361318793020

Jaswal, V. K., & Akhtar, N. (2019). Being versus appearing socially uninterested: Challenging assumptions about social motivation in autism. *Behavioral and Brain Sciences*, *42*, e82.

Katzman, D. K., Christensen, B., Young, A. R., & Zipursky, R. B. (2001). Starving the brain: Structural abnormalities and cognitive impairment in adolescents with anorexia nervosa. *Seminars in Clinical Neuropsychiatry*, *6*(2), 146–152. https://doi.org/10.1053/scnp.2001.22263

Kenny, L., Hattersley, C., Molins, B., Buckley, C., Povey, C., & Pellicano, E. (2016). Which terms should be used to describe autism? Perspectives from the UK autism community. *Autism*, *20*(4), 442–462. https://doi.org/10.1177/1362361315588200

Kerr-Gaffney, J., Halls, D., Harrison, A., & Tchanturia, K. (2020). Exploring relationships between autism spectrum disorder symptoms and eating disorder symptoms in adults with anorexia nervosa: A network approach [Original Research]. *Frontiers in Psychiatry*, *11*. https://doi.org/10.3389/fpsyt.2020.00401

Kinnaird, E., Norton, C., Stewart, C., & Tchanturia, K. (2019). Same behaviours, different reasons: What do patients with co-occurring anorexia and autism want from treatment? *International Review of Psychiatry*, *31*(4), 308–317. https://doi.org/10.1080/09540261.2018.1531831

Koskina, A., & Schmidt, U. (2019). Who am I without anorexia? Identity exploration in the treatment of early stage anorexia nervosa during emerging adulthood: a case study. *The Cognitive Behaviour Therapist*, *12*, e32.

Krumm, A., Ferraro, F. R., & Ingvalson, B. (2017). Exploring the relationship between autistic traits and body image, body satisfaction, and body competence. *Journal of Psychology*, *151*(6), 566–579. https://doi.org/10.1080/00223980.2017.1372343

Lai, M.-C., Kassee, C., Besney, R., Bonato, S., Hull, L., Mandy, W., . . . Ameis, S. H. (2019). Prevalence of co-occurring mental health diagnoses in the autism population: A systematic review and meta-analysis. *The Lancet Psychiatry*, *6*(10), 819–829. https://doi.org/10.1016/S2215-0366(19)30289-5

Leedham, A., Thompson, A. R., Smith, R., & Freeth, M. (2019). "I was exhausted trying to figure it out": The experiences of females receiving an autism diagnosis in middle to late adulthood. *Autism*, *24*(1), 135–146. https://doi.org/10.1177/1362361319853442

Leedham, A., Thompson, A. R., Smith, R., & Freeth, M. (2020). 'I was exhausted trying to figure it out': The experiences of females receiving an autism diagnosis in middle to late adulthood. *Autism*, *24*(1), 135–146.

Leppanen, J., Sedgewick, F., Halls, D., & Tchanturia, K. (2022). Autism and anorexia nervosa: Longitudinal prediction of eating disorder outcomes [Original Research]. *Frontiers in Psychiatry*, *13*. https://doi.org/10.3389/fpsyt.2022.985867

Lilley, R., Lawson, W., Hall, G., Mahony, J., Clapham, H., Heyworth, M., . . . Pellicano, E. (2021). "A way to be me": Autobiographical reflections of autistic adults diagnosed in mid-to-late adulthood. *Autism*, *26*(6), 1395–1408. https://doi.org/10.1177/13623613211050694

Livingston, L. A., Shah, P., & Happé, F. (2019). Compensatory strategies below the behavioural surface in autism: A qualitative study. *The Lancet Psychiatry*, *6*(9), 766–777. https://doi.org/10.1016/S2215-0366(19)30224-X

Longhurst, P. (2023). Body image and autism: A scoping review. *Research in Autism Spectrum Disorders*, *105*, 102170. https://doi.org/https://doi.org/10.1016/j.rasd.2023.102170

Longhurst, P., Aspell, J., Todd, J., & Swami, V. (2024). "There's no separating my view of my body from my autism": A qualitative study of positive body image in autistic individuals. *Body Image*, *48*, 101655. https://doi.org/https://doi.org/10.1016/j.bodyim.2023.101655

Mandy, W. (2023). The old and the new way of understanding autistic lives: Reflections on the life of Donald Triplett, the first person diagnosed as autistic. *Autism*, *27*(7), 1853–1855. https://doi.org/10.1177/13623613231194476

Mandy, W., & Tchanturia, K. (2015). Do women with eating disorders who have social and flexibility difficulties really have autism? A case series. *Molecular Autism*, *6*(1), 6. https://doi.org/10.1186/2040-2392-6-6

Mansour, S., Rozenblat, V., Fuller-Tyszkiewicz, M., Paganini, C., Treasure, J., & Krug, I. (2016). Emotions mediate the relationship between autistic traits and disordered eating: A new autistic-emotional model for eating pathology. *Psychiatry Research*, *245*, 119–126. https://doi.org/https://doi.org/10.1016/j.psychres.2016.08.021

Margari, L., Palumbi, R., Peschechera, A., Craig, F., de Giambattista, C., Ventura, P., & Margari, F. (2019). Sex-gender comparisons in comorbidities of children and adolescents with high-functioning autism spectrum disorder [Original Research]. *Frontiers in Psychiatry*, *10*. https://doi.org/10.3389/fpsyt.2019.00159

May, K. (2018). *The electricity of every living thing: One woman's walk with Asperger's*. Trapeze at Orion Books.

Mesa, S., & Hamilton, L. G. (2022). "We are different, that's a fact, but they treat us like we're different-er": Understandings of autism and adolescent identity development. *Advances in Autism*, *8*(3), 217–231. https://doi.org/10.1108/AIA-12-2020-0071

Meyer, I. H. (2003). Prejudice, social stress, and mental health in lesbian, gay, and bisexual populations: Conceptual issues and research evidence. *Psychological Bulletin*, *129*(5), 674–697. https://doi.org/10.1037/0033-2909.129.5.674

Miller, D., Rees, J., & Pearson, A. (2021). "Masking is life": Experiences of masking in autistic and nonautistic adults. *Autism in Adulthood*, *3*(4), 330–338. https://doi.org/10.1089/aut.2020.0083

Milton, D., & Bracher, M. (2013). Autistics speak but are they heard? (BSA Medical Sociology Online). *7*, 61–69.

Nazar, B. P., Peynenburg, V., Rhind, C., Hibbs, R., Schmidt, U., Gowers, S., . . . Treasure, J. (2018). An examination of the clinical outcomes of adolescents and young adults with broad autism spectrum traits and autism spectrum disorder and anorexia nervosa: A multi centre study. *International Journal of Eating Disorders*, *51*(2), 174–179. https://doi.org/https://doi.org/10.1002/eat.22823

Newman, B. M., Newman, P. R., Brady, E. B., & Morgan, K. (2006). *Development through life: A psychosocial approach*. Thomson/Wadsworth Belmont, CA.

Nielsen, S., Dobrescu, S. R., Dinkler, L., Gillberg, C., Gillberg, C., Råstam, M., & Wentz, E. (2022). Effects of autism on 30-year outcome of anorexia nervosa. *Journal of Eating Disorders*, *10*(1), 1–14.

Nilsson, E. W., Gillberg, C., Gillberg, I. C., & Råstam, M. (1999). Ten-year follow-up of adolescent-onset anorexia nervosa: Personality disorders. *Journal of the American Academy of Child & Adolescent Psychiatry*, *38*(11), 1389–1395. https://doi.org/10.1097/00004583-199911000-00013

Nimbley, E., Gillespie-Smith, K., Duffy, F., Maloney, E., Ballantyne, C., & Sharpe, H. (2023). "It's not about wanting to be thin or look small, it's about the way it feels": An IPA analysis of social and sensory differences in autistic and non-autistic individuals with anorexia and their parents. *Journal of Eating Disorders*, *11*(1), 89. https://doi.org/10.1186/s40337-023-00813-z

Oldershaw, A., Startup, H., & Lavender, T. (2019). Anorexia nervosa and a lost emotional self: A psychological formulation of the development, maintenance, and treatment of anorexia nervosa. *Frontiers in psychology*, *10*, 219.

Oredipe, T., Kofner, B., Riccio, A., Cage, E., Vincent, J., Kapp, S. K., . . . Gillespie-Lynch, K. (2022). Does learning you are autistic at a younger age lead to better adult outcomes? A participatory exploration of the perspectives of autistic university students. *Autism*, *27*(1), 200–212. https://doi.org/10.1177/13623613221086700

Page, T. (2009). *Parallel play: Growing up with undiagnosed Asperger's*. Anchor.

Pearson, A., & Rose, K. (2021). A conceptual analysis of autistic masking: Understanding the narrative of stigma and the illusion of choice. *Autism in Adulthood*, *3*(1), 52–60. https://doi.org/10.1089/aut.2020.0043

Pellicano, E., & den Houting, J. (2022). Annual research review: Shifting from "normal science" to neurodiversity in autism science. *Journal of Child Psychology and Psychiatry*, *63*(4), 381–396. https://doi.org/https://doi.org/10.1111/jcpp.13534

Perry, E., Mandy, W., Hull, L., & Cage, E. (2022). Understanding camouflaging as a response to autism-related stigma: A social identity theory approach. *Journal of Autism and Developmental Disorders*, *52*(2), 800–810. https://doi.org/10.1007/s10803-021-04987-w

Poulsen, R., Brownlow, C., Lawson, W., & Pellicano, E. (2022). Meaningful research for autistic people? Ask autistics! *Autism*, *26*(1), 3–5. https://doi.org/10.1177/13623613211064421

Riebel, M., Krasny-Pacini, A., Manolov, R., Rohmer, O., & Weiner, L. (2024). Compassion focused therapy for self-stigma and shame in autism: A single case pre-experimental study. *Frontiers in Psychiatry, 14*, 1281428. https://doi.org/10.3389/fpsyt.2023.1281428

Robison, J. E. (2008). *Look me in the eye: My life with Asperger's*. Random House.

Ruiz Calzada, L., Pistrang, N., & Mandy, W. P. L. (2012). High-functioning autism and asperger's disorder: Utility and meaning for families. *Journal of Autism and Developmental Disorders, 42*(2), 230–243. https://doi.org/10.1007/s10803-011-1238-5

Ryan, S., & Räisänen, U. (2008). "It's like you are just a spectator in this thing": Experiencing social life the "aspie" way. *Emotion, Space and Society, 1*(2), 135–143. https://doi.org/https://doi.org/10.1016/j.emospa.2009.02.001

Saure, E., Laasonen, M., Lepistö-Paisley, T., Mikkola, K., Ålgars, M., & Raevuori, A. (2020). Characteristics of autism spectrum disorders are associated with longer duration of anorexia nervosa: A systematic review and meta-analysis. *International Journal of Eating Disorders, 53*(7), 1056–1079. https://doi.org/https://doi.org/10.1002/eat.23259

Schmidt, U., Wade, T. D., & Treasure, J. (2014). The Maudsley Model of Anorexia Nervosa Treatment for Adults (MANTRA): development, key features, and preliminary evidence. *Journal of cognitive psychotherapy, 28*(1).

Schneid, I., & Raz, A. E. (2020). The mask of autism: Social camouflaging and impression management as coping/normalization from the perspectives of autistic adults. *Social Science & Medicine, 248*, 112826. https://doi.org/https://doi.org/10.1016/j.socscimed.2020.112826

Schneider, E. (1999). *Discovering my autism: Apologia pro vita sua* (with apologies to Cardinal Newman). Jessica Kingsley Publishers.

Sedgewick, F., Leppanen, J., & Tchanturia, K. (2021). Gender differences in mental health prevalence in autism. *Advances in Autism, 7*(3), 208–224. https://doi.org/10.1108/AIA-01-2020-0007

Sinclair, J. (1993). *Don't mourn for us*. Retrieved December 29, 2023, from https://autreat.com/dont_mourn.html

Sinclair, J. (2012). Why I dislike "person first" language. In T. A. S. A. Network (Ed.), *Loud hands: Autistic people, speaking* (pp. 223–224). The Autistic Press.

Singer, J. (1998). *Odd people in: The birth of community amongst people on the "autistic spectrum"*. Faculty of Humanities and Social Science, University of Technology, Sydney.

Skorikov, V. B., & Vondracek, F. W. (2011). Occupational identity. In S. J. Schwartz, K. Luyckx, & V. L. Vignoles (Eds.), *Handbook of identity theory and research* (pp. 693–714). Springer New York. https://doi.org/10.1007/978-1-4419-7988-9_29

Tajfel, H., & Turner, J. C. (1979). An integrative theory of intergroup conflict. In W. G. Austin & S. Worchel (Eds.), *The social psychology of intergroup relations* (pp. 33–47). Brooks/Cole.[Google Scholar].

Tchanturia, K., Adamson, J., Leppanen, J., & Westwood, H. (2019). Characteristics of autism spectrum disorder in anorexia nervosa: A naturalistic study in an inpatient treatment programme. *Autism, 23*(1), 123–130. https://doi.org/10.1177/1362361317722431

Tchanturia, K., Smith, K., Glennon, D., & Burhouse, A. (2020). Towards an improved understanding of the anorexia nervosa and autism spectrum comorbidity: PEACE pathway implementation. *Frontiers in Psychiatry, 11*, 640.

Tchanturia, K., Smith, E., Weineck, F., Fidanboylu, E., Kern, N., Treasure, J., & Baron Cohen, S. (2013). Exploring autistic traits in anorexia: A clinical study. *Molecular Autism*, *4*, 1–8.

Tierney, S., Burns, J., & Kilbey, E. (2016). Looking behind the mask: Social coping strategies of girls on the autistic spectrum. *Research in Autism Spectrum Disorders*, *23*, 73–83. https://doi.org/https://doi.org/10.1016/j.rasd.2015.11.013

Treasure, J. (2013). Coherence and other autistic spectrum traits and eating disorders: Building from mechanism to treatment. The Birgit Olsson lecture. *Nordic Journal of Psychiatry*, *67*(1), 38–42. https://doi.org/10.3109/08039488.2012.674554

Treasure, J., Oyeleye, O., Bonin, E.-M., Zipfel, S., & Fernandez-Aranda, F. (2021). Optimising care pathways for adult anorexia nervosa. What is the evidence to guide the provision of high-quality, cost-effective services? *European Eating Disorders Review*, *29*(3), 306–315. https://doi.org/https://doi.org/10.1002/erv.2821

Turk, F., & Waller, G. (2020). Is self-compassion relevant to the pathology and treatment of eating and body image concerns? A systematic review and meta-analysis. *Clinical Psychology Review*, *79*, 101856. https://doi.org/10.1016/j.cpr.2020.101856

Turnock, A., Langley, K., & Jones, C. R. (2022). Understanding stigma in autism: A narrative review and theoretical model. *Autism in Adulthood*, *4*(1), 76–91.

van Schalkwyk, G. I., & Dewinter, J. (2020). Qualitative research in the journal of autism and developmental disorders. *Journal of Autism and Developmental Disorders*, *50*(7), 2280–2282. https://doi.org/10.1007/s10803-020-04466-8

Wainscot, J. J., Naylor, P., Sutcliffe, P., Tantam, D., & Williams, J. V. (2008). Relationships with peers and use of the school environment of mainstream secondary school pupils with Asperger syndrome (high-functioning autism): A case-control study. *International Journal of Psychology and Psychological Therapy*, *8*(1), 25-38.

Westwood, H., Mandy, W., & Tchanturia, K. (2017). Clinical evaluation of autistic symptoms in women with anorexia nervosa. *Molecular Autism*, *8*, 12. https://doi.org/10.1186/s13229-017-0128-x

Westwood, H., & Tchanturia, K. (2017). Autism spectrum disorder in anorexia nervosa: An updated literature review. *Current Psychiatry Reports*, *19*(7), 41. https://doi.org/10.1007/s11920-017-0791-9

Williams, C. D., Byrd, C. M., Quintana, S. M., Anicama, C., Kiang, L., Umaña-Taylor, A. J., . . . Whitesell, N. (2020). A lifespan model of ethnic-racial identity. *Research in Human Development*, *17*(2–3), 99–129. https://doi.org/10.1080/15427609.2020.1831882

Williams, D. (2010). Theory of own mind in autism: Evidence of a specific deficit in self-awareness? *Autism*, *14*(5), 474–494. https://doi.org/10.1177/1362361310366314

Wood, C., & Freeth, M. (2016). Students' stereotypes of autism. *Journal of Educational Issues*, *2*(2), 131–140.

Zahavi, D. (2010). Complexities of self. *Autism*, *14*(5), 547–551. https://doi.org/10.1177/1362361310370040

Chapter 6

Longstanding Anorexia Nervosa

Janet Conti, Laura Kiely, and Phillipa Hay

Introduction

Living with anorexia nervosa (AN) for many years has impacts on a person's identity or who they understand themselves to be. This chapter focuses on the question of identity in the experience of severe and enduring AN (SE-AN) or longstanding AN. The chapter begins with an introduction of the concept of SE-AN and its diagnostic challenges. From here, we discuss how longstanding anorexia may entrap the person into an anorexic identity that may obscure more than it reveals about the person. We then explore some of the diverse ways that people recover their identities from AN to inform a greater understanding of SE-AN and its treatments. Finally, we examine the extent to which current evidence-based treatments focus on identity, and what more can be done, including ways to keep hope alive in therapeutic conversations when AN progresses to a longstanding and severe course.

What Is SE-AN? Introduction to SE-AN and Diagnostic Considerations

The term SE-AN (or longstanding AN) derives from the broader concept of severe and enduring eating disorder (SEED; Robinson, 2009). SE-AN is a major source of distress and compromised quality of life for people experiencing it, including carers and families, with impacts extending to health services and the wider community.

Estimates vary but most studies conclude that longstanding AN occurs in up to 20% of people experiencing AN. For example, a major study of the outcomes of AN (Steinhausen, 2009) reported persistent illness in 20% of people with AN, leading to death in 5% of cases. Similarly, Eddy et al. (2017) reported long-term outcomes in a clinical cohort of people with AN. Although recovery continued in a small proportion, it was evident that many were still living with AN up to 20 years later. Whilst such studies support the reality of SE-AN, the concept has not been without controversy. This is particularly the case as many studies have found that duration of illness in itself does not predict outcomes for treatment of people with AN and that treatment delay is associated with poorer outcomes (Austin et al., 2021). These studies, however, do not take into account other aspects of the

DOI: 10.4324/9781003468189-7

conceptualisation of SE-AN, and there remains an incomplete understanding of its defining characteristics.

Hay and Touyz (2018) proposed three criteria for SE-AN: symptoms that are (1) significantly burdensome, persistent, and unremitting, (2) long in duration, and (3) resistant to treatment. Whilst there is no consensus on what qualifies as a minimum duration, the authors noted the minimum that has been documented in the literature—three years (Broomfield et al., 2017). This was based on early studies of family therapy for people with AN (Russell et al., 1987), where those with more than three years of illness duration had a poorer outcome than those who were younger and had experienced a shorter illness duration. Since this study, other research has proposed durations of seven and ten years (Broomfield et al., 2017). The third criterion was modelled on Pilowsky's (1975) concept of treatment responsiveness and thus specified a number (at least two) of previous evidence-based treatments that had been provided at a sufficient level of intensity and duration. This aspect is, however, very difficult to apply in practice.

It is often problematic to understand if a person is truly treatment "intractable" when they are experiencing AN. This is likely in part because of variability in the expertise of therapists and lack of precision in tailoring treatments to the individual. Further, the nature of AN is usually affirming for the person, and many describe it as their major source of a sense of purpose and identity. This egosyntonic aspect of AN makes it understandable that people may be ambivalent about treatment, come late to treatment, and leave treatment early. Indeed, in qualitative research studies, people often describe a "battle" (Jarman et al., 1997) with the illness and with healthcare professionals, particularly those who do not understand the degree to which AN provides security and safety for the person.

A fourth or complementary dimension in the conceptualisation of SE-AN has been proposed: the global impoverishment of both a sense of self outside the AN identity and of interpersonal relationships and meaningful lifetime activities (Kiely et al., 2023). It is reflected in the marked contrast between ability and educational attainment and workplace function that is often reported in studies describing sociodemographic features of people with SE-AN (e.g., Touyz et al., 2013). It is one of the most striking aspects for people experiencing SE-AN in addition to the known and notable impairments in mental and physical health and health-related quality of life. The mental health-related quality of life impact for people with SE-AN is as high as that of any other mental health disorder, including psychotic disorders such as schizophrenia (Ágh et al., 2016). However, this is a complex area and the reporting of quality of life varies across studies and even within studies where it can fluctuate over time. For example, a recent study by Newton et al. (2024) found that eating disorder health-related quality of life (EDQoL) appeared to worsen during a cognitive behavioural treatment that was part of a randomised controlled trial. The study also reported that early change in EDQoL, whether for the better or worse, was associated with improvements in mental health-related quality of life at the end of treatment.

Research on the conceptualisation of SE-AN highlights the complexity of attempting to formulate defining features. Indeed, there is even debate as to the preferred term, with the most commonly used being SE-AN, longstanding AN (Downs, 2024), or chronic AN (Broomfield et al., 2017; Broomfield et al., 2021). One study has suggested people with lived experience prefer the term longstanding AN (Broomfield et al., 2021), but there is less agreement amongst other experts (Broomfield et al., 2021). There is more consistency from the literature of clinical experience and expertise regarding assessment and treatment (e.g., Hay et al., 2014; Yager, 2020; Wonderlich et al., 2020). This literature agrees that too many people with AN experience a persistent and debilitating illness for which there is an incomplete understanding. There is also some agreement that the treatment approach may need to be modified and that continuing to apply treatment models used in first or earlier presentations is unlikely to engage people and may do harm by adding to failure experiences (Zhu et al., 2023). Treatments need to be person-centred (Schmidt et al., 2025) and recovery-oriented, where hope is not lost and social and interpersonal relationships, including from peers (Pellizzer & Wade, 2023), are strengthened. Therapy should also acknowledge the internal conflict people experience in both wanting and not wanting to live with AN.

Identity in Shaping the AN Trajectory

Ambivalence about living with AN may, at least in part, be influenced by the extent to which individuals value the anorexic identity. This perspective is hardly new. For example, Hilde Bruch (1977) proposed that the "basic issues [in AN] center around their frantic effort to establish a sense of control and identity" and that "the focus of psychotherapy and family interventions ... should be on helping the patient develop a personal identity and a sense of self-reliance" (p. 110). Thirty-five years on from Bruch's foundation lecture in 1982, Treasure and Cardi (2017) extend her three key treatment foci of addressing interpersonal and familial relationships, the person's intra-personal factors that include addressing their sense of self, and their nutritional restitution. Treatments to date have focused on nutritional restoration in the early phases followed by addressing questions related to identity and self in the latter phases. We will return to this later in the chapter.

People with lived experience also repeatedly tell us that recovery from AN is more than reaching an endpoint signposted by a remitting of symptoms (Dawson et al., 2014a), and is rather a process imbued with meaning and identity shifts (Croce et al., 2024). A recent meta-synthesis of the literature on AN and identity found a theme of identity in recovery from anorexia that included notions such as "letting go of the AN" and "reclamation of self" (Croce et al., 2024). This was also illustrated by one participant in research conducted by the author (Janet):

> *Recovery isn't so much about the disease process, or recovering from it, it's about recovering yourself; it's about reclaiming your place in the world.*
>
> (Avalon; Conti, 2018)

Identity has been referred to as "one's sense of self" (Croce et al., 2024); however, the question of how this sense of oneself is understood is a philosophical one. On the writing of this chapter, we have taken up the following positions on the question of self and identity. Janet has taken the position that identity is a person's awareness of who they understand themselves to be, and that a person's sense of identity is constructed through the stories of their lives where "over developmental time, selves create stories, which in turn create selves" (McAdams & McLean, 2013). In the words of Jerome Bruner, "We become the autobiographical narratives by which we 'tell about' our lives" (Bruner, 1987). This position understands that our sense of ourselves is held together over time in narrative form that is constructed and reconstructed within a social and interpersonal context; this accounts for the role of micro- and macro-culture in processes of identity formation (Burr, 2015). These stories are not merely descriptive but also performative—that is, we perform the meaning of the stories of our lives (White, 2007).

Laura has a perspective of "self," informed by phenomenology and Gestalt theory (Perls et al., 1994). This is underpinned by two concepts—that a person's sense of self is not static but constantly evolving (emergent self) and that self is a relational entity, understood to exist in relation to "other" in the broadest sense. Philippson (2009) terms this "otherness." Gestalt theory posits that a person's true, authentic self can be obscured and interrupted by key processes. For example, formatively, the "gullible" child obediently swallows every word whole from their "field" of influence, i.e., authority figures/society. These become internalised messages or "introjects," a filter through which a person perceives themselves. In Gestalt therapy, to know who one truly is requires therapeutic re-examination of introjects through "adult eyes" (relationally) to assimilate and re-integrate aspects of self that are truly one's own via an embodied, phenomenological approach.

Phillipa's position on identity is informed by her training in psychodynamic therapy and broader developmental and biopsychosocial traditions, including psychoanalytic and lifespan models as articulated and integrated by Adler (2009) and others. This was extended by understandings of the role of AN in providing the self with a sense of control by Bruch (1978) and as extended to evidence-based forms of dynamic therapy, e.g., focal psychodynamic psychotherapy (Friederich et al., 2019).

Rather than speak from a singular definition of identity and self and their interrelationship, we have chosen instead to dialogue between our varying viewpoints. This chapter is our collective, dialogical understanding of the processes of losing and reclaiming identity and sense of self in the SE-AN experience. We have prioritised lived experience research as we seek to continue the conversation about innovative and meaningful ways of working with people living with AN, including those with a longstanding experience. Therefore, in this chapter we aim to present how people with a longstanding lived experience of AN describe and make sense of their experiences of losing identity and a sense of themselves to the anorexic identity, reclaiming lost and rebuilding new identities outside of the anorexic identity, and treatments that may scaffold these identity negotiations.

We hope that our diverse positionings on the question of self and identity, and their relationship, may translate into a chapter that has some resonances for you as the reader. What we agree on is that the question of self, identity, and their inter-relationship is unlikely to be resolved with a single explanation. And so too for those living with longstanding AN. We therefore move into this chapter with curiosity and the hope that we convey something meaningful to those with lived experience, their loved ones, clinicians, and researchers, whilst fostering opportunities for further meaningful conversations and hope.

Losing Identity in Longstanding AN

The extent to which a person loses a sense of identity to AN may be informed by the extent to which AN is perceived to be part of themselves. The anorexic identity may become an idealised version of the self that includes the sense of being able to exist without needs, ordered and controlled, and embodying a feminine subjectivity. Paradoxically, the anorexic identity may also be an expression of shame and disconnection from self, informed by "a vulnerable sense of self and identity, as well as interpersonal sensitivity" (Kiely et al., 2025).

A loss of a sense of oneself in SE-AN was evident in our recent SE-AN meta-synthesis that combined the voices of 382 participants across 36 extracted papers (Kiely et al., 2023). Through this process, an overarching four-phase, recursive model was constructed to depict how AN might progress to a longstanding experience. A person's sense of themselves was described as being interrupted across all phases of this model.

Overview of the SE-AN Recursive Model

The first phase (*vulnerable sense of self: hesitance to exist*) encompassed the complex inter- and intra-personal aspects compromising a person's relationship with themselves. Phase 1 of the recursive model captured the voices expressing a "vulnerable sense of self" and "hesitance to exist" whereby discomfort was described in taking space in the world. Participants talked about a fragile sense of self in the world that was characterised by struggles with a sense of belonging, sense of oneself as a burden, unworthy and alienated, underpinned by shame processes. Implicit in each of these dimensions of selfhood were the social and relational contexts within which troubled identities were constructed. For example, what were they struggling to belong to? Unworthy of what? Burdening whom? Alienated from whom? And shame in relation to what? The answer to each of these questions was undoubtedly as unique as the individual social and interpersonal contexts within which they lived. Nevertheless, interpersonal contexts within which a vulnerable sense of self was constructed included those that perpetuated stigma, stereotypes, and feeling misunderstood by others, including in treatment.

The AN performed meaningful functions for participants, including protecting them by concealing these vulnerable senses of self from themselves and others. This was understood to paradoxically further a person's disconnection from themselves, their bodies, and others, towards phase 2, *the disappearing self.* This was exemplified in the following extract:

> *I think just that anorexia gives you a sense of being that you wouldn't have otherwise [...] and I think without that you wouldn't be, well, I wouldn't feel like a person at all.*
>
> (Participant 1; Williams et al., 2016, p. 221)

Within this second phase, there appeared to be a progressive loss of identity to the anorexia. Participants described AN subsuming their sense of self to the point of "making me feel invisible" (Thoresen et al., 2021), "more like a shell" (Williams et al., 2016), "a ghost", and "voiceless" (Foye et al., 2019). These senses of invisibility and disappearance from life have been described elsewhere (e.g., Berry et al., 2024; Malson, 2003; White, 1987). Paralleling these was a loss of social and interpersonal opportunities to construct alternative identities outside of what had become the dominant anorexic identity. This identity was characterised by a disconnection from self and others and contributed to the loss of a sense of place in the world, for example: "more and more alien and difficult to remain in" (Arkell & Robinson, 2008) and "Like you're slipping into a whole different world" (Rance et al., 2017).

The chosen metaphors conveyed an internal emptiness ("a shell") and exemplified the sense of a loss of self ("ghost") to the AN experience. Further complicating this experience was a sense of loss of what was, for example, "I have lost everything through the eating disorder—absolutely everything…" (Stockford et al., 2018) and for some, a perceived loss of control, for example "this monster takes over… it has all the control; you have none" (King-Murphy, 1997). This resonated with our previous longitudinal research findings where the longstanding nature of AN had the effect of being traumatic in and of itself (Berry et al., 2024).

Paralleling a loss of control over the AN, participant narratives found stability around the AN experience. Within this context, there was talk of struggles to reimagine a life and identity outside of the AN experience. As such, from our outsider perspectives, there was a sense that the participants became entrapped in the anorexic identity that we termed *global impoverishment* (phase 3). Participants depicted this experience of entrapment into SE-AN through the use of a number of metaphors. One of these was a spider: "…[anorexia] builds a web so no one can come close to the real him, because alone he stands […] wary […] yes, it's not enough with just the spider […] needs to have something around himself" (Thoresen et al., 2021, p. 187). This metaphor was chosen as a visual representation in our expanded SE-AN conceptualisation (Kiely et al., 2025; see Figure 3 in that paper).

Global impoverishment captured the real effects of SE-AN and can be understood as an identity performance of a disappearing self. It was at this point that participants described what we conceptualised as the entrapment into SE-AN whereby piece by piece, parts of themselves were lost to the anorexic identity. This was exemplified by one participant: "I have lost everything through the eating disorder—absolutely everything" (Sarah; Stockford et al., 2018, p. 133). This included, for some, performing to a diagnostic identity (O'Connell, 2023). Furthermore, the participants experienced ambivalence in shifting their relationship with AN with the perception that it held their identity intact. These identity struggles have been talked about in the AN literature more broadly (Croce et al., 2024), and there is a need to understand in more detail some of the ways that people shift from this loss of identity to the anorexic identity over time. For example, Hilde Bruch proposed that AN interrupts a consistent sense of self over time as indicated by a sense of identity, whereby the person experiences difficulty ordering their life into a coherent life narrative of the self (Amianto et al., 2016). We agree and also propose that the embodied and relational impacts of longstanding AN erode quality of life and a sense of personal agency as well as interrupting social and occupational contexts available for identity (re)construction.

Participant narratives of the SE-AN experience, however, did not stay entrapped. Over time, several participants talked about moving towards a more integrated sense of themselves. This was characterised by more coherent life narratives, including the sense of having been shaped, and at times strengthened, through the AN experience. These temporal shifts were captured in the fourth distinctive phase of the SE-AN conceptualisation: interpsychic, temporal processes of change and recovery.

Before moving on to how participants talked about rebuilding and reclaiming lost identities from the SE-AN experience, we pause to draw your attention to the analysis of the artwork and poetry of a woman who left the legacy of her artwork and prose in book form to Laura to analyse. This was offered as a gesture of hope to those living with (and dying from) SE-AN, to inform treatments that walk alongside the person in ways that support and preserve their identities, regardless of where they are in the SE-AN experience.

The artist's work took us on a journey of her own self-inquiry, through to her death (Kiely et al., 2025). She communicated her sense of self through painted metaphor and colour, which she used to make meaning within the prose offered. Evident at the late stages of the AN is the perceived impossibility to disentangle a sense of self from the AN, and the artist offers a poignant clay self-portrait, engineered to crumble and disintegrate, representing a disappearing self that kinetically "diffuses" from the canvas. The artist correspondingly stated, "The eating disorder has taken over me completely now. It's taken over me" (Kiely et al., 2025).

Alongside this perceived loss of self were glimmers of seeing and reconciling a sense of identity through her art. In the process of understanding herself as subsumed to the AN, and the loss and grief incurred to it, this acceptance brought a paradoxical freedom. The artist's works became larger, more colourful, and "free."

The artist also spoke more generously of her own work, reflecting growing self-acceptance. Her autobiographical legacy became a comforting and coherent story, offering a sense of unity, purpose, and meaning-making in the face of imminent death. The artist reclaimed her disappearing self through art whereby an interpretivist self was created (and immortalised), leaving her mark through her book. Thus, hope metamorphosed into sharing and leaving a legacy for those with lived experience, rather than being tied to her own recovery, which she perceived to have eluded her.

Reclaiming Lost and Rebuilding New Identities Outside of the AN Identity

Given the descriptions of the profound impacts SE-AN had on participants across the studies comprising our first meta-synthesis (Kiely et al., 2023), it was unsurprising that meeting predetermined, medicalised definitions of recovery was perceived by the participants to be unimaginable (Kiely et al., 2023). In our second meta-synthesis with an additional 63 voices (Kiely et al., 2025), there was an increased focus of participant narratives on ways in which pathways could be reconstructed towards hope for a life less dominated by AN. These clearer themes of hope from the voice of lived experience were frequently articulated in response to, and arguments against, the proposal for a category of "terminal anorexia" that was argued to erode hope (Gaudiani et al., 2022). This part of the SE-AN conceptualisation is illustrated in Kiely et al. (2025, see Figure 4 in that paper).

These participant experiences joined with those in our earlier meta-synthesis where a total of 445 voices of people who experienced SE-AN expanded our conceptualisation of SE-AN. This expansion occurred particularly through recovery processes that interwove with a person's relationship with hope. These recovery processes were characterised by identity shifts, including experiences of a greater connection with the self. For example, Elwyn (2023) described recovery as "a continuing process of personal transformation, reclamation of power, reconnection with the self and changing navigation of socio-cultural political domains" (p. 7). This exemplified how recovering oneself is a transformative experience and, rather than an individual pursuit, an identity journey (Conti, 2018) that occurs within the process of navigating the broader terrain of the social-cultural and political context.

The participant narratives positioned hope as central to maintaining their engagement in building a life and sense of identity outside of AN. These hopes were antidotes to the "global impoverishment" (Phase 3) that was evoked by unrelenting physical, psychological, and psychosocial suffering of SE-AN. Pathways to hope were also multiple (as depicted in Figure 4 in Kiely et al., 2025) and included those that were shaped by social and interpersonal opportunities for the person to engage in the reconstruction of new and preferred identities. These contexts provided dialogical space for a person to reconstruct meanings for their life, including reconnection with a sense of self and identity outside of the AN identity. Making sense of the AN experience also included grieving for losses through its impacts over time, experiencing moments of joy, and connecting with a sense of meaning and purpose, including a vision of a life worth living—or, as Downs stated, "what to recover for" (Downs et al., 2023, p. 3). It is on this basis that it makes sense that effective treatments in longstanding AN are those that have focused on reclaiming a quality of life and a life worth living, underpinned by the hope that this is possible (Touyz et al., 2013). We will return to treatment implications later in this chapter.

Phase 4 of the recursive SE-AN model, interpsychic, temporal processes of changes and recovery, involved two aspects: opening the self to other(s) (the relational self) and reconnection with self. SE-AN was understood as a relational illness whereby the disconnected self and valuing of self-sufficiency risked further isolation and alienation and limited the interpersonal contexts within which a sense of identity could be re-authored and expanded. Thus several processes were associated with recovery. First, some of the participants described the need to re-connect with themselves and establish a sense of self ("it is hard to connect with others when you can't connect with yourself"; Foye, Hazlett, & I., 2019) and then confront their need for self-sufficiency, which was underpinned by disgust in perceived neediness ("urg [...] so needy"; Blackburn, O'Connor, & Parsons, 2021) and pain of the vulnerable sense of self ("All my life I was made to feel like a nobody. I was moulded by [others]"; King-Murphy, 1997). This process involved the person connecting with a sense of themselves. There were multiple ways that participants talked about how they reclaimed a sense of themselves including (a) resisting prioritising others' needs over their own because of the sense of being undeserving (White, 1987)—"...feel assertive enough to meet their [my] own needs and feel entitled to meet [my] own needs and accept responsibility for doing that, rather than meet someone else's needs" (Blackburn et al., 2021); (b) developing insight into how they had come to be who they were in the world: "I finally realized what had happened and I had a reason for the anorexia. With this understanding came some closure and I could get on with my life now" (Dawson, Rhodes, & Touyz, 2014b); and (c) through meaning-making that included a reconnection with their bodies as part of reintegration towards an embodied sense of self: "Within the state of surviving chronic AN, we may be profoundly disconnected or desensitised to our ability to continue walking on a knife's edge" (Elwyn, 2023).

In the way that identity formation is iterative, the same could be said of recovery. People with lived experience described recovery not as a final destination but a continual process of self-discovery, unique to each person. Rather than eliminating AN, recovery was conceptualised as reclaiming hope to re-engage with a sense of meaning and purpose that contributed to a sense that life was worth living. For example, Alykhan Asaria explained: "I now hope that I can have a purpose that makes life worth living, even if anorexia is always in my life—which is fundamentally different to it being my life (and death)" (Asaria, 2023). This finding was consistent with one of the authors' (Janet) previous research with a community sample of women, the majority of whom reported living with SE-AN (Conti, 2018). Analysis of the women's narratives, some over 10 years, found recovery was less about separating AN and erasing it from their identities (separation externalisation) and more about shifting their relationship with anorexia and in doing so, recovering aspects of themselves that had been obscured by the anorexic identity (relational externalisation) (Conti, 2018). Rather than seeking to erase AN through returning to some sort of pre-morbid state, the women did not want to forget. AN continued to be experienced as part of their identity, much like the notion of "history in person" (Holland & Lave, 2001), because it was part of their life story. This history was within them, shaping and informing their sense of themselves—something they could and would not forget.

What More Can Be Done in Treatments?

Current research evidence-based therapies for AN, including longstanding AN, include partial focus in some therapeutic modules on questions of identity and self-concept. For example, CBT-E has a module that focuses on self-esteem (Fairburn, 2008), Maudsley Anorexia Nervosa Treatment for Adults (MANTRA; Schmidt et al., 2019) and Family Based Treatment (FBT; Lock & Le Grange, 2013) focus on the person developing a sense of identity that is separate from the AN, with modules focused on identity in the final treatment phases, and cognitive behaviour therapy for anorexia nervosa (CBT-AN) (Pike et al., 2004) explores how a person's identity or self-concept becomes overtaken by what is termed an eating disorder schema.

Where these interventions focus on identity, this is usually in the latter stages of treatment once the person has engaged in substantial change around their eating behaviour and weight restoration. That means for people who do not restore their eating and weight, identity is not a focus of their treatment. Assumed in these treatments is the imperative for eating and weight restoration prior to addressing questions of identity and self. There is also a paucity of research that focuses on identity shifts in therapeutic interventions for AN and eating disorders more broadly.

Our research analysed the key in-session identity negotiations from therapy transcripts of participants in Hay et al.'s randomized controlled trial (RCT) (Hay et al., 2018) where all participants engaged in CBT-AN with some randomised to a group that included a module focused on compulsive exercise (Compulsive Exercise Activity Therapy) (Heywood et al., 2024). This analysis found that CBT-AN went some way in addressing the anorexic identity, particularly focusing on separating anorexia from a person's identity. Furthermore, in the latter stage of treatment, there was some focus on building new identities in ways that aligned with the CBT schema therapy practice of building new roles to support new self-concepts (Heywood et al., 2024).

Self-concept is addressed throughout the phases of focal dynamic psychotherapy for AN (Friederich et al., 2019) that at the outset addresses low self-esteem and negative self-perceptions within an empathic therapeutic framework through the therapeutic relationship (Friederich et al., 2019). As with Interpersonal Psychotherapy (IPT; McIntosh et al., 2000), focal dynamic psychotherapy also focuses on interpersonal relationships. The processes by which change emerges through improvements in interpersonal connections, although largely unknown, may at least be in part due to the interpersonal opportunities for identity reconstruction that may arise in the context of supportive relationships.

Further, a surprising finding at the time was that Specialist Supportive Clinical Management (SSCM) for AN, originally included as a "control" therapy group for comparison with CBT and IPT, emerged to be the most effective intervention for both the primary outcome, which was a global rating of AN symptom severity, and the secondary outcome of the DSM-IV Global Assessment of Function (McIntosh et al., 2005). Since then, three RCTs have been conducted with SSCM as a treatment group. Similar outcomes have been found regarding the efficacy of SSCM compared with MANTRA (Schmidt et al., 2012) with a larger trial reporting similar findings apart from a patient preference for MANTRA (Schmidt et al., 2015). SSCM has a dual focus on clinical management and supportive psychotherapy (Hay et al., 2016). It has been adapted for SE-AN (SSCM-SE) by Phillipa and colleagues with the focus on reducing the impact of AN on a person's quality of life rather than the treatment-as-usual that focuses on symptom reduction, particularly in the earlier phases. SSCM-SE thus far has promising findings with similar outcomes to CBT-AN (Touyz et al., 2013). What was interesting about this research was that when the focus was taken away from eating and weight restoration, those living with longstanding AN experienced not only improved quality of life but also paradoxically reduced eating disorder symptoms, including gaining weight.

Given that those with lived experience repeatedly talk about themes relevant to identity, there is a need to more comprehensively understand and address identity in treatment. These conversations need to extend beyond the anorexic identity, through practices such as externalisation, to finding and reclaiming identities that have been obscured by, and lost to, the anorexic identity. We also co-designed research with mixed methodologies investigating the putative features that prevent AN progressing to a longstanding course and address what people living with longstanding AN say, that is, to address more comprehensively problematic identities in AN.

We have been researching Michael White's narrative therapy for AN to understand the experiences and outcomes of an intervention that specifically focuses on questions of identity from the outset of treatment. Our systematic review of papers published on narrative therapy interventions for eating disorders found that all the interventions described a focus on questions of identity (Heywood et al., 2022). Interventions went beyond the more commonly implemented narrative practice of externalisation of the problem. Specifically, the practice of deconstructing or unpacking meaning, including the cultural and social contexts within which dominant meanings are derived (White, 2007), was highlighted as a key method for revealing identities obscured by problematic ones. We concluded that, first, there is a need to improve understanding about how these new and revealed identities are then performed or lived out, including as evidenced by shifts in a person's relationship with eating and their bodies. Second, given the potential medical complications with eating disorders, there is a need for narrative interventions to more fully describe how safety is established within a narrative world view that positions the person as the expert of their life. We then reviewed outcomes reported from these narrative therapy interventions (Conti et al., 2022). Of the published research, there was practice-based evidence for narrative therapy but a paucity of systematic outcomes reported.

There are other emerging treatments for AN that focus on self-concept and identity, such as the SPEAKS intervention that has been found to have feasibility for the treatment of AN (Oldershaw et al., 2024). This intervention focuses on aspects of our SE-AN recursive model (Kiely et al., 2025) with an initial focus on global distress and struggles for the person to see their life outside of AN (Oldershaw et al., 2022). Phases of this intervention shift in focus to address shame, guilt and sense of self as defective to grief. This then moves to addressing feelings of sadness, grief, and anger related to a sense of abandonment and attachment fears, then towards cultivating self-compassion and self-acceptance, and then self-efficacy and agency.

Given that treatments have been found to be effective in the longer term for around half of people living with an eating disorder (Murray et al., 2017), there is a need to think outside the box of the current evidence-based treatments that have failed those living with longstanding AN and other eating disorders. There is a need for greater consideration of the impacts of interventions whose urgency to remit eating disorder symptoms improvement is out of synchrony with the person (and thereby risks the person feeling traumatised by treatment). Personalising therapeutic interventions (Schmidt et al., 2025; Norcross & Cooper, 2021) through addressing the how of treatment, not just the what, is vital. This includes the critical consideration of tailoring treatment to a person's readiness to change (Norcross et al., 2022) as proposed by Geller and colleagues with the Short Treatment Allocation Tool for Eating Disorders, or STATED (Geller et al., 2018). This tool focuses on the development of treatments that are informed by the three dimensions of medical stability, interference in life, and tailored to a person's readiness to change (Geller et al., 2018).

The ambivalence people describe in the AN experience permeates treatment initiation and engagement, and lived experience perspectives have asserted that understanding the role of AN in their life was essential to moving towards self-led experimentation with "giving it up." It is understandable, given the high risk of sudden death and morbidity to AN, and the distress experienced in witnessing the impacts of AN on a person, that clinicians and families are anxious to see hasty physical restoration. Added to this is the evidence that symptom interruption and weight restoration can improve chances of recovery, and this is likely not just due to the physiological impact but also providing opportunities for people to re-engage in life outside of the AN. However, a false economy of sorts exists in rapid and impressive change, as opposed to a pace that more closely aligns to a person's own readiness to engage in physical symptom change. The shift in the less visible inter- and intra-psychic processes necessary to (re)building a sense of self and identity outside the anorexic identity likely takes time. Walking alongside the person to address issues that they perceive to be pertinent in their own recovery, sitting with them in ambivalence around change, holding hope that change is possible, and working with the person to reclaim identities that have been lost to the anorexic identity, are all aspects of eating disorder care that need greater consideration and research.

We have some way to go in limiting the progression of AN to longstanding AN and learning to walk alongside those who experience longstanding AN with hope that they will recover their life and identity from AN. We need to rethink, research, and be permitted to work with people who experience AN in ways that meet their needs and preferences rather than assuming that we as clinicians and researchers know what is best. Those living with longstanding AN are leading the way in asking us to rethink and expand therapeutic options for treatment, and they continue to implore us to do so.

References

Adler, R. H. (2009). Engel's biopsychosocial model is still relevant today. *Journal of Psychosomatic Research, 67*(6), 607–611. https://doi.org/10.1016/j.jpsychores.2009.08.008

Ágh, T., Kovács, G., Supina, D., Pawaskar, M., Herman, B. K., Vokó, Z., & Sheehan, D. V. (2016). A systematic review of the health-related quality of life and economic burdens of anorexia nervosa, bulimia nervosa, and binge eating disorder. *Eating and Weight Disorders – Studies on Anorexia, Bulimia and Obesity, 21*(3), 353–364. https://doi.org/10.1007/s40519-016-0264-x

Amianto, F., Northoff, G., Abbate-Daga, G., Fassino, S., & Tasca, G. A. (2016). Is anorexia nervosa a disorder of the self? A psychological approach. *Frontiers in Psychology, 7*, 869. https://doi.org/10.3389/fpsyg.2016.00849

Arkell, J., & Robinson, P. (2008). A pilot case series using qualitative and quantitative methods: Biological, psychological and social outcome in severe and enduring eating disorder (anorexia nervosa). *International Journal of Eating Disorders, 41*(7), 650–656. https://doi.org/10.1002/eat.20546

Asaria, A. (2023). "Terminal anorexia": A lived experience perspective. *Journal of Eating Disorders, 11*(1), 63. https://doi.org/10.1186/s40337-023-00823-x

Austin, A., Flynn, M., Richards, K., Hodsoll, J., Duarte, T. A., Robinson, P., Kelly, J., & Schmidt, U. (2021). Duration of untreated eating disorder and relationship to outcomes: A systematic review of the literature. *European Eating Disorders Review, 29*(3), 329–345. https://doi.org/10.1002/erv.2745

Berry, S., Hay, P., & Conti, J. (2024). "Once again it becomes a friend in times of adversity": A qualitative exploration of interrelationships between anorexia nervosa and trauma over ten years. *Psychiatry International, 5*(2), 188–204. https://doi.org/10.3390/psychiatryint5020013

Blackburn, B., O'Connor, J., & Parsons, H. (2021). Becoming needless: A psychoanalytically informed qualitative study exploring the interpersonal and intrapsychic experiences of longstanding anorexia nervosa. *International Journal of Applied Psychoanalytic Studies, 18*(4), 428–442. https://doi.org/10.1002/aps.1679

Bruch, H. (1977). Anorexia nervosa and its treatment. *Journal of Paediatric Psychology, 2*(3), 109–112. https://doi.org/10.1093/jpepsy/2.3.110

Bruch, H. (1978). *The golden cage: The enigma of anorexia nervosa.* Harvard University Press.

Bruner, J. (1987). Life as narrative. *Social Research, 54*(1), 11–32.

Broomfield, C., Noetel, M., Stedal, K., Hay, P., & Touyz, S. (2021). Establishing consensus for labelling and defining the later stage of anorexia nervosa: A Delphi study. *International Journal of Eating Disorders, 54*(11), 1865–1874. https://doi.org/10.1002/eat.23600

Broomfield, C., Stedal, K., Touyz, S., & Rhodes, P. (2017). Labelling and defining severe and enduring anorexia nervosa: A systematic review and critical analysis. *International Journal of Eating Disorders, 50*(6), 611–623. https://doi.org/10.1002/eat.22715

Burr, V. (2015). *Social constructionism* (3rd ed.). Routledge.

Conti, J. E. (2018). Recovering identity from anorexia nervosa – Women's constructions of their experiences of recovery from anorexia nervosa over 10 years. *Journal of Constructivist Psychology, 31*(1), 72–94. https://doi.org/10.1080/10720537.2016.1251366

Conti, J., Heywood, L., Hay, P., Shrestha, R. M., & Perich, T. (2022). Paper 2: A systematic review of narrative therapy treatment outcomes for eating disorders—Bridging the divide between practice-based evidence and evidence-based practice. *Journal of Eating Disorders, 10*(1), 138. https://doi.org/10.1186/s40337-022-00636-4

Croce, S. R., Malcolm, A. C., Ralph-Nearman, C., & Phillipou, A. (2024). The role of identity in anorexia nervosa: A narrative review. *New Ideas in Psychology, 72*, 101060. https://doi.org/10.1016/j.newideapsych.2023.101060

Dawson, L., Rhodes, P., & Touyz, S. W. (2014a). The recovery model and anorexia nervosa. *Australian and New Zealand Journal of Psychiatry, 48*(11), 1009–1016. https://doi.org/10.1177/0004867414539398

Dawson, L., Rhodes, P., & Touyz, S. W. (2014b). "Doing the impossible": The process of recovery from chronic anorexia nervosa. *Qualitative Health Research, 24*(4), 494–505. https://doi.org/10.1177/1049732314524029

Downs, J. (2024). Care pathways for longstanding eating disorders must offer paths to recovery, not managed decline. *BJPsych Bulletin, 48*(3), 177–181. https://doi.org/10.1192/bjb.2023.38

Downs, J., Ayton, A., Collins, L., Baker, S., Missen, H., & Ibrahim, A. (2023). Untreatable or unable to treat? Creating more effective and accessible treatment for long-standing and severe eating disorders. *The Lancet Psychiatry, 10*(2), 146–154. https://doi.org/10.1016/S2215-0366(22)00400-X

Eddy, K. T., Tabri, N., Thomas, J. J., Murray, H. B., Keshaviah, A., Hastings, E., Edkins, K., Krishna, M., Herzog, D. B., & Keel, P. K. (2017). Recovery from anorexia nervosa and bulimia nervosa at 22-year follow-up. *Journal of Clinical Psychiatry, 78*(2), 184–189. https://doi.org/10.4088/JCP.15m10393

Elwyn, R. (2023). A lived experience response to the proposed diagnosis of terminal anorexia nervosa: Learning from iatrogenic harm, ambivalence and enduring hope. *Journal of Eating Disorders, 11*(1), 18. https://doi.org/10.1186/s40337-022-00729-0

Fairburn, C. G. (2008). *Cognitive behaviour therapy and eating disorders*. Guilford Press.

Foye, U., Hazlett, D. E., & Irving, P. (2019). "The body is a battleground for unwanted and unexpressed emotions": Exploring eating disorders and the role of emotional intelligence. *Eating Disorders: Journal of Treatment and Prevention, 27*(4), 321–342. https://doi.org/10.1080/10640266.2018.1517520

Friederich, H., Wild, B., Zipfel, S., Schauenburg, H., & Herzog, W. (2019). *Anorexia nervosa: Focal psychodynamic psychotherapy*. Hogrefe.

Gaudiani, J. L., Bogetz, A., & Yager, J. (2022). Terminal anorexia nervosa: Three cases and proposed clinical characteristics. *Journal of Eating Disorders, 10*(1), 1–14. https://doi.org/10.1186/s40337-022-00548-3

Geller, J., Isserlin, L., Seale, E., Iyar, M. M., Coelho, J. S., Srikameswaran, S., & Norris, M. (2018). The Short Treatment Allocation Tool for Eating Disorders: current practices in assigning patients to level of care. *Journal of Eating Disorders*, *6*(1), 45.

Hay, P., Chinn, D., Forbes, D., Madden, S., Newton, R., Sugenor, L., Touyz, S., & Ward, W. (2014). Royal Australian and New Zealand College of Psychiatrists clinical practice guidelines for the treatment of eating disorders. *Australian and New Zealand Journal of Psychiatry, 48*(11), 977–1008. https://doi.org/10.1177/0004867414555814

Hay, P., McIntosh, G., & Bulik, C. (2016). Specialist supportive clinical management for severe and enduring anorexia nervosa: A clinician's manual. In *Managing severe and enduring anorexia nervosa* (pp. 112–127). Routledge.

Hay, P., & Touyz, S. (2018). Classification challenges in the field of eating disorders: can severe and enduring anorexia nervosa be better defined?. *Journal of eating disorders*, *6*(1), 41.

Hay, P., Touyz, S., Arcelus, J., Pike, K., Attia, E., Crosby, R. D., ... & Meyer, C. (2018). A randomized controlled trial of the compuLsive Exercise Activity TheraPy (LEAP): A new approach to compulsive exercise in anorexia nervosa. *International Journal of Eating Disorders*, *51*(8), 999–1004.

Heywood, L., Conti, J., & Hay, P. (2022). Paper 1: a systematic synthesis of narrative therapy treatment components for the treatment of eating disorders. *Journal of eating disorders*, *10*(1), 137.

Heywood, L., Conti, J., Touyz, S., Madden, S., & Hay, P. (2024). Key-in-session identity negotiations in a first line treatment for adult anorexia nervosa. *Journal of Eating Disorders*, *12*(1), 20.

Holland, D., & Lave, J. (2001). History in person: Enduring struggles, contentious practice, intimate identities. School of American Research Press.

Jarman, M., Smith, J. A., & Walsh, S. U. E. (1997). The psychological battle for control: A qualitative study of health-care professionals' understandings of the treatment of anorexia nervosa. *Journal of Community & Applied Social Psychology*, *7*(2), 137–152.

King-Murphy, L. M. (1997). *The lived experience of anorexia nervosa: A phenomenological study* (Master's thesis). Memorial University of Newfoundland, St John's, Newfoundland.

Kiely, L., Conti, J., & Hay, P. (2023). Conceptualisation of severe and enduring anorexia nervosa: A qualitative meta-synthesis. *BMC Psychiatry, 23*(1), 26. https://doi.org/10.1186/s12888-023-05098-9

Kiely, L., Conti, J., & Hay, P. (2025). Severe and enduring anorexia nervosa and the proposed "terminal anorexia" category: An expanded meta-synthesis. *Eating Disorders: The Journal of Treatment & Prevention, 32*(4), 1–32. https://doi.org/10.1080/10640266.2024.2379635

Lock, J., & Le Grange, D. (2013). *Treatment manual for anorexia nervosa: A family-based approach* (2nd ed.). Guilford Press.

Malson, H. (2003). Women under erasure: Anorexic bodies in postmodern context. *Australian Journal of Psychology, 55*(1), 52–52.

McAdams, D. P., & McLean, K. C. (2013). Narrative identity. *Current Directions in Psychological Science, 22*(3), 233–238. https://doi.org/10.1177/0963721413475622

McIntosh, V. V., Bulik, C. M., McKenzie, J. M., Luty, S. E., & Jordan, J. (2000). Interpersonal psychotherapy for anorexia nervosa. *International Journal of Eating Disorders, 27*(2), 125–139. https://doi.org/10.1002/(SICI)1098-108X(200003)27:2<125::AID-EAT1>3.0.CO;2-4

McIntosh, V. W., Jordan, J., Carter, F., Luty, S. E., McKenzie, J. M., Bulik, C. M., Frampton, C. M. A., & Joyce, P. (2005). Three psychotherapies for anorexia nervosa: A randomized controlled trial. *American Journal of Psychiatry, 162*(4), 741–747. https://doi.org/10.1176/appi.ajp.162.4.741

Murray, S. B., Pila, E., Griffiths, S., & Le Grange, D. (2017). When illness severity and research dollars do not align: Are we overlooking eating disorders? *World Psychiatry, 16*(3), 321. https://doi.org/10.1002/wps.20465

Newton, E. D., Liu, L., Conti, J., Touyz, S., Arcelus, J., Madden, S., Pike, K., & Hay, P. (2024). Early change in quality of life in the treatment of anorexia nervosa. *Psych, 6*(1), 288–304. https://doi.org/10.3390/psych6010018

Norcross, J. C., & Cooper, N. (2021). *Personalising psychotherapy: Assessing and accommodating patient preference*. American Psychological Association.

Norcross, J. C., Cook, D. M., & Fuertes, J. N. (2022). Patient readiness to change: What we know about their stages and processes of change. In J. N. Fuertes (Ed.), *The other side of psychotherapy: Understanding clients' experiences and contributions in treatment* (pp. 73–97). American Psychological Association.

O'Connell, L. (2023). Being and doing anorexia nervosa: An autoethnography of diagnostic identity and performance of illness. *Health, 27*(3), 263–278. https://doi.org/10.1177/13634593211017190

Oldershaw, A., Basra, R. S., Lavender, T., & Startup, H. (2024). Specialist psychotherapy with emotion for anorexia in Kent and Sussex: An intervention development and non-randomised single arm feasibility trial. *European Eating Disorders Review, 32*(2), 215–229. https://doi.org/10.1002/erv.3034

Oldershaw, A., Lavender, T., & Basra, R. (2022). SPEAKS study: Study protocol of a multisite feasibility trial of the Specialist Psychotherapy with Emotion for Anorexia in Kent and Sussex (SPEAKS) intervention for outpatients with anorexia nervosa or otherwise specified feeding and eating disorders, anorexia nervosa type. *BMJ Open, 12*(1), e050350. https://doi.org/10.1136/bmjopen-2021-050350

Perls, F. S., Goodman, P., & Hefferline, R. E. (1994). *Gestalt therapy: Excitement and growth in the human personality*. Gestalt Journal Press.

Pellizzer, M. L., & Wade, T. D. (2023). The effectiveness of lived experience involvement in eating disorder treatment: A systematic review. *International Journal of Eating Disorders, 56*(3), 331–349. https://doi.org/10.1002/eat.23847

Philippson, P. (2009). *The emergent self: An existential-Gestalt approach*. Routledge.

Pike, K., Carter, J., & Olmsted, M. (2004). *Cognitive behavioral therapy manual for anorexia nervosa* [Unpublished manual].

Pilowsky, I. (1975). Dimensions of abnormal illness behaviour. *Australian and New Zealand Journal of Psychiatry, 9*(2), 141–147. https://doi.org/10.3109/00048677509159839

Rance, N., Clarke, V., & Moller, N. (2017). The anorexia nervosa experience: Shame, solitude and salvation. *Counselling and Psychotherapy Research, 17*(2), 127–136. https://doi.org/10.1002/capr.12097

Robinson, P. (2009). *Severe and enduring eating disorder (SEED): Management of complex presentations of anorexia and bulimia nervosa.* Wiley.

Russell, G. F., Szmukler, G. I., Dare, C., & Eisler, I. (1987). An evaluation of family therapy in anorexia nervosa and bulimia nervosa. *Archives of General Psychiatry, 44*(12), 1047–1056. https://doi.org/10.1001/archpsyc.1987.01800240021004

Schmidt, U., Claudino, A., Fernández-Aranda, F., Giel, K., Griffiths, J., Hay, P., Kim, Y.-R., Marshall, J., Micali, N., Monteleone, A. M., ... & Treasure, J. (2025). The current clinical approach to feeding and eating disorders aimed to increase personalisation of management. *World Psychiatry, 24*(1), 4–31. https://doi.org/10.1002/wps.21263

Schmidt, U., Magill, N., Renwick, B., Keyes, A., Kenyon, M., Dejong, H., Lose, A., Broadbent, H., Loomes, R., Yasin, H., ... & Treasure, J. (2015). The Maudsley Outpatient Study of Treatments for Anorexia Nervosa and Related Conditions (MOSAIC): Comparison of the Maudsley Model of Anorexia Nervosa Treatment for Adults (MANTRA) with Specialist Supportive Clinical Management (SSCM) in outpatients with broadly defined anorexia nervosa: A randomized controlled trial. *Journal of Consulting and Clinical Psychology, 83*(4), 796–807. https://doi.org/10.1037/ccp0000019

Schmidt, U., Oldershaw, A., Jichi, F., Sternheim, L., Startup, H., McIntosh, V., Jordan, J., Tchanturia, K., Wolff, G., Rooney, M., ... & Treasure, J. (2012). Outpatient psychological therapies for adults with anorexia nervosa: Randomised controlled trial. *British Journal of Psychiatry, 201*(5), 392–399. https://doi.org/10.1192/bjp.bp.112.112078

Schmidt, U., Startup, H., & Treasure, J. (2019). *A cognitive-interpersonal therapy workbook for treating anorexia nervosa: The Maudsley Model.* Routledge.

Steinhausen, H. C. (2009). Outcome of eating disorders. *Child and adolescent psychiatric clinics of North America, 18*(1), 225–242.

Stockford, C., Kroese, B. S., Beesley, A., & Leung, N. (2018). Severe and enduring anorexia nervosa: The personal meaning of symptoms and treatment. *Women's Studies International Forum, 68*, 129–138. https://doi.org/10.1016/j.wsif.2018.03.003

Thoresen, L. H. K., Thørnquist, H. H., Stänicke, E., & McLeod, J. (2021). Shift in representation and symbolisation of affective experience: A paradoxical outcome in therapy. *European Journal of Psychotherapy and Counselling, 23*(2), 177–200. https://doi.org/10.1080/13642537.2021.1923048

Touyz, S. W., Le Grange, D., Lacey, J. H., Hay, P., Smith, R., Maguire, S., Bamford, B., Pike, K., & Crosby, R. (2013). Treating severe and enduring anorexia nervosa: A randomized controlled trial. *Psychological Medicine, 43*(12), 2501–2511. https://doi.org/10.1017/S0033291713000949

Treasure, J., & Cardi, V. (2017). Anorexia nervosa, theory and treatment: Where are we 35 years on from Hilde Bruch's foundation lecture? *European Eating Disorders Review, 25*(3), 139–147. https://doi.org/10.1002/erv.2511

White, M. (1987). Anorexia nervosa: A cybernetic perspective. In J. Elka-Harkaway (Ed.), *Eating disorders* (pp. 65–75). Aspen.

White, M. (2007). *Maps of narrative practice.* Norton.

Williams, K., King, J., & Fox, J. R. (2016). Sense of self and anorexia nervosa: A grounded theory. *Psychology and Psychotherapy: Theory, Research and Practice*, *89*(2), 211-228.

Wonderlich, S. A., Bulik, C. M., Schmidt, U., Steiger, H., & Hoek, H. W. (2020). Severe and enduring anorexia nervosa: Update and observations about the current clinical reality. *International Journal of Eating Disorders, 53*(8), 1303–1312. https://doi.org/10.1002/eat.23283

Yager, J. (2020). Managing patients with severe and enduring anorexia nervosa: When is enough, enough? *Journal of Nervous and Mental Disease, 208*(4), 277–282. https://doi.org/10.1097/NMD.0000000000001124

Zhu, J., Hay, P., Yang, Y., Le Grange, D., Lacey, J. H., Lujic, S., Smith, C., & Touyz, S. (2023). Specific psychological therapies versus other therapies or no treatment for severe and enduring anorexia nervosa. *Cochrane Database of Systematic Reviews, 8*, CD011570. https://doi.org/10.1002/14651858.CD011570.pub2

Part II

The Social Self

The Interplay Between Anorexia Nervosa and Social Experience: Emotional Expression, Loneliness, Belonging, Group Identity, Gender, and Culture

Chapter 7

Emotions in a Social Context

Marc O. Williams and John R.E. Fox

Summary

The first part of this volume has explored how identity takes shape – and sometimes struggles to take shape – in the context of anorexia nervosa (AN). Drawing on a range of perspectives, the chapters have considered the influence of early relationships, self-conscious emotions, the anorexic voice, and neurodiversity. Despite their different lenses, a common theme has run through them all: that AN can take root where a clear and accepted sense of self has not yet had the space or support to grow. In these conditions, AN can offer something deceptively solid – clarity, control – in the face of uncertainty and confusion. But like a fast-growing plant that overshadows neighbouring shoots, it can block light from reaching other parts of the self, stifling the development of other aspects of one's identity. Over time, AN can begin to dominate, making the idea of recovery feel more complicated and more distant. Many therapeutic approaches, each in their own way, try to help individuals reconnect with who they are beyond the eating disorder.

In Part II, we widen the focus from the inner world to the social world, where identity is shaped in connection with others. Social identity – the sense of who we are and our roles in relation to others – plays a powerful role in how our sense of overall identity unfolds. But navigating the social world can be fraught, especially for those with AN. Forming or deepening the very relationships that could offer a path out of AN requires authentic emotional expression and the willingness to show vulnerability, often in the context of shame, stigma, and long-established strategies for emotional avoidance.

This chapter begins by exploring emotional regulation and its implications for identity in interpersonal contexts. Later chapters in Part II consider how stigma, loneliness, gender identity, and cultural experience interact with AN. Together, they highlight the powerful role of social and cultural contexts in shaping how AN is experienced, understood, and addressed.

DOI: 10.4324/9781003468189-9

Anorexia Nervosa and Emotional Regulation

Anorexia nervosa (AN) is not only a condition of the body, but one that also reaches into the emotional lives of those affected, and their loved ones. Those with AN often report that it does something emotionally important: providing a distinct identity and a feeling of specialness, enhancing self-confidence, giving control over emotions, and signalling distress to others (Serpell et al., 1999, 2004). These emotional functions come at a cost. What once felt like a coping strategy becomes constraining, even suffocating. "You suffocated all my natural emotions, clouded all my responses," one person with AN reflected (Serpell et al., 1999, p. 181), capturing the emotional blunting that often results from AN.

This chapter explores the emotional dimension of AN, especially in the context of how emotions are regulated in social contexts. We begin by outlining the literature on emotional regulation, followed by what the research tells us about how these processes might play a role in the development and maintenance of AN. We then consider how emotional regulation strategies may play a causal role in the development of AN, particularly in the context of early interpersonal experiences. We then turn to the social implications of emotional avoidance and suppression, including how they can affect one's sense of self and connectedness with others. Finally, we consider what all this means for treatment and recovery, focusing on therapeutic models that place emotion at the heart of their work.

Theoretical Foundations and Empirical Findings

Emotions help us make sense of the world. They guide our decisions, signal our needs, and – perhaps most importantly – draw us into connection with others. As Keltner and Gross (1999) remind us, emotions evolved not just for survival, but for belonging. They shape how we respond to life's recurring challenges and serve as social signposts, communicating what matters to us.

But emotion doesn't always flow freely. How we regulate emotions – how we respond to them, shape them, or shut them down – is just as important as the emotions themselves. Gross's (1998) model of emotion regulation outlines five key stages at which this regulation can happen. We might steer ourselves away from situations likely to trigger strong feelings, or try to change those situations once we're in them. We might distract ourselves, reframe what's happening, or suppress our responses entirely. Some of these strategies are proactive and adaptive; others are more reactive and defensive.

In the case of AN, many of these strategies seem to become skewed toward avoidance and suppression. A meta-analysis by Oldershaw et al. (2015) found that individuals with AN were more likely to avoid emotionally charged situations and struggled to modify them in helpful ways. Instead of confronting problems directly, many turned inward – ruminating, comparing themselves unfavourably to others, and silencing their emotional responses. They used fewer adaptive strategies like reappraisal and acceptance, and more often tried to suppress what they felt, especially in the presence of others.

These aren't just abstract patterns – they echo what many people with AN say about their lived experience. Worry, rumination, and self-criticism often reach far beyond food and body image. Many describe AN-related behaviours – such as restriction or overexercise – as ways to dull distress, cope with uncertainty, or manage feelings of shame and inadequacy.

Neuroscientific findings further support these patterns. For instance, Steward et al. (2022) found altered connectivity between areas of the brain involved in emotion regulation (namely, the prefrontal cortex and the amygdala) when participants with AN tried to reframe distressing situations. Reduced connectivity in this network was linked to greater eating disorder severity and more pronounced difficulties with emotion regulation. Other studies have shown atypical patterns of autonomic nervous system response (Jenkins et al., 2021): heartrate variability responses (HRV) to emotional stimuli suggest atypical parasympathetic and sympathetic nervous system activity, and the authors note that HRV is different in acute AN than in lean controls without AN, suggesting that this is not solely attributable to low weight. Together, these findings support the view that emotional regulation difficulties are integral to AN and may underpin its cognitive, behavioural, and interpersonal features, including common comorbidities like depression and anxiety (Jagielska & Kacperska, 2017).

Cause or Consequence?

Whether difficulties with emotional regulation can *explain* AN is a topic of debate, and the answer is obscured by the biological effects of the acute starvation state, which themselves could disturb emotional regulation. Oldershaw et al. (2015) summarised findings from studies comparing healthy controls with individuals who had recovered from AN: while some emotional regulation capacities appear to normalise at least somewhat following recovery, including reduced avoidance of emotion-inducing situations and reduced social comparisons and submissiveness, relatively high levels of emotional suppression remain.

Without longitudinal studies of individuals prior to AN onset, it is difficult to ascertain the role of emotional regulation traits preceding the development of AN as opposed to a "scar" caused by starvation (Harrison et al., 2010). Two lines of evidence, however, suggest trait vulnerability prior to AN onset. First, starvation does not seem to reliably cause deficits in emotional regulation, and evidence suggests that lower Body Mass Index (BMI) in AN is, to the contrary, associated with better emotional regulation (Brockmeyer et al., 2012; Racine & Wildes, 2013). Munro et al. (2017) argued that any improvements in emotional regulation following recovery likely reflect psychological changes, rather than being merely due to physical recovery. Second, anxiety disorders often precede the onset of AN (Lloyd et al., 2017), suggesting that anxiety – and perhaps difficulties with regulating anxiety – may play a role in the disorder's development.

Developmentally, difficulties could emerge from adverse childhood experiences. Molendijk et al. (2017) performed meta-analyses to examine differences between AN subtypes and healthy controls in the experience of childhood maltreatment, showing an association between childhood physical abuse and both AN subtypes (restricting and binge-purge), sexual abuse and AN (only for the binge-purge subtype), and emotional abuse and AN (subtypes were not analysed separately due to lack of data). On the other hand, Caslini et al. (2016) found no significant link between childhood sexual abuse and AN when controlling for publication bias, and no evidence linking childhood emotional abuse to AN, though childhood physical abuse was associated with the disorder. Emotional and physical neglect are also commonly reported in general eating disorder samples (Pignatelli et al., 2017), but few studies have looked at this in AN specifically.

Morrison et al. (2022) present findings from a qualitative study of women with AN, who described characteristics of their "anorexic voice" (an internal critical voice that encourages eating disorder behaviours; Pugh, 2016) that mirrored those of their childhood abusers and bullies (see Chapter 4 for a fuller discussion on the anorexic voice). This supports the idea that, for some individuals, restriction serves as a means of coping with unmanageable emotions associated with childhood adversity (Caslini et al., 2016). While this is a plausible mechanism explaining the association between trauma and AN, further longitudinal work would be needed in order to draw definitive causal conclusions.

Emotional Features and Their Social Implications

Emotions are not just fleeting reactions, but are deeply tied to how we understand ourselves and connect with others. As Damasio (2003) argued, emotions are central to the sense of self, acting as signals that guide us in navigating our internal and external world. Chapter 2 considers how, in AN, this signal is often muted through emotional suppression which, coupled with deficits in emotional and interoceptive awareness, may interfere with identity development, leading to vulnerability to AN. But these strategies don't just affect how someone feels internally – they ripple outward, influencing their social reactions and, in turn, how others relate to them.

While Munro et al. (2017) proposed that attempts to mute emotional expression in AN may reflect a fear of rejection (appearing "too needy" or vulnerable), Gross and John (2003) presented evidence that emotional suppression has its own negative social consequences for identity, as it leads to painful awareness of one's own inauthenticity and is associated with finding intimacy difficult. Masking emotions can also lead to being *perceived* as inauthentic or untrustworthy, making relationships harder to form and maintain (Lynch et al., 2015).

Lynch et al. (2015) posited that AN is a disorder of over-control in which excessive self-control (a tendency to inhibit emotions and impulses in the pursuit of longer-term goals) impairs social signalling of warmth, openness, and cooperation, preventing the formation of deep social bonds (emotional loneliness); indeed, AN is associated with high levels of loneliness (Levine, 2012). If AN is a means of managing emotions, such as suppressing difficult emotional experiences and managing how we are perceived by others (Munro et al., 2017; Serpell et al., 2004), one of its unintended consequences might be the removal of emotional closeness and intimacy with others (Lynch et al., 2013).

Even basic forms of emotional communication can be affected. For instance, research shows that individuals with AN are more likely to avoid eye contact than people without the disorder (Harrison et al., 2019). While this might seem like a small detail, eye contact plays a vital role in signalling trust and connection. If this signal is missing, others may not feel invited in – and the person with AN may miss out on the warmth that genuine connection can bring.

Other emotional traits common in AN add to these challenges. Alexithymia (difficulty in identifying and describing emotions) and social anhedonia (reduced ability to find pleasure in social interactions) often persist even after recovery (Oldershaw et al., 2019). Together, they may inhibit the ability to form deep social connections. Without shared emotional experiences, relationships may feel shallow or effortful, and the individual may struggle to build the kind of social identity that is formed through mutual understanding and shared emotional resonance. More research is needed to determine whether these features predict the onset of AN and what their relationship is with adversity (particularly trauma experienced in social relationships).

Treatment Implications

If emotional suppression in AN disrupts both social intimacy and the capacity to know oneself in relation to others, then this has significant consequences for how treatment is conceptualised and delivered. Emotion regulation should not be regarded as a peripheral issue or a byproduct of starvation; rather, it is a core developmental process that shapes identity, interpersonal connection, and the sense of self. As Damasio (1999) observed, emotions function as fundamental signals – guiding us toward or away from particular courses of action and providing feedback on our relationship to the world around us. Similarly, Power (2010) highlighted the centrality of emotion to self-regulation, goal pursuit, and meaning-making. In AN, chronic suppression or avoidance of emotion can be seen as a defensive adaptation: it blunts painful self-awareness, but at the cost of deep loneliness, alienation from others, and a constricted sense of identity.

Cognitive Behaviour Therapy for Eating Disorders (CBT-E)

Among the most widely used and well-evidenced approaches is cognitive behaviour therapy (CBT), and specifically CBT for eating disorders (CBT-E; Fairburn, 2008), recommended by NICE (2017) for the treatment of AN. CBT-E has impressive outcomes: in controlled studies, around two-thirds of individuals with AN who complete the programme achieve sustained improvements in weight and symptoms (Fairburn et al., 2013). However, treatment completion rates are variable, and across the broader AN literature – not limited to CBT-E – relapse following treatment remains common, with up to 50% of patients experiencing a return of symptoms (Sala et al., 2023).. These findings suggest that, while CBT-E can be highly effective for many, there is a pressing need to improve engagement, sustain recovery, and address underlying processes that contribute to the onset and persistence of AN.

CBT-E does recognise that intolerance of emotion can play a role in maintaining the disorder for some, and it addresses the emotional consequences of starvation alongside other maintaining mechanisms. Within its structure, difficulties with emotion regulation are generally treated as secondary concerns, addressed more explicitly only in those who meet criteria for significant mood intolerance, in which case an optional module is provided. While this flexibility can be useful, it risks underestimating the possibility that emotion regulation difficulties are not solely consequences of starvation but often pre-date the illness, contributing to its onset and persistence. Evidence suggests that emotional suppression and avoidance can emerge well before restrictive eating behaviours, meaning that emotion regulation might require more systematic attention from the outset of therapy rather than being treated as an add-on.

From a relational perspective, CBT-E may face particular challenges in building therapeutic rapport when clients have difficulty with the reciprocal expression and recognition of emotion. As Oldershaw et al. (2019) note, if clients with AN suppress their emotional signals, therapists may struggle to respond in a way that feels attuned and congruent. This mismatch can leave both parties feeling disengaged or frustrated. Oyer et al. (2016) report that people with AN sometimes experience therapists as emotionally unresponsive, which they identify as unhelpful to recovery. While CBT-E's central target (to reduce the overvaluation of eating, weight, and shape as the primary source of self-worth) often involves encouraging engagement in other life domains, the emotional barriers to such re-engagement may be underexplored in standard delivery. Strengthening the emotional component within CBT-E, for example by embedding more experiential or interpersonal work, could enhance both its relational depth and its impact on identity reconstruction.

The Maudsley Model of Anorexia Nervosa Treatment for Adults (MANTRA)

Another NICE-recommended treatment, the Maudsley Model of Anorexia Nervosa Treatment for Adults (MANTRA; Schmidt et al., 2015), places greater emphasis on the emotional and social processes described in this chapter. MANTRA was developed specifically for adults with AN and is grounded in the idea that maintaining factors such as cognitive rigidity, emotional avoidance, and an identity fused with the disorder are central to its persistence. The model explicitly addresses emotion regulation difficulties, particularly high levels of avoidance and suppression, and invites patients to reflect on the emotional functions served by AN. Through personalised case formulations, motivational interviewing techniques, experiential tasks, and compassionate mind training, MANTRA works to improve emotional awareness and interpersonal functioning.

One of MANTRA's particular strengths is its focus on enhancing social connection. By helping individuals to develop emotional insight and re-engage in relationships, it directly supports identity development beyond the illness. This makes it potentially well-suited for those experiencing alexithymia or social anhedonia. However, like CBT-E, its effectiveness relies heavily on patient engagement with emotionally evocative tasks – a process that may be challenging for those with high avoidance. Further research is also needed to understand which individuals are most likely to benefit from its specific mechanisms.

Emotion-Focused Therapy (EFT)

Other approaches have moved even further toward placing emotion at the heart of treatment. Chapter 2 in this volume describes in detail an approach to addressing emotional regulation difficulties in AN drawing on the principles of Emotion-Focused Therapy (EFT; Greenberg, 2006). EFT offers a framework for understanding different types of emotional responses, including how painful, "primary maladaptive" emotions – often rooted in early unmet attachment, identity, or safety needs – can remain stuck into adulthood. In AN, such core emotional pain is frequently masked by secondary emotions or by global distress, leaving individuals disconnected from adaptive emotional signals. From an EFT perspective, therapy becomes a process of re-learning to access, symbolise, and transform these underlying emotions (Greenberg & Pascual-Leone, 2024). In the context of AN this emphasis on transforming maladaptive emotion is particularly relevant to addressing the interpersonal and identity-related difficulties described in this chapter. Although evidence for EFT in AN is still emerging (Sala et al., 2016), its direct targeting of emotional avoidance makes it theoretically compelling.

Compassion-Focused Therapy (CFT) and CFT-E

Compassion-focused therapy (CFT; Gilbert, 2014) and its adaptation for eating disorders (CFT-E; Goss & Allan, 2014) further highlight the role of social and affiliative emotions in recovery. CFT is based on the premise that emotion regulation evolved within three interacting systems: threat, drive, and soothe. In AN, regulation is often dominated by threat-based processes, with restriction and self-control serving as defensive strategies against perceived social rejection or inadequacy. CFT interventions, such as compassionate mind training and imagery exercises, aim to cultivate affiliative emotions and social safeness. This may help to displace defensive, threat-driven regulation with more balanced and socially connected patterns. Research indicates that early reduction in shame and improvements in self-compassion in eating disorder treatment are associated with better outcomes (Kelly et al., 2014) and that CFT may be superior to CBT in long-term outcomes for those with a history of trauma (Vrabel et al., 2024), though further high-quality trials are needed.

Radically-Open Dialectical Behaviour Therapy (RO-DBT)

As noted earlier, excessive self-control in AN can interfere with interpersonal functioning, leading to emotional loneliness (Lynch et al., 2013). Radically-open dialectical behaviour therapy (RO-DBT) is designed specifically for disorders of over-control, including AN. RO-DBT emphasises that emotions are not just signals to be managed but valuable information about needs, values, and social intentions. Treatment aims to foster openness, flexibility, and trust through strategies such as loving-kindness meditation and social signalling training. By directly targeting emotional loneliness and encouraging prosocial risk-taking, RO-DBT seeks to counteract the isolation that often maintains AN. While feasibility and acceptability studies (Hempel et al., 2018; Sala et al., 2016) have been promising, the approach remains in the early stages of evidence development for AN.

Concluding Synthesis

Across the treatments reviewed in this section, there is broad – though not uniform – recognition that difficulties in emotion regulation play a role in the onset or persistence of AN. Some models, such as MANTRA, Emotion-Focused Therapy, Compassion-Focused Therapy, and RO-DBT, place emotional processes at the centre of their formulations, viewing them as key mechanisms through which identity, interpersonal connection, and self-worth are rebuilt. These approaches actively target emotional awareness, expression, and tolerance as primary therapeutic goals, often embedding them in relational or experiential work.

Others, such as CBT-E, acknowledge that emotional intolerance can maintain the eating disorder but tend to position it as secondary to the central task of reducing the overvaluation of weight and shape. In such models, emotion regulation work may be offered selectively, for example when significant mood intolerance is present, rather than being seen as universally necessary.

Taken together, these approaches differ in emphasis but share a recognition that for many individuals with AN, change requires some engagement with emotional experience, whether as a direct target or as a means to facilitate other therapeutic aims. Strengthening emotional capacities, in turn, can help open the way to more flexible self-appraisals, richer social connection, and the development of a sense of self less constrained by the disorder. More work is needed to determine whether systematically integrating emotion regulation insights into mainstream treatments could enhance their efficacy, and to strengthen the evidence base for interventions that explicitly centre emotions as a foundation for recovery.

Conclusion

Emotional regulation difficulties are a consistent and multifaceted feature of AN, shaping not only how distress is internally managed but also how individuals relate to others and construct a sense of self. From early avoidance of emotion-inducing situations to entrenched habits of suppression, these strategies may initially serve protective functions but ultimately restrict emotional expression, impair social connection, and limit identity development. Features such as alexithymia and social anhedonia further compound these effects, dampening the rewards of social interaction and potentially disrupting relational signals that support the formation of a coherent self. Treatments that centre on emotional expression, social engagement, and identity reconstruction (such as RO-DBT, Emotion-Focused Therapy, CFT, and MANTRA) offer promising avenues for addressing these patterns. Ultimately, understanding emotional regulation as not only an internal process but a deeply social one is key to supporting individuals with AN in moving toward a more authentic and developed sense of self.

References

Brockmeyer, T., Holtforth, M. G., Bents, H., Kammerer, A., Herzog, W., & Friederich, H. C. (2012). Starvation and emotion regulation in anorexia nervosa. *Comprehensive Psychiatry, 53*, 496–501. https://doi.org/10.1016/j.comppsych.2011.09.003

Caslini, M., Bartoli, F., Crocamo, C., Dakanalis, A., Clerici, M., & Carrà, G. (2016). Disentangling the association between child abuse and eating disorders: A systematic review and meta-analysis. *Psychosomatic Medicine, 78*(1), 79–90.

Damasio, A. (1999). The feeling of what happens: Body and emotion in the making of consciousness. Harcourt College Publishers.

Damasio, A. (2003). Feelings of emotion and the self. *Annals of the New York Academy of Sciences, 1001*(1), 253–261.

Fairburn, C. G. (2008). *Cognitive behavior therapy and eating disorders*. Guilford Press.

Fairburn, C. G., Cooper, Z., Doll, H. A., O'Connor, M. E., Palmer, R. L., & Dalle Grave, R. (2013). Enhanced cognitive behaviour therapy for adults with anorexia nervosa: A UK–Italy study. *Behaviour Research and Therapy, 51*(1), R2–R8.

Gilbert, P. (2014). The origins and nature of compassion focused therapy. *British Journal of Clinical Psychology, 53*(1), 6–41.

Goss, K., & Allan, S. (2014). The development and application of compassion-focused therapy for eating disorders (CFT-E). *British Journal of Clinical Psychology, 53*(1), 62–77.

Greenberg, L. (2006). Emotion-focused therapy: A synopsis. *Journal of Contemporary Psychotherapy, 36*, 87–93.

Greenberg, L., Pascual-Leone, J., & Johnson, J. (2024). Schematic processing and emotional change: Implications for treatment. *New Ideas in Psychology, 73*, 1–9.

Gross, J. J. (1998). The emerging field of emotion regulation: An integrative review. *Review of General Psychology, 2*(3), 271–299.

Gross, J. J., & John, O. P. (2003). Individual differences in two emotion regulation processes: Implications for affect, relationships, and well-being. *Journal of Personality and Social Psychology, 85*(2), 348–362.

Harrison, A., Tchanturia, K., & Treasure, J. (2010). Attentional bias, emotion recognition, and emotion regulation in anorexia: State or trait? *Biological Psychiatry, 68*(8), 755–761.

Harrison, A., Watterson, S. V., & Bennett, S. D. (2019). An experimental investigation into the use of eye-contact in social interactions in women in the acute and recovered stages of anorexia nervosa. *International Journal of Eating Disorders, 52*(1), 61–70.

Hempel, R., Vanderbleek, E., & Lynch, T. R. (2018). Radically open DBT: Targeting emotional loneliness in anorexia nervosa. *Eating Disorders, 26*(1), 92–104.

Jagielska, G., & Kacperska, I. (2017). Outcome, comorbidity and prognosis in anorexia nervosa. *Psychiatria Polska, 51*(2), 205–218.

Jenkins, Z. M., Eikelis, N., Phillipou, A., Castle, D. J., Wilding, H. E., & Lambert, E. A. (2021). Autonomic nervous system function in anorexia nervosa: A systematic review. *Frontiers in Neuroscience, 15*, 682208.

Kelly, A. C., Carter, J. C., & Borairi, S. (2014). Are improvements in shame and self-compassion early in eating disorders treatment associated with better patient outcomes?. *International Journal of Eating Disorders*, *47*(1), 54–64.

Keltner, D., & Gross, J. J. (1999). Functional accounts of emotions. *Cognition & Emotion, 13*(5), 467–480.

Levine, M. P. (2012). Loneliness and eating disorders. *The Journal of Psychology, 146*(1–2), 243–257.

Lloyd, E. C., Frampton, I., Verplanken, B., & Haase, A. M. (2017). How extreme dieting becomes compulsive: A novel hypothesis for the role of anxiety in the development and maintenance of anorexia nervosa. *Medical Hypotheses, 108*, 144–150.

Lynch, T. R., Gray, K. L., Hempel, R. J., Titley, M., Chen, E. Y., & O'Mahen, H. A. (2013). Radically open-dialectical behavior therapy for adult anorexia nervosa: Feasibility and outcomes from an inpatient program. *BMC Psychiatry, 13*(1), 1–17.

Lynch, T. R., Hempel, R. J., & Dunkley, C. (2015). Radically open-dialectical behavior therapy for disorders of over-control: Signaling matters. *American Journal of Psychotherapy, 69*(2), 141–162.

Molendijk, M. L., Hoek, H. W., Brewerton, T. D., & Elzinga, B. M. (2017). Childhood maltreatment and eating disorder pathology: A systematic review and dose-response meta-analysis. *Psychological Medicine, 47*(8), 1402–1416.

Morrison, J., Williams, M. O., & Fox, J. R. (2022). Negative childhood events and the development of the anorexic voice: A grounded theory. *Psychology and Psychotherapy: Theory, Research and Practice*, *95*(4), 1018–1035.

Munro, C., Randell, L., & Lawrie, S. M. (2017). An integrative bio-psycho-social theory of anorexia nervosa. *Clinical Psychology & Psychotherapy, 24*(1), 1–21.

National Institute for Health and Care Excellence. (2017). *Eating disorders: Recognition and treatment* [NICE Guideline No. 69]. https://www.nice.org.uk/guidance/ng69

Oldershaw, A., Lavender, T., Sallis, H., Stahl, D., & Schmidt, U. (2015). Emotion generation and regulation in anorexia nervosa: A systematic review and meta-analysis of self-report data. *Clinical Psychology Review, 39*, 83–95.

Oldershaw, A., Startup, H., & Lavender, T. (2019). Anorexia nervosa and a lost emotional self: A psychological formulation of the development, maintenance, and treatment of anorexia nervosa. *Frontiers in Psychology*, *10*, 219.

Oyer, L., O'Halloran, M. S., & Christoe-Frazier, L. (2016). Understanding the working alliance with clients diagnosed with anorexia nervosa. *Eating Disorders, 24*(2), 121–137.

Pignatelli, A. M., Wampers, M., Loriedo, C., Biondi, M., & Vanderlinden, J. (2017). Childhood neglect in eating disorders: A systematic review and meta-analysis. *Journal of Trauma & Dissociation, 18*(1), 100–115.

Power, M. (2010). Emotion-focused cognitive therapy. Wiley Blackwell.

Pugh M, Waller G. The anorexic voice and severity of eating pathology in anorexia nervosa *Int J Eat Disord. 2016 Jun*; *49*(6): 22-5. doi: 10.1002/eat.22499.

Racine, S. E., & Wildes, J. E. (2013). Emotion dysregulation and symptoms of anorexia nervosa: The unique roles of lack of emotional awareness and impulse control difficulties when upset. *International Journal of Eating Disorders, 46*, 713–720. https://doi.org/10.1002/eat.22145

Sala, M., Heard, A., & Black, E. A. (2016). Emotion-focused treatments for anorexia nervosa: A systematic review of the literature. *Eating and Weight Disorders–Studies on Anorexia, Bulimia and Obesity, 21*, 147–164.

Sala, M., Keshishian, A., Song, S., Moskowitz, R., Bulik, C. M., Roos, C. R., & Levinson, C. A. (2023). Predictors of relapse in eating disorders: A meta-analysis. *Journal of Psychiatric Research, 158*, 281–299.

Schmidt, U., Magill, N., Renwick, B., Keyes, A., Kenyon, M., Dejong, H., ... & Landau, S. (2015). The Maudsley Outpatient Study of Treatments for Anorexia Nervosa and Related Conditions (MOSAIC): Comparison of the Maudsley Model of Anorexia Nervosa Treatment for Adults (MANTRA) with specialist supportive clinical management (SSCM) in outpatients with broadly defined anorexia nervosa: A randomized controlled trial. *Journal of Consulting and Clinical Psychology, 83*(4), 796.

Serpell, L., Treasure, J., Teasdale, J., & Sullivan, V. (1999). Anorexia nervosa: Friend or foe? *International Journal of Eating Disorders, 25*(2), 177–186.

Serpell, L., Teasdale, J. D., Troop, N. A., & Treasure, J. (2004). The development of the P-CAN, a measure to operationalize the pros and cons of anorexia nervosa. *International Journal of Eating Disorders, 36*(4), 416–433.

Steward, T., Martínez-Zalacaín, I., Mestre-Bach, G., Sánchez, I., Riesco, N., Jiménez-Murcia, S., ... & Fernandez-Aranda, F. (2022). Dorsolateral prefrontal cortex and amygdala function during cognitive reappraisal predicts weight restoration and emotion regulation impairment in anorexia nervosa. *Psychological Medicine, 52*(5), 844–852.

Vrabel, K. R., Waller, G., Goss, K., Wampold, B., Kopland, M., & Hoffart, A. (2024). Cognitive behavioral therapy versus compassion focused therapy for adult patients with eating disorders with and without childhood trauma: A randomized controlled trial in an intensive treatment setting. *Behaviour Research and Therapy, 174*, 104480.

Chapter 8

Social Identity

Niamh McNamara

Introduction

The health and well-being of people living with anorexia (AN) (or indeed, any eating disorder) is inescapably associated with the degree to which they are socially connected (McNamara et al., 2022). Loneliness is a key risk factor for the development of AN, often serves to worsen symptoms, and acts as a precursor to relapse following treatment (Harney et al., 2014; Richardson et al., 2017; Cardi et al., 2018; Cockell et al., 2004). Equally, the presence of supportive relationships, a feeling of connection and belonging, and having diverse social networks (i.e., with connections unrelated to the eating disorder) are linked to sustained recovery outcomes (Linville et al., 2012; Rowlands et al., 2021). These social factors feature prominently in definitions of 'personal' recovery generated from individual lived experiences but tend to rarely, if at all, feature in understandings of 'clinical' recovery and are relatively neglected in research and acute treatment (Wetzler et al., 2020). Understanding and tackling the social elements of AN development and recovery may go some way to addressing the relatively high rate of relapse – estimated at 41% in the first year post-treatment (Venturo-Conerly et al., 2020). This chapter will outline the role that social relationships, specifically group memberships (and their associated social identities), play in the development, maintenance, and treatment of eating disorders[1] and will argue that social identity considerations may potentially bridge the gap between personal and clinical recovery.

The Importance of Supportive Social Relationships in Recovery

There is no real consensus on how recovery from AN should be defined and clinical conceptualisations often fail to accord with lived experiences of recovery (McDonald et al., 2021). It is proposed that recovering from any form of mental illness encompasses 'subjective' or 'personal' elements of 'internal transformation' (Wetzler et al., 2020, p. 1189) including identity change, hope, empowerment, and increased social connectedness and that recovery itself can be experienced in the presence of continuing symptoms (Leamy et al., 2011). While the concept

DOI: 10.4324/9781003468189-10

of personal recovery has featured in the mental health literature for some time, it is only recently that there have been efforts to understand its application to eating disorders. One framework, developed by Wetzler et al. (2020) based on a qualitative meta-synthesis of 20 studies with those with lived experience, proposes that personal recovery comprises six fundamental elements (with associated sub-elements), namely: *Supportive Relationships*, *Identity*, *Hope*, *Meaning and Purpose*, *Empowerment*, and *Self-Compassion*. The authors calculated intensity effect sizes for each of their framework's 14 sub-elements to understand their relative importance which revealed the most fundamental component to be *support and encouragement from others* (Wetzler et al., 2020).

While the importance of social support to sustained recovery is recognised, the link between social relationships, particularly non-familial relationships, and eating disorders is an under-researched topic (Linville et al., 2012; Pearce et al., 2023) and there is a lack of evidence-based interventions to help those in recovery broaden their social networks and access appropriate recovery support (Davies, 2004). The absence of social support is a significant problem for people living with an eating disorder. They tend to have small, poor-quality social networks (Patel et al., 2016) and believe that there is less support available to them compared to general population controls (Arcelus et al., 2013; Makri et al., 2022). Over the course of the illness, difficulties developing and maintaining social connections lead to severe isolation (Rowlands et al., 2021). The resultant feelings of loneliness are exceptionally difficult during the acute stages of an eating disorder (Levine, 2012) and may trigger relapse during recovery (Cardi et al., 2018; Stewart, 2004). During the COVID-19 pandemic, strict lockdown and 'social distancing' protocols contributed to heightened loneliness, worse eating disorder symptomatology and related psychopathology, increased hospital admissions and higher than usual proportions of suicidal ideation and attempted suicide among those with an established eating disorder (Devoe et al., 2023; Taquet et al., 2022).

Conversely, there tends to be an increase in social group memberships (Streete, 2020) and perceived social support among those who have recovered (Cockell et al., 2004). Maintaining connections with supportive others, particularly family, may go some way to addressing eating disorder-related loneliness (McNamara et al., 2022). Even the COVID-19 pandemic was not exclusively negatively experienced by those living with an eating disorder. Increased time spent at home and the ability to provide more support were valued by carers (Clark Bryan et al., 2020) and those in recovery noted the beneficial impacts of greater connectivity with family and friends during this time (Termorshuizen et al., 2020). Indeed, the family group was shown to act as a protective resource against loneliness and eating disorder-related impacts of lockdowns, which in turn were associated with reduced eating disorder symptomatology and anxiety (McNamara et al., 2022). Thus, social relationships enhanced resilience during times of exceptional challenge and crisis. Despite the clear importance of social relationships to both the development of, and recovery from, an eating disorder, Pearce et al. (2023, p. 29) note 'we are still further from a clear understanding of causal relationships, and high-quality research elucidating pathways between social relationships and conditions such as … eating disorders.' The Social Identity Approach to Health (SIAH; Haslam et al., 2018) can go some way to bridging that lacuna.

The Social Identity Approach to Health: Understanding How Social Relationships Impact Health and Well-being

Within Psychology, discussions of the self and identity tend to take an individualistic focus – orienting to the attributes that make one unique (Haslam et al., 2018). However, we also define ourselves in terms of the groups we belong to, such as our family, local community, favourite sports team, or profession. The Social Identity Approach (SIA) in Social Psychology (Tajfel & Turner, 1979) – comprising social identity theory and self-categorisation theory – provides a framework that articulates when, why, and how we come to self-define as group members rather than as unique individuals and the implications that has for our behaviour (and, more recently, our health). Social identification (i.e., the psychological experience of group membership) represents our knowledge that we belong to a particular group as well as the emotional and value significance we attach to that group (Tajfel, 1982). When we identify with a group, we internalise it as part of our self-concept and it guides our values, beliefs, and actions (Turner, 1982). Of course, we tend to have more than one social identity and whether we identify in terms of any specific group membership depends on the social context we find ourselves in. For example, the workplace might make our professional identity salient, while moving to a new country might cue our national identity. In addition, our perception of the *fit* of a particular identity and our *readiness* to adopt that identity will also make it more likely that we will act in terms of that group membership in relevant social situations (Turner, 1982). In short, we are more likely to think of ourselves in terms of a particular social identity to the extent that that identity helps us to understand who we are in that situation as well as how to successfully navigate it. Therefore, group memberships help us understand ourselves, provide us with a sense of purpose, guide our actions, and influence how we relate to others in the social environment (Haslam et al., 2018; Tajfel & Turner, 1979).

Originally, the SIA was used as a framework to explore intergroup behaviour (for a historical overview, see Hornsey, 2008). More recently, however, social psychologists began to consider the implications of group memberships for individual health as part of a paradigm that is known as the 'Social Cure' (Jetten et al., 2012). Researchers in this field argue that understanding the precise psychological mechanisms through which social relationships influence health is essential for the development of appropriate and effective interventions to tackle issues such as loneliness and isolation and to support individuals in building social networks that enhance health and well-being (Jetten et al., 2012).

Over the last 15 years, research within the SIAH (SIAH, Haslam et al., 2018), has uncovered key insights into how group processes impact individual and collective health. First, social identities act to influence group members' appraisal of situations as stressful or not, as well as their appraisal of their ability to cope with adversity (Haslam et al., 2005). Second, social identities satisfy global psychological needs (Greenaway et al., 2016) and provide members with a range of social psychological resources that enhance group members' physical and mental health, such as social support, collective efficacy, and a sense of belonging, meaning and purpose (Haslam et al., 2018). These benefits have been shown across a range of groups and contexts, such as residents of disadvantaged neighbourhoods (McNamara et al., 2013), older adults (Gleibs et al., 2011), people with long-term mental health problems (Cruwys et al., 2014), migrants (McIntyre et al., 2016), and those living in post-conflict societies (Stevenson et al., 2020). Furthermore, these health benefits are enhanced through membership of multiple groups (Iyer et al., 2009).

The importance of groups for health is particularly apparent when they are lost – typically during significant life events or transitions. The ways in which group memberships buffer the negative effects of transitions by supporting adjustment to the new life stage and protecting health are articulated in the Social Identity Model of Identity Change (SIMIC, Haslam, Haslam et al., 2021). While there are several factors impacting health and adjustment to change, the loss of groups specifically has been shown to predict poorer quality of life and increase mortality risk in retirees (Steffens et al., 2016) and predict depression in new mothers (Seymour-Smith et al., 2017). However, multiple group memberships provide a rich social landscape that can help counter these adverse health consequences (Haslam, Haslam et al., 2021) through either maintaining pre-transition groups or acquiring new groups post-transition. Group memberships that are maintained during the transition have the potential to provide a sense of identity continuity and support during times of change, both of which contribute to positive health outcomes. Maintaining groups has been evidenced to enhance health in stroke victims (Haslam et al., 2008), to support perceptions of personal control in retired elite athletes (Haslam, Lam et al., 2021), and enhance academic performance and life satisfaction in university students (Cruwys et al., 2021).

Existing groups can also scaffold the acquisition of new identities. For instance, access to multiple groups can support professional identity development in doctoral students (Bentley et al., 2019) and asylum seekers' connection to their new host country (Panagiotopoulos & Pavlopoulos, 2024). New groups acquired during the transition can then offer appropriate, identity-based support in adjusting to the new life stage that other existing groups might not be able to provide. For example, Seymour-Smith et al. (2017) found that identification as a new mother was predictive of better mental health while increased preference for a recovery identity among those in treatment for addiction predicted abstinence and reduced occurrences of relapse (Buckingham et al., 2013). There are, of course, limits to these benefits and group memberships are not always associated with positive outcomes. To determine their relative impact on health, we need to consider (1) the group's identity content, (2) the relationships between groups in an individual's social identity network, and (3) the circumstances of the group.

First, all groups possess a specific identity content, that is, the norms, values, and behaviours that are typical of that group (Cruwys & Gunasaleen, 2016). In any given social context, when a social identity is salient, group members (particularly high identifiers) will perceive, think, and behave in terms of those norms (Turner, 1991). Whether group membership benefits (rather than undermines) health depends on the nature of these norms and behaviours (Tarrant et al., 2012). For instance, some groups (e.g., a walking club, mindfulness group) may promote health-enhancing norms and behaviours while others (e.g., relating to substance misuse or university students) might facilitate unhealthy beliefs and behaviours. In relation to eating healthily, Liu et al. (2019) found that increasing fruit and vegetable or reducing junk food consumption in university students depended on group healthy eating norms and how strongly participants identified with the norm referent group. In relation to health-damaging behaviours, Willis et al. (2020) found that university students were more likely to both endorse and engage in binge drinking to the degree that this activity was perceived to be important to the student group identity. Adhering to these group norms can, in turn, increase a sense of identification with the group, thereby strengthening the importance of the group to the individual (Rathbone et al., 2023).

The second instance whereby groups might act to undermine health is the nature of the relationships *between* groups in an individual's social network. Earlier we noted that health benefits of group memberships are cumulative. However, this is only the case to the extent to which the groups one identifies with are compatible with each other (i.e., there is some form of overlap or harmony between the members, values, norms, and behaviours of these groups) (Iyer et al., 2009). Incompatibility between groups can cause tension within the network and act as a stressor, negatively impacting health. For instance, UK university students from lower socioeconomic backgrounds and from ethnic minority backgrounds tend to see their identities as incompatible with the university student identity, which can impact their adjustment to university life, health and well-being, and attainment (Iyer et al., 2009; Frings et al., 2020). In addition, addiction recovery can be hampered to the extent that individuals identify more strongly with a 'using' group than with a recovery group (Best et al., 2016).

Last, the circumstances of the group also impact the degree to which identification serves to either enhance or undermine members' health through the group's capacity to furnish its members with a positive sense of identity (Haslam et al., 2018). Ultimately, group members wish their groups to be positively viewed (by themselves and others) as this enhances individual self-esteem, which has positive implications for health (Haslam et al., 2018). The health and well-being of group members are compromised in cases where the group is threatened (e.g., through status loss) or stigmatised in some way. Stigma can act as a corrosive process that undermines social cure processes, effectively turning group membership into a 'social curse' (Kellezi et al., 2019; Stevenson et al., 2014).

This has been investigated in relation to socially disadvantaged groups such as those with a mental illness diagnosis (Cruwys & Gunasaleen, 2016), low socioeconomic status neighbourhoods (McNamara et al., 2013), and ethnic minority groups (Schmitt & Branscombe, 2002). In some instances, group membership is associated with poor health outcomes. In these cases, groups tend to have some form of stigma conferred upon them and consequently experience the social environment as hostile towards them based on that group membership. Possessing a low status or stigmatised identity can result in poor health and well-being outcomes either because its concealment acts as a barrier to support seeking (McKenna & Bargh, 1998), group members internalise negative stereotypes associated with the group (Cruwys & Gunasaleen, 2016), or possessing that identity leads to ostracism from other important groups (Kellezi et al., 2019). However, identification with low status or stigmatised groups is not always associated with poor outcomes (Schmitt & Branscombe, 2002). Even in instances when the group is stigmatised, group members can still reap the health benefits of group membership through a sense of collective efficacy (McNamara et al., 2013) or stigma resistance (Crabtree et al., 2010).

Overall, according to the SIAH, we will only benefit from our social group memberships to the extent that (1) we identify with multiple compatible groups, (2) these groups possess health-enhancing norms and behaviours, and (3) they are not stigmatised in some way. To that end, it has significant promise as a potential lens through which to identify and explore the precise mechanisms through which social relationships impact eating disorder symptomatology and recovery outcomes. In particular, the SIAH can help to pinpoint pathways through which AN and other eating disorders might develop, how particular groups may support their maintenance and how social identities might inspire and support recovery.

How Might Social Group Memberships Contribute to the Development of Anorexia Nervosa?

The Role of Group Norms

While suggesting that social relationships may prompt the development of AN or influence its maintenance is not new (e.g., Schmidt & Treasure, 2006), very little work in this area has considered the role of group memberships and social identities (McNamara & Parsons, 2016). To broaden our understanding of the sociocultural factors impacting eating disorder development, it is essential that we move beyond an individualistic focus to consider other important aspects of the self and social environment. The Situated Identity Enactment Model (SIE; Cruwys et al., 2016), drawing from the SIA, provides a theoretical model which proposes that disordered eating is influenced by three key social elements. Specifically, the *social context* signals the salience of particular *social identities* and associated *norms*. Norms can indicate what behaviours group members are perceived to endorse (i.e., injunctive norms) and/or indicate how group members behave (i.e., descriptive norms). Thus, disordered eating results from the individual being in a social context that cues or makes salient a specific social group with which they identify along with group-endorsed disordered eating behaviours (Cruwys et al., 2016).

Previous research has identified some groups with potentially problematic normative attitudes and behaviours that place members at higher risk of disordered eating. For example, sports such as gymnastics, dance, diving, and wrestling are associated with higher levels of disordered eating in women and men as they endorse certain appearance-related ideals as well as potentially disordered eating behaviours (Mancine et al., 2020; Chapman & Woodman, 2016). Groups such as family and friends may also endorse problematic norms (McNamara et al., 2024). For instance, family beliefs and attitudes around eating and body image can lead to body dissatisfaction and disordered eating (Kluck, 2010). People's level of perfectionism may also be shaped by family interactions that communicate ideals which are then incorporated into personal identity (Bouguettaya et al., 2019).

The norms of the groups mentioned above can be as problematic as groups that more traditionally cause concern in relation to eating disorders – so-called 'pro-eating disorder' communities. In a study exploring the norms of important groups in the social networks of young adults in recovery, no difference was found in perceptions of how strongly thinness-related injunctive norms were espoused by participants' friendship groups and online pro-eating disorder groups – both were equally problematic and much more so than those espoused by family and recovery groups (McNamara et al., 2024). Ultimately, membership of any groups that endorse or engage in disordered eating behaviours may delay detection of an eating disorder as such behaviours are potentially seen by the individual and others as 'normative' or acceptable rather than indicating a problem requiring intervention (Cruwys et al., 2016). The perceived benefits from the individual's perspective that act to maintain these behaviours relate to fulfilling social psychological needs such as cultivating feelings of self-worth, success, and positive distinctiveness (Schmidt & Treasure, 2006; Jenkins & Ogden, 2012) as well as fuelling feelings of belonging and connection to others (Schmidt & Treasure, 2006; Rathbone et al., 2023).

From Disordered Eating to an Eating Disorder: A Chronically Salient Identity

There comes a point at which disordered eating behaviours become entrenched and compulsive and progress to an eating disorder (Schmidt & Treasure, 2006). Alongside this, people socially withdraw, with relationships such as friendships becoming less important and more difficult to maintain (Patel et al., 2018). This results in restricted networks and a loss of social support alongside an increasingly important illness identity (Makri et al., 2022; Ison & Kent, 2010). From a social identity perspective, when an identity becomes progressively self-defining, it is more likely to be readily accessible across social contexts, becoming a 'central' social identity that is chronically salient. It then acts as a lens through which the entire social world is experienced (Crane et al., 2018). A central eating disorder identity might accentuate differences between the individual and others who would normally be perceived as in-group members, undermining a previously valued social identity. This, in addition to within-group tensions resulting from the illness (Linville et al., 2012) and the stigma associated with it (Akey et al., 2013), might lead that individual to psychologically withdraw or *disidentify* from valued groups because they begin to perceive them as in some way threatening to, (i.e., not supportive of), the eating disorder identity (Becker & Tausch, 2014). This, in turn, fuels social isolation and loneliness that may worsen intrusive thoughts or increase reliance on maladaptive behaviours as a coping strategy (Harney et al., 2014).

Individuals rarely seek support from their existing network when trying to cope with their disorder (Akey et al., 2013), preferring instead to connect with similar others (McNamara & Parsons, 2016). This can be for several reasons, including concerns around negative judgement, feeling misunderstood, or not wishing to relinquish what they see as a vital coping mechanism (Akey et al., 2013; O'Connor et al., 2021). Recognising that this illness identity is not something unique to oneself but is one that is also shared with others, the individual may actively seek out groups that support this identity and that facilitate the formation of identity-based connections (McNamara et al., 2024; McNamara & Parsons, 2016). As noted earlier, the impact of these connections in terms of whether they act to maintain the eating disorder will depend on the group's identity content (McNamara & Parsons, 2016).

During acute stages of the illness (prior to any motivation to pursue recovery), one form of group people typically access is 'Pro-Ana' groups – online communities widely perceived to take an anti-recovery position. These connections are likely to contribute to the maintenance of the disorder through the provision of social psychological resources such as alleviating isolation, identity-related support, and the normalisation of disordered beliefs and behaviours (Csipke & Horne, 2007; McNamara et al., 2024). The feelings of acceptance and belonging offered by such communities might compensate for the loss of other groups (Greenaway et al., 2016). In addition, such groups may engage in efforts to derive a positive sense of self-esteem from an anorexic identity in the face of external stigmatisation (O'Connor et al., 2021). Ultimately, such connections might be difficult to break – even in the face of increased symptomatology and worsening health (McNamara et al., 2024). This is particularly true of those online groups that strongly endorse disordered behaviours as normative for the group (McNamara et al., 2024).

While there is a point at which disordered eating becomes an eating disorder, there is also a turning point towards recovery (Ison & Kent, 2010). It is thought that this might be partly motivated by important groups such as family and friends (Robinson et al., 2017; Venturo-Conerly et al., 2020) and that it also signals a shift in social identity – whereby the costs of self-defining in terms of an eating disorder begin to outweigh the benefits (Ison & Kent, 2010). It is this issue we turn to next.

How Might Social Group Memberships Support Recovery from Anorexia?

Recovery as a Process of Social Identity Change

Retaining a positively valued eating disorder identity undermines motivation to change as well as contributing to poor treatment outcomes and relapse (Abbate-Daga et al., 2013). Consequently, psychologically disconnecting (or disidentifying) from the eating disorder is essential for sustainable recovery (McNamara & Parsons, 2016). Preliminary evidence suggests that for those in recovery, increases in recovery identification over time are associated with positive outcomes for health (Streete, 2020). However, this identity change process is challenging in that it requires a re-definition of the self, a revision of personal beliefs and values, and abandonment of valued coping strategies and behaviours (Abbate-Daga et al., 2013; Jenkins & Ogden, 2012). While identity change is recognised as an essential part of recovery – how this can be achieved is not well understood. There have been calls for clinicians to support clients' development of a 'more mature personality' (Abbate-Daga et al., 2013, p. 307) or a non-anorexic identity (Schmidt et al., 2023). These approaches locate the aetiology of the eating disorder within the person (Malson et al., 2011) with the result that they omit a significant source of recovery support – social groups (McNamara & Parsons, 2016).

The idea that group memberships can successfully support the identity change needed during recovery has already been investigated in the context of addiction recovery (Best et al., 2016; Buckingham et al., 2013; Frings et al., 2019). Here, recovery is conceptualised as a process of social identity change (Best et al., 2016). The Social Identity Model of Recovery (SIMOR; Best et al., 2016) emphasises two elements in this process: (1) the development of a recovery identity (to replace the addict identity) and (2) the creation of a social identity network comprising groups that will promote (rather than undermine) recovery. The former requires connecting with peers committed to recovery. The latter requires resolution of the incompatibility associated with networks comprising groups with competing norms around recovery by maintaining ties with groups that promote recovery and severing ties with those that support the addict identity (Best et al., 2016). The Social Identity Model of Cessation Maintenance (SIMCM, Frings et al., 2019) also highlights the important role of recovery peers and associated recovery identity. This model postulates that a preference for the recovery over the addict identity drives positive outcomes such as increases in self-efficacy and abstinence (Buckingham et al., 2013). Over time, the developing recovery identity supports good health and well-being by providing group members with a belief in their ability to maintain cessation, a guide for how to navigate daily life, and norms prescribing how to behave when confronted with situations in which there is the potential for relapse (Frings et al., 2019).

Although both SIMOR and SIMCM were developed and tested in the context of addiction recovery, the processes they describe are likely to be applicable to the case of eating disorder recovery (McNamara & Parsons, 2016; McNamara et al., 2024). We will examine this first in relation to peers and the task of developing a recovery identity before exploring the challenges associated with building recovery-supportive networks.

Recovery Peers: Moving from an Illness to a Recovery Identity

While peer support is common practice in other domains of mental healthcare, it has yet to be fully incorporated into treatment pathways for those in recovery from an eating disorder (Beveridge et al., 2019). The limited evidence on the influence of treatment peers on recovery outcomes is mixed – these relationships are only viewed as helpful to the extent that others are similarly committed to recovery (Bezance & Holliday, 2013; Venturo-Conerly et al., 2020). In those circumstances, building relationships with others in inpatient settings can provide social support and shared understanding as well as opportunities to practise new recovery-relevant skills (Ison & Kent, 2010; Venturo-Conerly et al., 2020).

Online recovery groups offer similar resources (Hastings et al., 2016; McNamara & Parsons, 2016). Those in recovery are often motivated to join these groups to access what they see as 'appropriate' social support that more closely matches their needs than that provided by those who do not share their lived experience (Hastings et al., 2016; McNamara & Parsons, 2016; McNamara et al., 2024). In addition, qualitative research suggests that these connections provide resources central to personal recovery such as belief in recovery, hope, motivation to change, and self-efficacy (Hastings et al., 2016; McNamara & Parsons, 2016). However, the health benefits of these connections are dependent on the presence of a shared recovery identity and a community expectation that group members will cultivate a safe, recovery-supportive space (Hastings et al., 2016; McNamara & Parsons, 2016; McNamara et al., 2024). In the absence of such group regulation, some recovery spaces could act to undermine members' recovery.

On balance, it would be advisable to harness the positive aspects of peer support – particularly in group-based settings (Bezance & Holliday, 2013; McNamara & Parsons, 2016). Providing a positive group experience is essential for people to develop the social skills and confidence to support their ability to grow their social networks beyond the treatment or support setting (Davies, 2004). More research is needed, however, to understand how to effectively deliver this in a group setting and establish whether the associated identity supports sustained recovery over time. The question remains as to the composition of such groups and whether it is best to include those who are further along in their recovery journey or whether peer support should take the form of individual mentoring by a recovered peer.

Recovered role models are judged by those in recovery to be especially helpful – more so than treatment peers (Venturo-Conerly et al., 2020). While lived experience mentoring relationships are experienced as interpersonal encounters (i.e., as one person offering support to another), these interactions are likely made more meaningful through a sense of shared recovery identity. This social identity should provide identity-based resources such as 'appropriate' social support and belief and hope in recovery, which in turn, should have positive consequences for health and treatment adherence. Recent reviews have found preliminary support for this. Positive benefits for participants of peer-mentoring programmes included improvements in treatment engagement, weight, BMI, mood, and reduced eating disorder symptomatology (Pellizzer & Wade, 2023). Qualitative research with mentees revealed that these relationships inspired hope in recovery, motivation, and a sense of agency as well as supporting the navigation of treatment and recovery and re-engagement with others beyond the eating disorder world (Beveridge et al., 2019; Lewis & Foye, 2022; Fogarty et al., 2016). Of course, it should be noted that this evidence base is limited and there is a need for higher-quality grade evidence (including randomised controlled trials) as well as the examination of long-term outcomes for mentee as well as mentor recovery (Pellizzer & Wade, 2023).

Clearly, there are preliminary indications that peer engagement and the associated recovery identity might positively impact clinical as well as personal recovery outcomes. However, these connections might be best thought of as transitional rather than an end-point (McNamara & Parsons, 2016). It is likely that extending one's network beyond eating disorder-related groups and creating a recovery-supportive network is essential for sustained recovery (Rowlands et al., 2021). Therefore, recovery in the longer term might best be understood as an ability to navigate daily life and address ongoing needs through a variety of diverse (yet recovery-supportive) groups rather than through eating disorder-related groups (McNamara et al., 2024). The final section outlines the challenges faced when creating such a network including group (in)compatibility and the consequences of disclosing an eating disorder.

Building Recovery-Supportive Social Networks

The second key task in recovery is to maintain existing (or develop new) connections with groups whose norms support recovery and disidentify from those that undermine it (Best et al., 2016; Frings et al., 2019). As noted previously, the social networks of those living with an eating disorder tend to be small (Patel et al., 2018). Acute treatment decreases these networks further, which presents significant difficulties on discharge (Patel et al., 2018). Therefore, (re)establishing supportive relationships is something that needs to begin as early as possible in the recovery process.

As noted in the previous section, new connections with peers can support recovery, but it is also beneficial to maintain existing groups – providing their norms are compatible with recovery. Maintaining close friendships before, during, and after acute treatment can support a sense of 'normality' for those in recovery (Bezance & Holliday, 2013). For many, family can also be an important recovery resource. Greater family identification has been found to alleviate eating disorder-related loneliness and predict normative eating self-efficacy (McNamara et al., 2022; McNamara et al., 2024). However, disconnecting from unsupportive groups and expanding one's social identity network is extremely challenging, and there are two key contributors to this that are likely to impact an individual's ability to achieve sustainable recovery.

First is the issue of individual ambivalence towards recovery which acts as a significant barrier to positive outcomes (Abbate-Daga et al., 2013). Recent research suggests that this ambivalence may be reflected in, and fuelled by, the social networks of those living with an eating disorder (McNamara et al., 2024). A high proportion of individuals tend to belong to both recovery and pro-eating disorder online groups (McNamara et al., 2024). These groups have distinct and incompatible norms in relation to recovery (McNamara et al., 2024; McNamara & Parsons, 2016). While it is generally hypothesised that incompatibility within a network is experienced as stressful and acts as a motivator for change (Best et al., 2016; Haslam et al., 2021), this is not always the case. In those living with an eating disorder, these incompatible groups facilitate strategic support-seeking in times of stress (McNamara et al., 2024). Therefore, for someone who is not yet committed to recovery, a relapse may not always be managed by engaging with recovery-supportive groups but with pro-eating disorder groups with associated negative consequences for health (McNamara et al., 2024). While those in McNamara et al.'s (2024) study at a later stage of recovery recognised the costs of belonging to harmful groups and disidentified from them, it is not yet clear what could activate these changes at an earlier stage.

Second is the issue of stigmatisation. This can have an impact early in recovery as well as being a consideration post-treatment. In the initial stages of recovery, the person must seek support from family members and health services; however, a fear of judgement and feelings of shame often prevent them from doing so (Akey et al., 2013). Research has shown that eating disorders are stigmatised to a greater extent than other mental illnesses among the public, health professionals, and even within the families of those diagnosed (O'Connor et al., 2021). When compared with those living with other mental illnesses such as depression, people with eating disorders are perceived as attention-seeking, more responsible for the development of their illness, are assigned more negative traits, and considered less pleasant to interact with (O'Connor et al., 2021). Those contemplating recovery are aware of these stereotypes (McNamara & Parsons, 2016) and they can lie at the root of a decision to conceal the illness and avoid help-seeking (Akey et al., 2013; O'Connor et al., 2021).

Stigma can also present itself as misunderstanding the nature of recovery and the level of control individuals have over its progression (McNamara & Parsons, 2016). Family members or close supporters might not be fully informed as to recovery's non-linear trajectory, for example, or may comment on an individual's appearance believing this to be supportive. This is often experienced as unhelpful by those in recovery who may choose to conceal difficulties experienced during recovery so as not to place a burden on their social groups or due to a fear of disappointing them (Akey et al., 2013; Hastings et al., 2016; McNamara & Parsons, 2016). Some also report feeling that even when recovered their behaviours continue to be excessively monitored by family and friends to the extent that they withdraw from those relationships to support their recovery (Streete, 2020).

Given the stigmatisation associated with eating disorders, building one's network requires a decision to be made around whether to disclose an ongoing or past eating disorder. Such disclosure can be experienced negatively; however, it might also provide the individual with an important guide as to which group memberships should be maintained and which should be severed (Akey et al., 2013; Streete, 2020). While concealment of the disorder tends to be discouraged to facilitate recovery, there may be instances where it supports a return to 'normal' (Streete, 2020). For instance, joining a diverse range of groups as a prototypical group member (rather than as someone with an eating disorder) might be especially helpful in sustaining recovery in the longer term (Rowlands et al., 2021; Streete, 2020). Further research is needed to investigate this, however.

Conclusion

Loneliness precedes the development of AN, prolongs its duration, and triggers relapse (Levine, 2012). Sustained recovery therefore is predicated on the presence of supportive social relationships (Linville et al., 2012). Despite this, the topic remains relatively neglected in research and in treatment pathways (Davies, 2004; Pearce et al., 2023). This chapter argues that this knowledge and practice gap can be addressed by drawing on the SIAH (Haslam et al., 2018). This approach offers an established theoretical framework that articulates how social relationships, specifically group memberships (and their associated social identities), can contribute to the development and maintenance of AN as well as how these same processes can be harnessed to promote its recovery.

These relationships can assist the identity change central to the recovery process, provided individuals can be supported to psychologically disconnect from unsupportive groups with norms that are incompatible with recovery maintenance. The social and psychological resources 'unlocked' through identification with recovery-supportive groups mirror those identified as essential to personal recovery, including social support, efficacy, belief in recovery, and connectedness. There is growing evidence to suggest that social identities enhance the health and well-being of those in eating disorder recovery through these resources. This includes preliminary evidence proposing an association between group memberships (such as family) and reduced loneliness, ED symptomatology and related psychopathology as well as greater recovery self-efficacy (Hastings et al., 2016; McNamara & Parsons, 2016; McNamara et al., 2022; McNamara et al., 2024). Overall, this suggests that social identities may bridge the gap between clinical and personal recovery.

While further research in this area is needed, the existing literature suggests several recommendations for clinical practice. Rather than almost exclusively focusing on eliminating disordered behaviours, clinical interventions should address the social component of these disorders (Davies, 2004). This should include the safe incorporation of peer support into treatment pathways. It should be noted that eating disorder-related groups are not inherently harmful to recovery but only in instances where group norms promote disordered behaviours and a clear commitment to recovery is absent (McNamara et al., 2024). When engaging with peer support, individuals should be mindful of protecting their own health by limiting their exposure to harmful peer-based interactions or settings. Peer support groups should develop a collective commitment to ensuring they create a recovery-supportive space and an expectation that all group members adhere to this commitment (Hastings et al., 2016; McNamara & Parsons, 2016). Finally, social networks should be collaboratively discussed in treatment at the earliest opportunity with a view to equipping them with the ability to evaluate the quality of their social connections, assess their impact (positive and negative) on their recovery, and empower them to disconnect from harmful groups as well as identify new and meaningful groups to join.

Note

1 While the term AN will be used in this chapter, it should be noted that most research in this area takes a transdiagnostic approach and so the processes described are likely to apply to all forms of eating distress.

References

Abbate-Daga, G., Amianto, F., Delsedime, N., De-Bacco, C., & Fassino, S. (2013). Resistance to treatment and change in anorexia nervosa: A clinical overview. *BMC Psychiatry*, *13*, 294–311. https://doi.org/10.1186/1471-244-13-294

Akey, J. E., Rintamaki, L. S., & Kane, T. L. (2013). Health belief model determinants of social support seeking among people coping with eating disorders. *Journal of Affective Disorders*, *145*, 246–252. https://doi.org/10.1016/j.jad.2012.04.045

Arcelus, J., Haslam, M., Farrow, C., & Meyer, C. (2013). The role of interpersonal functioning in the maintenance of eating psychopathology: A systematic review and testable model. *Clinical Psychology Review*, *33*, 156–167. https://doi.org/10.1016/j.cpr.201210.009

Becker, J. C., & Tausch, N. (2014). When group memberships are negative: The concept, measurement, and behavioural implications of psychological disidentification. *Self & Identity*, *13*, 294–321. https://doi.org/10.1080/15298868.2013.819991

Bentley, S. V., Peters, K., Haslam, S. A., & Greenaway, K. H. (2019). Construction at work: Multiple identities scaffold professional identity development in academia. *Frontiers in Psychology*, *10*. https://doi.org/10/3389/fpsyg.2019.00628

Best, D., Beckwith, M., Haslam, C., Haslam, S. A., Jetten, J., Mawson, E., & Lubman, D. I. (2016). Overcoming alcohol and other drug addiction as a process of social identity transition: The social identity model of recovery (SIMOR). *Addiction Research and Theory*, *24*, 111–123. https://doi.org/10.3109/16066359.2015.1075980

Beveridge, J., Phillipou, A., Jenkins, Z., Newton, R., Brennan, L., Hanly, F., Torrens-Witherow, B., Warren, N., Edwards, K., & Castle, D. (2019). Peer mentoring for eating disorders: Results from the evaluation of a pilot program. *Journal of Eating Disorders*, *7*, 13.

Bezance, J., & Holliday, J. (2013). Adolescents with anorexia have their say: A review of qualitative studies on treatment and recovery from anorexia nervosa. *European Eating Disorders Review*, *21*, 352–360. https://doi.org/10.1002/erv.2239

Buckingham, S. A., Frings, D., & Albery, I. P. (2013). Group membership and social identity in addiction recovery. *Psychology of Addictive Behaviours*, *27*, 1132–1140. https://doi.org/10.1037/ a0032480

Bouguettaya, A., Klas, R., King, R., & Knight, T. (2019). Perfectionism as a social identity in eating disorders: A qualitative investigation of identity navigation. *Australian Psychologist*, *54*, 347–357. https://doi.org/10.1111/ap.12379

Cardi, V., Mallorqui-Bague, N., Albano, G., Monteleone, A. M., Fernández-Aranda, F., & Treasure, J. (2018). Social difficulties as risk and maintaining factors in anorexia nervosa. *Frontiers in Psychiatry*, *9*. https://doi.org/10.3389/fpsyt.2018. 00012

Chapman, J., & Woodman, T. (2016). Disordered eating in male athletes: A meta-analysis. *Journal of Sports Sciences*, *34*, 101–109. https://doi.org/10.1080/02640414.2015.1040824

Clark Bryan, D., Macdonald, P., Ambwani, S., Cardi, V., Rowlands, K., Willmott, D., & Treasure, J. (2020). Exploring the ways in which COVID-19 and lockdown has affected the lives of adult patients with anorexia nervosa and their carers. *European Eating Disorders Review*, *28*, 826–835. https://doi.org/10.1002/erv.2762

Cockell, S. J., Zaitsoff, S. L., & Geller, J. (2004). Maintaining change following eating disorder treatment. *Professional Psychology: Research & Practice*, *35*, 527–534. https://doi.org/10.1037/0735-0728.35.5.527

Crabtree, J. W., Haslam, S. A., Postmes, T., & Haslam, C. (2010). Mental health support groups, stigma, and self-esteem: Positive and negative implications of group identification. *Journal of Social Issues*, *66*, 553–569. https://doi.org/10.1111/j.1540-4560.2010.01662.x

Crane, M. F., Louis, W. F., Phillips, J. K., Amiot, C. E., & Steffens, N. K. (2018). Identity centrality moderates the relationship between acceptance of group-based stressors and well-being. *European Journal of Social Psychology*, *48*, 866–882. https://doi.org/10.1002/ejsp.2367

Csipke, E., & Horne, O. (2007). Pro-eating disorder websites: Users' opinions. *European Eating Disorders Review*, *15*, 196– 206. https://doi.org/10.1002/erv.789

Cruwys, T., & Gunaseelan, S. (2016). "Depression is who I am": Mental illness identity, stigma, and well-being. *Journal of Affective Disorders*, *189*, 36–42. https://doi.org/10.1016/j.jad.2015.09.012

Cruwys, T., Ng, N. W. K., Haslam, S. A., & Haslam, C. (2021). Identity continuity protects academic performance, retention, and life satisfaction among international students. *Applied Psychology*, *70*, 931–954. https://doi.org/10.1111/apps.12254

Cruwys, T., Platow, M. J., Rieger, E., Bryne, D. G., & Haslam, S. A. (2016). The social psychology of disordered eating: The situated identity enactment model. *European Review of Social Psychology*, *27*, 160–195. https://doi.org/10.1080/10463283.2016.1229891

Cruwys, T., Haslam, S. A., Dingle, G. A., Jetten, J., Hornsey, M. J., Chong, E. M., & Oei, T. P. S. (2014). Feeling connected again: Interventions that increase social identification reduce depression symptoms in community and clinical settings. *Journal of Affective Disorders*, *159*, 139–146.

Davies, S. (2004). A group-work approach to addressing friendship issues in the treatment of adolescents with eating disorders. *Clinical Child Psychology & Psychiatry*, *9*, 519–531. https://doi.org/10.1177/1359104504046157

Devoe, D. J., Han, A., Anderson, A., Katzonen, D. K., Patten, S. B., Soumbasis, A., Flanagan, J., Paslakis, G., Vyver, E., Marcoux, G., & Dimitropoulos, G. (2023). The impact of the COVID-19 pandemic on eating disorders: A systematic review. *International Journal of Eating Disorders*, *56*, 5–25. https://doi.org/10.1002/eat.23704

Fogarty, S. Ramjam, L., & Hay, P. (2016). A systematic review and meta-synthesis of the effects and experience of mentoring in eating disorders and disordered eating. *Eating Behaviors*, *21*, 66–75. https://doi.org/10.10161/j.eat.beh.2015.12.004

Frings, D., Gleibs, I. H., & Ridley, A. (2020). What moderates the attainment gap? The effects of social identity incompatibility and practical incompatibility on the performance of students who are or are not Black, Asian or Minority Ethnic. *Social Psychology of Education*, *23*, 171–188.

Frings, D., Wood, K. V., Lionetti, N., & Albery, I. P. (2019). Tales of hope: Social identity and learning lessons from others in alcoholics anonymous: A test of the social identity model of cessation maintenance. *Addictive Behaviors*, *93*, 204–211. https://doi.org/10.1016/j.addbeh.2019.02.004

Gleibs, I. H., Haslam, C., Haslam, S. A., & Jones, J. M. (2011). Water clubs in residential care: Is it the water or the club that enhances health and well-being? *Psychology & Health*, *26*, 1361–1377.

Greenaway, K. H., Cruwys, T., Haslam, S. A., & Jetten, J. (2016). Social identities promote well-being because they satisfy global psychological needs. *European Journal of Social Psychology*, *46*, 294–307.

Harney, M. B., Fitzsimmons-Craft, E. E., Maldonado, C. R., & Bardone-Cone, A. M. (2014). Negative affective experiences in relation to stages of eating disorder recovery. *Eating Behaviors*, *15*, 24–30. https://doi.org/10.1016/j.eatbeh.2013. 10.016

Haslam, C., Haslam, S. A., Jetten, J., Cruwys, T., & Steffens, N. K. (2021). Life change, social Identity, and health. *Annual Review of Psychology*, *72*, 635–661. https://doi.org/10.1146/annurev-psych-060120-111721

Haslam, C., Holme, A., Haslam, S. A., Iyer, A., Jetten, J., & Williams, W. H. (2008). Maintaining group memberships: Social identity continuity predicts well-being after stroke. *Neuropsychological rehabilitation*, *18*(5-6), 671-691.

Haslam, C., Lam, B. C. P., Yang, J., Steffens, N. K., S. A. Haslam, Cruwys, T., Boen, F., Mertens, N., De Brandt, K., Wang, X., Mallett, C. J., & Fransen, K. (2021). When the final whistle blows: Social identity pathways support mental health and life satisfaction after retirement from competitive sport. *Psychology of Sport & Exercise*, *57*, 102049. https://doi.org/10.1016/j.psychsport.2021.102049

Haslam, C., Jetten, J., Cruwys, T., Dingle, G. A., & Haslam, S. A. (2018). *The new psychology of health: Unlocking the social cure*. Routledge.

Haslam, S. A., O'Brien, A., Jetten, J., Vormedal, K., & Penna, S. (2005). Taking the strain: Social identity, social support and the experience of stress. *British Journal of Social Psychology*, *44*, 355–370.

Hastings, A., McNamara, N., Allan, J., & Marriott, M. (2016). The importance of social identities in the management of and recovery from "Diabulimia": A qualitative exploration. *Addictive Behaviors Reports*, *4*, 78–86. https://doi.org/10.1016/j.abrep.2016.10.043

Hornsey, M. J. (2008). Social identity theory and self-categorisation theory: A historical review. *Social & Personality Psychology Compass*, *2*, 204–222. https://doi.org/10.1111/j.1751-9004.2007.00066.x

Ison, J., & Kent, S. (2010). Social identity in eating disorders. *European Eating Disorders Review*, *18*, 475–485. https://doi.org/10.1002/erv.1001

Iyer, A., Jetten, J., Tsivrikos, D., Postmes, T., & Haslam, S. A. (2009). The more (and the more compatible) the merrier: Multiple group memberships and identity compatibility as predictors of adjustment after life transitions. *British Journal of Social Psychology*, *48*, 707–733. https://doi.org/10.1348/014466608X397628

Jenkins, J., & Ogden, J. (2012). Becoming "whole" again: A qualitative study of women's views of recovering from anorexia nervosa. *European Eating Disorders Review*, *20*, e23–e31. https://doi.org/10.1002/erv.1085

Jetten, J., Haslam, S. A., & Haslam, C. (2012). *The social cure: Identity, health and well-being*. Psychology Press.

Kellezi, B., Bowe, M., Wakefield, J. R. H., McNamara, N., & Bosworth, M. (2019). Understanding and coping with immigration detention: Social identity as cure and curse. *European Journal of Social Psychology*, *49*, 333–351. https://doi.org/10.1002/ejsp.2543

Kluck, A. S. (2010). Family influence on disordered eating: The role of body image dissatisfaction. *Body Image*, *7*, 8–14. https://doi.org/10.1016/j.bodyim.2009.09.009

Leamy, M., Bird, V., Le Boutillier, C., Williams, J., & Slade, M. (2011). Conceptual framework for personal recovery in mental health: Systematic review and narrative synthesis. *British Journal of Psychiatry*, *199*, 445–452. https://doi.org/10.1192/bjp.bp.110.083733

Levine, M. P. (2012). Loneliness and eating disorders. *The Journal of Psychology*, *146*, 243–257. https://doi.org/10.1080/00223980.2011.606435

Lewis, H. K., & Foye, U. (2022). From prevention to peer support: A systematic review exploring the involvement of lived-experience in eating disorder interventions. *Mental Health Review Journal*, *27*, 1–17. https://doi.org/10.1108/MHRJ-04-2021-0033

Linville, D., Brown, T., Sturm, K., & McDougal, T. (2012). Eating disorders and social support: Perspectives of recovered individuals. *Eating Disorders*, *20*, 216–231. https://doi.org/10.1080/10640266.2012.668480

Liu, J., Thomas, J. M., & Higgs, S. (2019). The relationship between social identity, descriptive social norms and eating intentions and behaviours. *Journal of Experimental Social Psychology*, *82*, 217–230. https://doi.org/10.1016/j.jesp.2019.02.002

Makri, E., Michopoulos, I. & Gonidakis, F. (2022). Investigation of loneliness and social support in patients with eating disorders: A case-control study. *Psychiatry International*, *3*, 142–157. https://doi.org/10.3390/psychiatryint3020012

Malson, H., Bailey, L., Clarke, S., Treasure, J., Anderson, G., & Kohn, M. (2011). Un/imaginable future selves: A discourse analysis of in-patients' talk about recovery from an "eating disorder". *European Eating Disorders Review*, *19*, 25–36. https://doi.org/10.1002/erv.1011

Mancine, R. P., Gusfa, D. W., Moshrefi, A., & Kennedy, S. F. (2020). Prevalence of disordered eating in athletes categorised by emphasis on leanness and activity type – A systematic review. *Journal of Eating Disorders*, *8*, 47.

McDonald, S., Williams, A. J., Barr, P. McNamara, N., & Marriott, M. (2021). Service user and eating disorder therapist views on anorexia nervosa recovery criteria. *Psychology & Psychotherapy: Theory, Research & Practice*, *94*, 721–736. https://doi.org/10.1111/papt.12340

McIntyre, J., Elahi, A., & Bentall, R. P. (2016). Social identity and psychosis: Explaining elevated rates of psychosis in migrant populations. *Social & Personality Psychology Compass*, *10*, 619–633.

McKenna, K. Y. A., & Bargh, J. A. (1998). Coming out in the age of the Internet: Identity "demarginalization" through virtual group participation. *Journal of Personality & Social Psychology*, *75*, 681–694. https://psycnet.apa.org/doi/10.1037/0022-3514.75.3.681

McNamara, N., & Parsons, H. (2016). "Everyone here wants everyone else to get better": The role of social identity in eating disorder recovery. *British Journal of Social Psychology*, *55*, 662–680. https://doi.org/10.1111/bjso.12161

McNamara, N., Stevenson, C., & Muldoon, O. T. (2013). Community identity as resource and context: A mixed method investigation of coping and collective action in a disadvantaged community. *European Journal of Social Psychology*, *43*, 393–403.

McNamara, N., Wakefield, J. R. H., Cruwys, T., Potter, A., Jones, B. A., & McDevitt, S. (2022). The link between family identification, loneliness, and symptom severity in people with eating disorders. *Journal of Community & Applied Social Psychology*, *32*, 949–962. https://doi.org/10.1002/casp.2606

McNamara, N., Wakefield, J. R. H., Mair, E., Rennoldson, M., Stevenson, C., & Fitzsimmons, W. (2024). Multiple group identifications and identity compatibility in eating disorder recovery: A mixed methods study. *Journal of Community & Applied Social Psychology*, *34*, e2720. https://doi.org/10.1002/casp.2720

O'Connor, C., McNamara, N., O'Hara, L. McNicholas, M., & McNicholas, F. (2021). How do people with eating disorders experience the stigma associated with their condition? A mixed-methods systematic review. *Journal of Mental Health*, *30*, 454–469. https://doi.org/10.1080/09638237.2019.1685081

Panagiotopoulos, A., & Pavlopoulos, V. (2024). Group belonging and social identities in the transition of asylum-seekers in Greece: Longitudinal pathways to adjustment. *Healthcare*, *12*, 55. https://doi.org/10.3390/healthcare12010055

Patel, K., Tchanturia, K., & Harrison, A. (2016). An exploration of social functioning in young people with eating disorders: A qualitative study. *PLoS One*, *11*, e0159910. https://doi.org/10.1371/journal.pone.0159910

Pearce, E., Birken, M., Pais, S., Tamworth, M., Ng, Y., Wang, J., Chipp, B., Crane, E., Schlief, M., Yang, J., Stamos, A., Cheng, L. K., Condon, M., Lloyd-Evans, B., Kirkbride, J. B., Osborn, D., Pitman, A., & Johnson, S. (2023). Associations between constructs related to social relationships and mental health conditions and symptoms: An umbrella review. *BMC Psychiatry*, *23*, 652. https://doi.org/10.1186/s12888-023-05069-0

Pellizzer, M. L., & Wade, T. D. (2023). The effectiveness of lived experience involvement in eating disorder treatment: A systematic review. *International Journal of Eating Disorders*, *56*, 331–349. https://doi.org/10.1002/eat.23847

Rathbone, J. A., Cruwys, T., Stevens, M., Ferris, L. J., & Reynolds, K. J. (2023). The reciprocal relationship between social identity and adherence to group norms. *British Journal of Social Psychology*, *62*, 1346–1362. https://doi.org/10.1111/bjso.12635

Richardson, T., Elliott, P., & Roberts, K. (2017). The relationship between loneliness and mental health in students. *Journal of Public Mental Health*, *16*, 48–54. https://doi.org/10.1108/JPMH-03-2016-0013

Rowlands, K. Willmott, D., Cardi, V., Clark Bryan, D., Cruwys, T., & Treasure, J. (2021). An examination of social group memberships in patients with eating disorders, carers, and healthy controls. *European Eating Disorders Review*, *29*, 733–743. https://doi.org/10.1002/erv.2840

Schmidt, U., & Treasure, J. (2006). Anorexia nervosa: Valued and visible. A cognitive-interpersonal maintenance model and its implications for research and practice. *British Journal of Clinical Psychology*, *45*, 343–366. https://doi.org/10.1348/014466505X53902

Schmidt, U., Treasure, J., & Allen, K. (2023). The Maudsley Model of Anorexia Nervosa Treatment for Adults (MANTRA). In P. Robinson, T. Wade, B. Herpertz-Dahlmann, F. Fernandez-Aranda, J. Treasure, & S. Wunderlich. (Eds.), *Eating disorders: An international comprehensive view* (pp. 1153-1167). Springer.

Schmitt, M. T., & Branscombe, N. R. (2002). The meaning and consequences of perceived discrimination in disadvantaged and privileged social groups. *European Journal of Social Psychology*, *12*, 167–199. https://doi.org/10.1080/14792772143000058

Seymour-Smith, M., Cruwys, T., S. A. Haslam, & Brodribb, W. (2017). Loss of group membership predicts depression in postpartum mothers. *Social Psychiatry & Psychiatric Epidemiology*, *52*, 201–210. https://doi.org/ 10.1007/s00127-016-1315-3

Steffens, N. K., Cruwys, T., Haslam, C., Jetten, J., & Haslam, S. A. (2016). Social group memberships in retirement are associated with reduced risk of premature death: Evidence from a longitudinal cohort study. *BMJ Open*, *6*, 1–9. https://doi.org/10.1136/bmjopen-2015- 010164

Stevenson, C., Costa, S., Easterbrook, M., McNamara, N., & Kellezi, B. (2020). Social cure processes help lower intergroup anxiety among neighbourhood residents. *Political Psychology*, *41*, 1093–1111.

Stevenson, C., McNamara, N., & Muldoon, O. (2014). Stigmatized identity and service usage in disadvantaged communities: Residents' community workers' and service providers' perspectives. *Journal of Community & Applied Social Psychology*, *24*, 453–466. https://doi.org/10.1002/ casp.2184

Stewart, W. (2004). The role of perceived loneliness and isolation in the relapse from recovery in patients with anorexia nervosa and bulimia nervosa. *Clinical Social Work Journal*, *32*, 185–196.

Streete, J. L. (2020). *The role of social identity in eating disorder recovery*. Unpublished PhD thesis. Nottingham Trent University.

Tarrant, M., Haggar, M. S., & Farrow, C. V. (2012). Promoting positive orientation towards health through social identity. In J. Jetten, C. Haslam, & S. A. Haslam (Eds.), *The social cure: Identity, health and well-being* (pp. 39–54). Psychology Press.

Taquet, M., Geddes, J. R., Luciano, S., & Harrison, P. J. (2022). Incidence and outcomes of eating disorders during the COVID-19 pandemic. *British Journal of Psychiatry*, *220*, 262–264. https://doi.org/10.1192/bjp.2021.105

Termorshuizen, J. D., Watson, H. J., Thornton, L. M., Borg, S., Flatt, R. E., MacDermod, C. M., … Bulik, C. M. (2020). Early impact of COVID-19 on individuals with self-reported eating disorders: A survey of 1000 individuals in the United States and The Netherlands. *International Journal of Eating Disorders*, *53*, 1780–1790. https://doi.org/10.1002/eat.23353

Tajfel, H. (1982). Social psychology of intergroup relations. *Annual Review of Psychology, 33*, 1–39. https://doi.org/10.1146/annurev.ps.33.020182.000245
Tajfel, H., & Turner, J. C. (1979). An integrative theory of intergroup conflict. In W. G. Austin & S. Worchel (Eds.), *The social psychology of intergroup relations* (pp. 33–47). Brooks/Cole.
Turner, J. C. (1982). Towards a cognitive redefinition of the social group. In H. Tajfel (Ed.), *Social identity and intergroup relations* (pp.15–40). Cambridge University Press.
Turner, J. C. (1991). *Social influence*. Open University Press.
Venturo-Conerly, K. E., Wasil, A. R., Dreier, M. J., Lipson, S. M., Shingleton, R. M., & Weisz, J. R. (2020). Why I recovered: A qualitative investigation of factors promoting motivation for eating disorder recovery. *International Journal of Eating Disorders, 53*, 1244–1251. https://doi.org/10.1002/eat.23331
Wetzler, S., Hackmann, C., Peryer, G., Clayman, K., Friedman, D., Saffran, K., Silver, J., Swarbrick, M., Magill, E., van Furth, E., & Pike, K. M. (2020). A framework to conceptualise personal recovery from eating disorders: A systematic review and qualitative meta-synthesis of perspectives from individuals with lived experience. *International Journal of Eating Disorders, 53*, 1188–1203. https://doi.org/10.1002/eat23260
Willis, L., Lee, E., Reynolds, K. J., & Kilk, K. A. (2020). The theory of planned behaviour and the social identity approach: A new look at group processes and social norms in the context of student binge drinking. *European Journal of Psychology, 16*, 357–383. https://doi.org/10.5964/ejop.v16i3.1900

Chapter 9

Gender Role Norms

Jaclyn A. Siegel

Introduction

Eating disorders have been described as one of the most sexually dimorphic psychiatric conditions (Murray, 2017). Across virtually every study, women are significantly more likely to report eating disorder symptoms than men (Hudson et al., 2008; Striegel-Moore et al., 2009; Udo & Grilo, 2018), and the disordered eating behaviors in which people engage often vary across gendered lines, with women, on average, engaging in more thinness-oriented disordered eating and men engaging in more muscularity-oriented disordered eating (Lavender et al., 2017; Murray, 2017). However, there is significant variability within gender categories, with some men and women engaging in thinness- *and* muscularity-oriented disordered eating (Bozsik et al., 2018; Convertino et al., 2022; Tiggemann et al., 2007). One potential explanation to account for the variability within gender categories is that this dimorphic presentation of symptoms is not necessarily biologically ingrained but rather reflects the gender roles – and gendered body ideals – prescribed to (cisgender) women and men (see Breton et al., 2023). Indeed, gender roles have been linked to virtually every element of eating disorders, from differences in body ideals to symptom presentation (Murray, 2017) to help-seeking (Raisanen & Hunt, 2014) to diagnosis (Griffiths et al., 2015) to stigmatization (Austen & Griffiths, 2019). In this chapter, we summarize the research on femininity, masculinity, and androgyny in relation to anorexia nervosa (AN).

It is important to note that femininity is not a quality inherent to women, and masculinity is not a quality inherent to men (van Anders, 2015). Women can have masculine characteristics, and men can have feminine characteristics, and there is more within-group variability in these traits than between-group variability (Hyde, 2005). Further, women and men are certainly not the only two gender categories. Yet, to keep this chapter focused, we primarily highlight research conducted with cisgender women and cisgender men. The experiences of transgender individuals, who are at elevated risk of experiencing eating disorders, are discussed in Chapter 10. It is also important to note that women and men are diverse groups, and femininity and masculinity are experienced differently based on age, sexual orientation, race, (dis)ability, and other characteristics and life experiences (Connell, 2020). Finally, in this chapter, we cite existing psychological literature on gender and

DOI: 10.4324/9781003468189-11

disordered eating, in which young, white participants are overrepresented, and in which operationalizations of femininity and masculinity largely reflect the perspectives and experiences of young, upwardly mobile, white, cisgender, heterosexual women and men. These various limitations – and their impact – are highlighted toward the end of this chapter.

Review of the Literature

Women, Femininity, and Anorexia Nervosa

Female gender role socialization encourages women to take up as little space as possible in social situations, in workplaces, and in relationships. Women are socialized to attend to the needs of those around them above their own needs (Helgeson & Fritz, 1998), and women are especially taught to prioritize their beauty and attractiveness over other elements of their lives, personalities, and accomplishments (Brownmiller, 1985; Engeln, 2017; Mahalik et al., 2005; Wolf, 1991). In this way, AN can be understood as an extension and consequence of rigid adherence to feminine gender role norms (Till, 2011). Rather than figuratively taking up less space by self-silencing and prioritizing the needs of others, women with AN quite literally take up less space by shrinking the size of their bodies. In a society in which thinness remains the dominant beauty ideal for women (Swami, 2015), in which dysregulated and disordered eating behaviors are normalized and even encouraged, and in which discontent surrounding women's body image is regarded as "normative" (Rodin et al., 1984), AN and femininity can be understood as intimately intertwined. Indeed, the "femininity hypothesis" of disordered eating suggests that women's conformity to feminine gender role norms places them at risk for restriction-oriented eating disorders (Lakkis et al., 1999). Below, we review the evidence supporting this hypothesis. Given different operationalizations of feminine gender role adherence, the following sections are divided by the instrument used to evaluate "femininity" in these studies.

Conformity to Feminine Norms and Gender Role Adherence

Conformity to Feminine Norms

One of the most popular instruments for evaluating femininity is Mahalik et al.'s (2005) Conformity to Feminine Norms Inventory (CFNI). The CFNI contains eight subscales: Invest in Appearance (e.g., "I spend more than 30 min a day doing my hair and make-up"), Thinness (e.g., "I would be happier if I was thinner"), Nice in Relationships (e.g., "It is important to let people know they are special"), Modesty (e.g., "I hate telling people about my accomplishments"), Sexual Fidelity (e.g., "I would feel guilty if I had a one night stand"), Domestic ("It is important to keep your living space clean"), Care for Children (e.g., "Taking care of children is extremely fulfilling"), and Romantic Relationship (e.g., "Having a romantic relationship is essential in life") (Mahalik et al., 2005). Abbreviated versions of this instrument contain nine subscales, splitting the Nice in Relationships subscale into Sweet and Nice and Relational (Parent & Moradi, 2011). It is important to note, however, that the CFNI was developed out of interviews with female students at a predominantly white university in the northeast of the United States. The "norms" of femininity identified in such an instrument likely reflect the dimensions of femininity as experienced by young, white women, and not necessarily the dimensions of femininity as experienced by the broader population. This is a point to which we will return later in the chapter.

Research on women's conformity to feminine norms as they relate to drive for thinness and AN symptoms has yielded mixed findings over the last two decades. In Mahalik et al.'s (2005) validation paper for the CFNI, the team identified significant links between the Thinness, Investment in Appearance, and Nice in Relationships subscale of the CFNI and the Eating Disorder Inventory (EDI; Garner et al., 1983) subscales (Drive for Thinness, Bulimia, and Body Dissatisfaction). The study also identified a significant correlation between the CFNI total score and all three subscales of the EDI. However, in a separate study with a small sample of women from a midwestern liberal arts college (Green et al., 2008), only the Thinness subscale of the CFNI was significantly correlated with EDI subscale scores. Given that Drive for thinness is a dimension of the EDI, this significant correlation is unsurprising. However, the absence of significant correlations between the EDI subscales and the other CFNI subscale scores complicates the assertion that femininity and AN are empirically linked. Further, scores on the full CFNI were unrelated to EDI scores, casting further doubt on the conceptual link between the two.

The CFNI has also been employed in relation to self-objectification, a strong predictor of eating disorders (for a review, see Schaefer & Thompson, 2018). Self-objectification refers to an internalization of the sexually objectifying male gaze on people's experiences of their bodies. Dimensions of the CFNI have consistently – across studies – been linked to self-objectification. For example, in Hurt et al.'s (2007) examination of conformity to feminine norms, self-objectification, and disordered eating in a sample of women recruited through a variety of sources, Thinness, Investment in Appearance, and Romantic Relationships were all significantly correlated with body shame, which was, in turn, connected to body surveillance, which was, in turn, connected to disordered eating. This study was conceptually replicated by Siegel and Calogero (2019), who identified the same associations between Thinness, Investment in Appearance, Romantic Relationships, and self-objectification. As such, there is support for the assertion that appearance- and romantic relationship-oriented dimensions of femininity may be associated with increased risk for eating disorders; however, various other factors of femininity (as operationalized by the CFNI) appear unrelated to these conditions.

Feminine Personal Attributes

The Personal Attributes Questionnaire (PAQ; Spence et al., 1975) has also been employed in relation to disordered eating attitudes in women. The PAQ asks participants to respond to items related to different elements of femininity (sometimes referred to as expressive traits), masculinity (sometimes referred to as instrumental traits), and some masculine-feminine traits (sometimes referred to as instrumental-expressive traits). In a sample of 45 female undergraduate students, scores on the PAQ were unrelated to eating disorder symptomatology; however, the importance of appearance was related to both femininity and disordered eating (Timko et al., 1987). These findings support the above point: femininity, absent of appearance-focused dimensions of the feminine gender role, is not strongly related to disordered eating. However, these findings – and many findings on this link – are limited by a very small sample size.

Femininity Ideology

Relatedly, *femininity* ideology is associated with poor body image, as well. Endorsement of femininity ideology is distinct from conformity to feminine norms in that conformity to feminine norms entails individual adherence to these norms, rather than a belief in the importance of these norms for all women. The Femininity Ideology Scale (FIS; Lehman, 2000) contains five subscales, each of which evaluate a distinct domain of femininity: Stereotypic Image and Activities (i.e., the belief that women should be thin and attractive; e.g., "A woman should have a petite body"), Dependency/Deference (i.e., the belief that women should be modest and subservient to men; e.g., "A woman should not be competitive"), Purity (e.g., women should not be vulgar and should dress conservatively; "A woman should not tell dirty jokes"), Caretaking (i.e., women should enjoy taking on caretaking roles; e.g., "An appropriate female occupation is nursing"), and Emotionality (i.e., women will be viewed as emotional; "It is expected that women will not think logically"). In a sample of women, the total femininity ideology score, as well as the FIS subscales of Purity and Stereotypic Images and Activities were significantly negatively associated with body appreciation (Swami & Abbasnejad, 2010). While low body appreciation is not equivalent to AN , body appreciation has an inverse relation with eating disorder symptoms (Tylka & Wood-Barcalow, 2015), and appreciating one's body can be protective against the development of these conditions (e.g., Ramos-Martins et al., 2022). This study reveals that supporting some beliefs about women's roles in society may be linked to poorer body image, a risk factor for eating disorders.

Feminine Gender Role Stress

Another element of femininity that has been linked to eating disorders is feminine gender role stress. Feminine gender role stress refers to the anxiety that a person feels in situations that are gender atypical. The most common measure to evaluate female gender role stress is the Feminine Gender Role Stress Scale (FGRSS; Gillespie & Eisler, 1992), which contains five subscales: Fear of Unemotional Relationships (i.e., fearing that one is failing to meet others' expectations and needs), Fear of Physical Unattractiveness (i.e., fearing that one is perceived as ugly), Fear of Victimization (i.e., fearing experiencing violence), Fear of Behaving Assertively (i.e., fearing setting boundaries), and Fear of Not Being Nurturant (i.e., fear of engaging in behaviors seen as non-nurturant). It is important to note that the FGRSS, much like the CFNI, contains items specifically related to appearance and weight loss.

Feminine gender role stress has been implicated in women's disordered eating in nonclinical samples. For example, in a study of women between the ages of 18 and 40, several dimensions of the FGRSS were significantly correlated with body dissatisfaction, dietary restraint, eating concern, and bulimic symptoms (i.e., bingeing and purging). Specifically, the Fear of Being Unattractive subscale of the FGRSS was correlated with all three subscales of the Eating Disorder Examination Questionnaire (i.e., dietary restraint, eating concern, and bingeing and purging; Mussap, 2007), as well as body dissatisfaction and overcontrol. The links between feminine gender role stress and eating disorder symptoms were mediated by body dissatisfaction and overcontrol. Relatedly, the FGRSS total score was significantly correlated with eating concern, suggesting that feminine gender role stress – broadly – is associated with disordered eating symptoms. However, it is unclear the degree to which the correlation between eating disorder symptoms and Fear of Unattractiveness drives this significant association.

Feminine gender role stress seems particularly relevant among individuals living with eating disorders. In one small study of women in inpatient psychiatric care and a larger sample of college-aged women, the FGRSS was able to distinguish between people with eating disorders and other psychiatric disorders, as well as distinguish between those with eating disorders and college-aged women (Martz et al., 1995). Specifically, women living with eating disorders scored statistically significantly higher on the full FGRSS, as well as the Fear of Physical Unattractiveness, Fear of Behaving Assertively, and Fear of Not Being Nurturant subscales, compared to psychiatric inpatients with other Axis 1 psychiatric disorders and comparison college students. Further, in a small sample of women with eating disorders and a small sample of women without eating disorders (Bekker & Boselie, 2002), those with eating disorders reported higher levels of feminine gender role stress, but also masculine gender role stress, and recent stressors. Women with an eating disorder scored significantly higher on the total FGRSS, as well as Fear of Nonemotional Relationships and, as expected, Fear of Physical Unattractiveness. However, women with eating disorders also scored significantly higher than women without eating disorders on the total Masculine Gender Role Stress Scale, as well as Fear of Physical Inadequacy, Fear of Emotional Expression, Fear of Intellectual Inferiority, and Fear of Performance Failure. Stress itself, rather than gender role stress specifically, seems to be common among women living with these conditions (Bekker & Boselie, 2002). In interpreting these studies, it is important to note the low sample sizes, limiting the interpretability of these findings.

Taken together, this research suggests that the dimensions of femininity related to appearance, thinness, and relationships are related to eating disorder symptomatology and risk factors. Relatedly, stress and fear of disappointing others or embarrassing oneself also seem to be related to disordered eating symptoms. However, given the multidimensionality of femininity, these links only provide moderate support for the femininity hypothesis of eating disorders.

Women, Masculinity, and Anorexia Nervosa

While there is more within-group than between-group variability among genders in the expression of traditionally gendered traits (Hyde, 2005), masculine and feminine gender role norms are positioned as oppositional. Given that femininity is (theoretically) a risk factor for AN among women, it would seem to follow that masculinity would be a protective factor for this disorder. When considering the stereotypes associated with the masculine gender role, which are positioned as complementary to those of the feminine gender role, the potential protective nature of masculinity for thinness-based eating disorders is also clear. Indeed, some research has found that, while femininity is positively associated with eating problems, masculinity is negatively associated with eating problems and positively associated with body satisfaction across genders and sexual orientations (Cella et al., 2013; Lampis et al., 2017; Meyer et al., 2001; Steele et al., 2019).

However, masculinity has also been linked to disordered eating in some samples. For example, in a sample of professional ballet dancers, who are at elevated risk for restriction-based eating disorders (Arcelus et al., 2014), those who endorsed higher levels of masculinity had higher scores on measures of eating disorder symptoms and body unease (Ravaldi et al., 2006). Further, among sexual minority women, masculinity has been linked to body shame (Massey et al., 2020). However, overall, the literature linking women, masculinity, and AN is scant and inconsistent. Across studies, general trends in the data suggest that masculinity is associated with better body image and reduced risk for disordered eating. However, masculinity is not necessarily protective for some groups (e.g., athletes and sexual minority women).

Women, Feminism, and Anorexia Nervosa

While not explicitly tied to femininity and masculinity, feminist scholars have positioned disordered eating as the internalization of sexist ideals for women (Fallon et al., 1996; Wolf, 1991). Indeed, the many elements of the feminine gender role may be conceptualized as appropriate reactions to consistent sexist treatment, routine and uncontrollable experiences of sexual objectification (Fredrick & Roberts, 1997), or a way to stay safe and gain resources in a patriarchal society

(Calogero et al., 2017). For example, investment in appearance may help women avoid appearance-based teasing and help them acquire resources. Feminine norms of caring for children and interest in domestic labor may reflect centuries of gender role norms in which one of women's primary roles in their relationships with men included childrearing and running the home. In feminist writings on eating disorders, some have concluded that keeping women obsessed with their food is an effective way to distract them from the oppression they experience (Wolf, 1991).

The idea that feminism may help women avoid the trappings of appearance-focused elements of femininity is supported in empirical research. Feminism in women – both feminist identity and feminist attitudes – has been shown to serve as a protective factor in some research on eating disorders. For example, in Murnen and Smolak's (2009) meta-analysis of feminist identity and eating disorder symptomatology, they found that women who endorse feminist ideology and particularly those who self-identify as feminists report lower levels of disordered eating in correlational research. Lesbian women are consistently more likely to identify as feminists compared to their heterosexual counterparts, and feminism in lesbian women has been shown to serve a protective function against the development of eating disorders in lesbian women (Guille & Chrisler, 2008). Given that women who identify as feminists are also less likely to endorse elements of traditional gender role norms (see Hurt et al., 2007; Siegel & Calogero, 2019), it is possible that feminist-identified women's lower scores on measures of disordered eating may be a function of reduced adherence to the feminine norms predictive of AN. Relatedly, listening to a feminist audiotape intervention has been shown to improve body image (Peterson et al., 2006). However, it is important to note that not all research has found that feminist identity and attitudes are protective against eating disorder behaviors (Borowsky et al., 2016; Siegel & Calogero, 2019), highlighting the complexity of these topics.

Men, Femininity, and Anorexia Nervosa

The bulk of research on men's disordered eating and gender roles has focused on muscularity-oriented disordered eating and drive for muscularity. This focus on muscularity is warranted, given that epidemiological studies consistently find that most men are concerned with their muscularity, not their body fat (Murray, 2017), and body ideals for men are often rather muscular and lean, rather than thin. This focus on muscularity is, in itself, consistently associated with masculinity, particularly the masculine norms of dominance and winning (Murnen et al., 2023), and masculine gender role strain is associated with muscularity concerns (Murnen et al., 2023). The "masculinity hypothesis" of disordered eating, the corollary to the femininity hypothesis, predicts that men's masculine gender role adherence places them at elevated risk for muscularity-oriented disordered eating, not thinness-oriented disordered eating (see Blashill, 2011). Further, the threatened masculinity hypothesis, which suggests that when men's masculinity is threatened or questioned, they will report higher levels of muscle dissatisfaction, has received preliminary – though mixed – support (Frederick et al., 2017; Hunt et al., 2013).

Over the last few years, there has been interest in the idea of "bigorexia," a masculine parallel to AN geared toward achieving the muscular male body ideal (Arslan et al., 2022; Vasiliu, 2023). Despite debate in the field (see Murray et al., 2010), muscularity-oriented disordered eating and "bigorexia" are not currently classified as eating disorders in the Diagnostic and Statistical Manual of Mental Disorders, 5th Edition (DSM-5) (though muscle dysmorphia is classified under body dysmorphia in the obsessive-compulsive and related disorders category), and given that the drive for muscularity is largely unrelated to the drive for thinness (McCreary & Sasse, 2000), research on the topic will not be highlighted in this chapter (though, for a review of the drive for muscularity and its links with masculinity, see Murnen et al., 2023).

Although roughly one in three disorder cases is attributed to men, the most common eating disorder among men is binge eating disorder. While some men are diagnosed with AN, there is comparatively little research on the experiences of these men, given the low prevalence of AN in this sample. Some research has found that sexual minority men may be at unique risk for body image dissatisfaction (Knight et al., 2022) and eating disorder development (Bell et al., 2019; Diemer et al., 2015; Feldman & Meyer, 2007; Russell & Keel, 2002; Strong et al., 2000; see also Parker & Harriger, 2020), given that body ideals for sexual minority men tend to be thinner than body ideals for heterosexual men (Tiggemann et al., 2007).

Indeed, preliminary research has revealed that femininity among men may place them at risk for AN and body dissatisfaction. For example, in a large sample of Italian adolescents, young men who scored higher on the femininity subscale of the Bem Sex-Role Inventory also scored higher on the bulimia and drive for thinness subscales of the EDI (Lampis et al., 2017). Further, in a small sample of men (21 men with muscle dysmorphia, 24 men with AN, and 30 control participants who attended a gym), those with AN scored higher on scales of femininity compared to men with muscle dysmorphia and those without a mental health condition (Murray et al., 2013). However, among men, femininity does not seem to be a primary driver of body and muscle dissatisfaction. In a meta-analysis of gender role norms, body dissatisfaction, and muscularity dissatisfaction among men, the role of femininity in men's body attitudes was not significantly different from zero (Blashill, 2011). Taken together, this research suggests that the role of femininity in men's risk for eating disorders is minimal and inconsistent.

Men, Masculinity, and Anorexia Nervosa

Very little research has linked men's masculinity to AN or risk factors for the disorder. However, in one qualitative study of men's participation in pro-ana (pro-anorexia) communities, the analysis revealed that men both refute and embrace masculinity in these spaces (Quiniones & Oster, 2019). In posts in which men embrace masculinity, they discuss the norms of power, control, and accomplishment associated with self-starvation.

More research, however, has focused on the role of masculinity in the stigmatization associated with AN. Notably, eating disorders in men are stereotyped as gender anomalous in news reporting on them (MacLean et al., 2015). Men with eating disorders are aware of this stigma (Griffiths et al., 2015) and actively try to avoid experiencing stigma grounded in a perceived masculinity deficit (see Siegel & Sawyer, 2020). Consistently, research has revealed that men endorse more stigma toward individuals with eating disorders (Mond & Arrighi, 2011). However, this discrepancy can be better accounted for by conformity to masculine norms, rather than gender. In a large study of young adults, participants' conformity to masculine norms was associated with stigmatization of individuals with eating disorders (particularly the masculine norms of self-reliance and heterosexual self-presentation; Austen & Griffiths, 2019). This stigma may prevent men from identifying anorexic symptoms within themselves and seeking help for these conditions.

Androgyny and Anorexia Nervosa

Research on androgyny and AN is in its nascency. However, one study including women with eating disorders found that women's endorsement of femininity, masculinity, and social desirability were all associated with EDI subscales. However, androgyny – having high levels of both femininity and masculinity, was associated with lower levels of eating disorder symptomatology, compared to having an undifferentiated orientation toward gender (Hepp et al., 2005). Relatedly, in a study comparing professional ballet dancers to non-dancer controls, those in the control group who had an undifferentiated orientation toward gender had the highest scores on measures of eating disorders and body unease (Ravaldi et al., 2006).

While very little literature exists on the topics of androgyny and undifferentiated gender orientation, the consistency between these two studies points to an interesting finding: while conformity to gender-congruent gender roles can put individuals at risk for eating disorders, so too cannot conforming to either set of gender role norms. This could potentially help to explain why transgender and nonbinary individuals are at elevated risk of developing eating disorders (McGreggor et al., 2023), compared to their cisgender counterparts. For more information on the experiences of transgender and nonbinary individuals, see Chapter 10.

Discussion

In the above section, the literature on gender role norms and AN was reviewed, highlighting the limitations of the existing literature. Here, those limitations are expanded on, calling attention to the influence of those limitations on our understanding of the relationships between gender role norms and AN.

First, our understanding of the relations between AN and gender role norms is limited by the instrumentation available to evaluate masculinity and femininity. Mahalik et al.'s (2003, 2005) gender role conformity scales have helped researchers to evaluate how gender-related stereotypes and pressures are linked to problematic mental health. However, when investment in appearance and drive for thinness are conceptualized as fundamental elements of the feminine gender role, and overemphasis on appearance and drive for thinness are predictors and elements of eating disorders, it is important to query the links between femininity and disordered eating in quantitative work using these instruments. In addition, the inclusion of Thinness and Investment in Appearance Subscales of Mahalik et al.'s (2003) CFNI, but no parallel appearance-focused subscales on the Conformity to Masculine Norms Inventory, prevents meaningful comparisons between masculinity and femininity conceptualized through these instruments as they relate to disordered eating. Given that the diagnostic criterion for AN includes the undue influence of weight and shape on self-evaluation, and most instruments used to capture disordered eating symptoms include scales for drive for thinness, the links between femininity and disordered eating may be, in fact, due to measurement overlap. Indeed, virtually every instrument employed to evaluate femininity contains at least a few items related to investment in appearance. If tools to evaluate masculinity contained equivalent subscales to evaluate drive for muscularity (arguably an appropriate parallel subscale to the Thinness subscale on the CFNI), it is possible that links between masculinity and AN may be stronger with that tool. Conversely, if measurements of femininity did not include appearance-related dimensions, this apparent link may meaningfully shrink.

Further, nearly all instruments used to evaluate gender role adherence that have been used in studies linking gender role norms to eating disorders were developed over two decades ago, and the norms were established based on the discussions of a few dozen young, highly educated, cisgender, white women. As the meaning of femininity changes over time and the field takes a more deliberately inclusive approach to the study of both gender role norms and eating disorders, it may be time for the field to consider new instruments to evaluate gender role adherence, grounded in the experiences and perspectives of a broader range of people who identify as feminine. A related issue with this literature is the overwhelming dependence on small, white, and college-aged samples for research on these associations. While eating disorders are often trivialized as conditions of skinny, white, affluent individuals (mostly women), eating disorders do not discriminate by gender, race, age, class, or sexual orientation (Schaumberg et al., 2017). The overreliance on samples that reflect stereotypes about these conditions limits our understanding of the links between gender role norms and eating disorder symptomatology in other groups. It is worth considering, also, that the bulk of research on this topic was conducted in the 1990s and early 2000s. As femininity evolves and changes – and the samples with which we conduct research diversify – it is possible that the studies cited here may not replicate in samples today.

Further, very few instruments exist to evaluate non-white understandings of masculinity and femininity. A few notable exceptions to this include the Machismo-Caballerismo scale (describing masculinity among Latino men; Arciniega et al., 2008), the Masculinity Inventory Scale for Black Men (Mincey et al., 2014), and the Multicultural Gender Role Scale for Asian American Women (Rooney, 2019). However, no literature using these instruments in relation to eating disorders has been published in peer-reviewed journals, and as such, no literature using these scales is cited here. Over the last decade, the field of masculinity studies has called attention to the fact that masculinity is not a monolith and that instrumentation that evaluates only dominant, white masculinity does not accurately capture the complexity of masculinity for men across cultures. As such, we cannot necessarily identify masculinity as protective against AN – and particularly against muscularity-oriented disordered eating – until we examine masculinity more comprehensively.

Despite an expansive and growing literature on the links between eating disorders and sexual minority men, the links between gender role norms and disordered eating among sexual minority women are scant. Although most studies find that sexual minority women – and bisexual women in particular (e.g., Hazzard et al., 2020) – are at elevated risk of developing eating disorders, there is virtually no literature linking gender and eating disorders in this population. The focus of this chapter was cisgender individuals; however, it should also be noted that literature is scant with transgender and nonbinary participants, as well, though this literature base – particularly the qualitative literature in this area – appears to be growing (see Springmann et al., 2022). Future research should explore the role of femininity and masculinity in sexual minority women's risk of eating disorders. Sexual minority women sometimes adhere to gendered categories (i.e., butch and femme). Given the alarmingly high rate of eating disorders among sexual minority women, an examination of these gendered subdivisions in relation to eating disorders is warranted. There is already some research to support the idea that femme lesbian women may be a higher risk group – in a small study of college-aged heterosexual and sexual minority men and women, femininity was linked to Eating Attitudes Test Scores in sexual minority women, but not heterosexual women (Meyer et al., 2001). It is important to note that this sample was quite small ($n = 20$ lesbian women, 30 heterosexual women), and more research is needed. Evaluating this hypothesis may require the creation of novel psychological instruments that reflect unique gendered experiences and attitudes of these groups. This chapter did not cover literature on transgender, intersex, and nonbinary participants' experiences, though more research should be conducted with these underrepresented populations, as well.

In addition to measurement and sample issues within the existing literature, the stigma attributed to men with eating disorders may prevent them from responding honestly to questions related to disordered eating in survey research. It is possible, then, that men are underreporting their eating disorder symptoms and negative body attitudes in survey research. Men with eating disorders are also less likely to engage in help-seeking behaviors related to their conditions, so literature on men living with diagnosed eating disorders is limited. Further, few treatment centers specialize or even permit men, increasing the difficulty of getting high-quality clinical data with this population.

It is important to consider the fact that the diagnostic criterion for AN was exclusive of cisgender men until the DSM-IV was released, given that amenorrhea (absence of a menstrual period) was an essential part of the diagnosis. Despite the removal of this diagnostic criterion in later editions of the DSM, the emphasis on women's experiences of AN lingers in the conceptualization. Though it is presently in a state of flux, the dominant feminine body ideal remains quite thin, and women's pursuit of the ideal often includes dieting behaviors, which can quickly turn to anorexia symptoms. Given that body ideals for men are not generally achieved through anorexic symptoms, it is unsurprising that men's masculinity and femininity are not as strongly linked to eating disorder symptoms as they are for women.

Conclusion

Eating disorders and gender role norms are linked in the literature, though inconsistently. Most commonly, women's and men's femininity is associated with higher levels of drive for thinness and eating disorder symptomatology. The role of masculinity in thinness-oriented and restriction-based eating disorders is more mixed. However, limitations of existing research and instrumentation on these topics prevent clear conclusions from being drawn from the extant literature. New scales that appropriately capture the complexity of modern, diverse forms of gender role norms are necessary for comprehensively understanding the role of gender roles in AN.

References

Arcelus, J., Witcomb, G. L., & Mitchell, A. (2014). Prevalence of eating disorders amongst dancers: A systemic review and meta-analysis. European eating disorders review: *The Journal of the Eating Disorders Association*, *22*(2), 92–101. https://doi.org/10.1002/erv.2271

Arciniega, G. M., Anderson, T. C., Tovar-Blank, Z. G., & Tracey, T. J. (2008). Toward a fuller conception of Machismo: Development of a Traditional Machismo and Caballerismo Scale. *Journal of Counseling Psychology*, *55*(1), 19.

Arslan, M., Ayhan, N. Y., Sariyer, E. T., Colak, H., & Cevik, E. (2022). The effect of bigorexia nervosa on eating attitudes and physical activity: A study on university students. *International Journal of Clinical Practice*, 6425860. https//doi.org/10.1155/2022/6325860

Austen, E., & Griffiths, S. (2019). Why do men stigmatize individuals with eating disorders more than women? Experimental evidence that sex differences in conformity to gender norms, not biological sex, drive eating disorders' stigmatization. *Eating Disorders*, *27*(3), 267–290. https://doi.org/10.1080/10640266.2018.1499337

Bekker, M. H. J., & Boselie, K. A. H. M. (2002). Gender and stress: Is gender role stress? A re-examination of the relationship between feminine gender role stress and eating disorders. *Stress and Health*, *18*, 141–149. https://doi.org/10.1002/smi.933

Bell, K., Rieger, E., & Hirsch, J. K. (2019). Eating disorder symptoms and proneness in gay men, lesbian women, and transgender and gender non-conforming adults: Comparative levels and a proposed mediational model. *Frontiers in Psychology*, *9*, 2692. https://doi.org/10.3389/fpsyg.2018.02692.

Blashill, A. J. (2011). Gender roles, eating pathology, and body dissatisfaction in men: A meta-analysis. *Body Image*, *8*(1), 1–11. https://doi.org/ 10.1016/j.bodyim.2010.09.002

Borowsky, H. M., Eisenberg, M. E., Bucchianeri, M. M., Piran, N., & Neumark-Sztainer, D. (2016). Feminist identity, body image, and disordered eating. *Eating disorders*, *24*(4), 297–311.

Bozsik, F., Whisenhunt, B. L., Hudson, D. L., Bennett, B., & Lundgren, J. D. (2018). Thin is in? Think again: The rising importance of muscularity in the thin ideal female body. *Sex Roles*, *79*, 609–615. https://doi.org/10.1007/s11199-017-0886-0

Breton, E., Juston, R.-P., & Booij, L. (2023). Gender and sex in eating disorders: A narrative review of the current state of knowledge, research gaps, and recommendations. *Brain and Behavior*, *13*(4), e2871. https://doi.org/10.1002/brb3.2871

Brownmiller, S. (1985). *Femininity*. Ballantine Books.

Calogero, R. M., Tylka, T. L., Donnelly, L. C., McGetrick, A., & Leger, A. M. (2017). Trappings of femininity: A test of the "beauty as currency" hypothesis in shaping college women's gender activism. *Body Image*, *21*, 66–70.

Cella, S., Iannaccone, M., & Cotrufo, P. (2013). Influence of gender role orientation (masculinity versus femininity) on body satisfaction and eating attitudes in homosexuals, heterosexuals, and transsexuals. *Eating and Weight Disorders*, *18*(2), 115–124. https://doi.org/10.1007/s40519-013-0017-z

Connell, R. W. (2020). Gender as a social practice. In S. Seidman & J. C. Alexander (Eds.), The new social theory reader (pp. 369–375). Routledge.

Convertino, A. D., Elbe, C. I., Mendoza, R. R., Calzo, J. P., Brown, T. A., Siegel, J. A., Jun, H.-J., Corliss, H. L., & Blashill, A. J. (2022). Internalization of muscularity and thinness ideals: Associations with body dissatisfaction, eating disorder symptoms, and muscle dysmorphic symptoms in at risk sexual minority men. *International Journal of Eating Disorders*, *55*(12), 1765–1776. https://doi.org/10.1002/eat.23829

Diemer, E. W., Grant, J. D., Munn-Chernoff, M. A., Patterson, D. A., & Duncan, A. E. (2015). Gender identity, sexual orientation, and eating-related pathology in a national sample of college students. Journal of Adolescent Health, 57(2), 144–149. https://doi.org/10.1016/j.jadohealth.2015.03.003

Engeln, R. (2017). *Beauty sick: How the cultural obsession with appearance hurts girls and women*. Harper.

Fallon, P., Katzman, M. A., & Wooley, S. C. (Eds.). (1996). *Feminist perspectives on eating disorders*. Guilford Press.

Feldman, M. B., & Meyer, I. H. (2007). Eating disorders in diverse lesbian, gay, and bisexual populations. *International journal of eating disorders*, *40*(3), 218–226.

Fredrickson, B. L., & Roberts, T. A. (1997). Objectification theory: Toward understanding women's lived experiences and mental health risks. *Psychology of Women Quarterly, 21*(2), 173–206. https://doi.org/10.1111/j.1471-6402.1997.tb00108.x

Frederick, D. A., Shapiro, L. M., Williams, T. R., Seoane, C. M., McIntosh, R. T., & Fischer, E. W. (2017). Precarious manhood and muscularity: Effects of threatening men's masculinity on reported strength and muscle dissatisfaction. *Body image, 22*, 156–165.

Garner, D. M., Olmstead, M. P., & Polivy, J. (1983). Development and validation of a multidimensional eating disorder inventory for anorexia nervosa and bulimia. *International journal of eating disorders, 2*(2), 15–34.

Gillespie, B. L., & Eisler, R. M. (1992). Development of the feminine gender role stress scale: A cognitive-behavioral measure of stress, appraisal, and coping for women. *Behavior Modification, 16*(3), 426–438. https://doi.org/10.1177/01454455920163008

Green, M. A., Davids, C. M., Skaggs, A. K., Riopel, C. M., & Hallengren, J. J. (2008). Femininity and eating disorders. *Eating Disorders: The Journal of Treatment & Prevention, 16*(4), 283–293. https://doi.org/10.1080/10640260802115829

Griffiths, S., Mond, J. M., Murray, S. B., & Touyz, S. (2015). The prevalence and adverse associations of stigmatization in people with eating disorders. *International Journal of Eating Disorders, 49*(6), 767–774. https://doi.org/10.1002/eat.22353

Guille, C., & Chrisler, J. C. (1999). Does feminism serve a protective function against eating disorders? *Journal of Lesbian Studies*.

Hazzard, V. M., Simone, M., Borg, S. L., Borton, K. A., Sonneville, K. R., Calzo, J. P., & Lipson, S. K. (2020). Disparities in eating disorder risk and diagnosis among sexual minority college students: Findings from the national Healthy Minds Study. *International Journal of Eating Disorders, 53*(9), 1563–1568.

Helgeson, V. S., & Fritz, H. L. (1998). A theory of unmitigated communion. *Personality and Social Psychology Review, 2*(3), 173–183. https://doi.org/10.1207/s15327957pspr0203_2

Hepp, U., Spindler, A., & Milos, G. (2005). Eating disorder symptomatology and gender role orientation. *International Journal of Eating Disorders, 37*, 227–233. https://doi.org/10.1002/eat.20087

Hudson, J. I., Hirpi, E., Pope, H. G., & Kessler, R. C. (2008). The prevalence and correlates of eating disorders in the national comorbidity survey replication. *Biological Psychiatry, 61*(3), 348–358. https://doi.org/10.1016/j.biopsych.2006.03.040

Hunt, C. J., Gonsalkorale, K., & Murray, S. B. (2013). Threatened masculinity and muscularity: An experimental examination of multiple aspects of muscularity in men. *Body Image, 10*(3), 290–299. https://doi.org/10.1016/j.bodyim.2013.02.007

Hurt, M. M., Nelson, J. A., Turner, D. L., Haines, M. E., Ramsey, L. R., Erchull, M. J., & Liss, M. (2007). Feminism: What is it good for? Feminine norms and objectification as the link between feminist identity and clinically relevant outcomes. *Sex Roles, 57*, 355–363. https://doi.org/10.1007/s11199-007-9272-7

Hyde, J. S. (2005). The gender similarities hypothesis. *American Psychologist, 60*(6), 581–592. https://doi.org/10.1037/0003-066X.60.6.581

Knight, R., Carey, M., Jenkinson, P., & Preston, C. (2022). The impact of sexual orientation on how men experience disordered eating and drive for muscularity. *Journal of Gay & Lesbian Mental Health*. https://doi.org/10.1080/19359705.2022.2118921

Lakkis, J., Ricciardelli, L. A., & Williams, R. J. (1999). Role of sexual orientation and gender-related traits in disordered eating. *Sex Roles: A Journal of Research, 41*(1–2), 1–16. https://doi.org/10.1023/A:1018829506907

Lampis, J., Cataudella, S., Busonera, A., De Simone, S., & Tommasi, M. (2017). The moderating effect of gender role on the relationships between gender and attitudes about body and eating in a sample of Italian adolescents. *Eating and Weight Disorders*, *24*, 3–11. https://doi.org/ 10.1007/s40519-017-0372-2

Lavender, J. M., Brown, T. A., & Murray, S. B. (2017). Men, muscles, and eating disorders: An overview of traditional and muscularity-oriented disordered eating. *Current Psychology Reports*, *19*(6), 32. https://doi.org/ 10.1007/s11920-017-0787-5

Lehman, P. (2000). *A validity study of the femininity ideology scale.* Master's thesis, Florida Institute of Technology.

MacLean, A., Sweeting, H., Walker, L., Patterson, C., Raisanen, U., & Hunt, K. (2015): "It's not healthy and it's decidedly not masculine": A media analysis of UK newspaper recommendations of eating disorders in males. *BMJ Open, 5*, 5. http://dx.doi.org/10.1136/ bmjopen-2014-007468

Mahalik, J. R., Locke, B. D., Ludlow, L. H., Diemer, M. A., Scott, R. P. J., Gottfried, M., & Freitas, G. (2003). Development of the conformity to masculine norms inventory. *Psychology of Men & Masculinity, 4*(1), 3–25. https://doi.org/10.1037/1524-9220.4.1.3

Mahalik, J. R., Morray, E. B., Coonerty-Femiano, A., Ludlow, L. H., Slattery, S. M., & Smiler, A. (2005). Development of the conformity to feminine norms inventory. *Sex Roles*, *52*, 417–435. https://doi.org/ 10.1007/s11199-005-3709-7

Martz, D. M., Handley, K. B., & Eisler, R. M. (1995). The relationship between feminine gender role stress, body image, and eating disorders. *Psychology of Women Quarterly*, *19*(4), 493–508. https://doi.org/10.1111/j.1471-6402.1995.tb00088.x

Massey, C. J., Keener, E., & McGraw, J. S. (2020). The role of masculinity and femininity in body objectification: Comparison of heterosexual and gay communities. *Gender Issues*, *38*, 180–199. https://doi.org/10.1007/s12147-020-09263-2

McCreary, D. R., & Sasse, D. K. (2000). An exploration of the drive for muscularity in adolescent boys and girls. *Journal of American College Health*, *48*(6), 297–304. https://doi.org/10.1080/07448480009596271

McGregor, K., McKenna, J. L., Barrera, E. P., Williams, C. R., Hartman-Munick, S. M., & Guss, C. E. (2023). Disordered eating and considerations for the transgender community: A review of the literature and clinical guidance for assessment and treatment. *Journal of Eating Disorders*, *11*, 75. https://doi.org/10.1186/s40337-023-00793-0

Meyer, C., Blissett, J., & Oldfield, C. (2001). Sexual orientation and eating psychopathology: the role of masculinity and femininity. *International Journal of Eating Disorders*, *29*(3), 314–318.

Mincey, K. D., Alfonso, M. L., Hackney, A. A., & Luque, J. S. (2014). Being a Black man: Development of the Masculinity Inventory Scale (MIS) for Black men. *The Journal of Men's Studies*. https://doi.org/ 10.3149/jms.2203.167

Mond, J. M., & Arrighi, A. (2011). Gender differences in perceptions of the severity and prevalence of eating disorders. *Early Intervention in Psychiatry*, *5*(1), 41–49. https://doi.org/10.1111/j.1751-7893.2010.00257.x.

Murray, S. B. (2017). Gender identity and eating disorders: The need to delineate novel pathways for eating disorder symptoms. *Journal of Adolescent Health*, *60*(1), 1–2. https://doi.org/10.1016/j.jadohealth.2016.10.004

Murnen, S. K., & Smolak, L. (2009). Are feminist women protected from body image problems? A meta-analytic review of relevant research. *Sex Roles, 60*(3), 186–197. https://doi.org/10.1007/s11199-008-9523-2

Murnen, S. K., Dunn, A. C., & Karazsia, B. T. (2023). Masculinity and men's drive for muscularity: A meta-analytic review. *Psychology of Men & Masculinities, 24*(4), 381–393. https://doi.org/10.1037/men0000431

Murray, S. B., Rieger, E., Karlov, L., & Touyz, S. W. (2013). Masculinity and femininity in the divergence of male body image concerns. *Journal of Eating Disorders, 11*, 1. https://doi.org/10.1186/2050-2974-1-11

Murray, S. B., Rieger, E., Touyz, S. W., & De la Garza Garcia Lic, Y. (2010). Muscle dysmorphia and the DSM-V conundrum: Where does it belong? A review paper. *International Journal of Eating Disorders, 43*(6), 483–491. https://doi.org/10.1002/eat.20828

Mussap, A. J. (2007). The relationship between feminine gender role stress and disordered eating symptomatology in women. *Stress and Health, 23*(5). https://doi.org/10.1002/smi.1152

Parent, M. C., & Moradi, B. (2011). An abbreviated tool for assessing feminine norm conformity: Psychometric properties of the Conformity to Feminine Norms Inventory–45. *Psychological Assessment, 23*(4), 958–969. https://doi.org/10.1037/a0024082

Parker, L. L.,& Harriger, J. A. (2020). Eating disorders and disordered eating behaviorsin the LGBT population: a review of the literature. *Journal of eatingdisorders, 8*(1), 51. https://doi.org/10.1186/s40337-020-00327-y

Quiniones, C., & Oster, C. (2019). Embracing or resisting masculinity: Male participation in the proeating disorders (proana) online community. *Psychology of Men & Masculinities, 20*(3), 368–378. https://doi.org/10.1037/men0000169

Peterson, R. D., Tantleff-Dunn, S., & Bedwell, J. S. (2006). The effects of exposure to feminist ideology on women's body image. *Body Image, 3*(3), 237-246.

Raisanen, U., & Hunt, K. (2014). The role of gendered constructions of eating disorders in delayed help-seeking in men: A qualitative interview study. *BMJ Open, 4*, e004342. https://doi.org/10.1136/bmjopen-2013-004342

Ramos-Martins, C., Oliveira, S., & Ferreira, C. (2022). Can body appreciation buffer the association between external and internal shame experiences with eating psychopathology? *Clinical Psychologist, 26*(1), 53–62. https://doi.org/10.1080/13284207.2021.1929142

Ravaldi, C., Vannacci, A., Bolognesi, E., Mancini, S., Faravelli, C., & Ricca, V. (2006). Gender role, eating disorder symptoms, and body image concern in ballet dancers. *Journal of Psychosomatic Research, 61*(4), 529–535. https://doi.org/10.1016/j.jpsychores.2006.04.016

Reba-Harrelson, L., Von Holle, A., Hamer, R. M., Swann, R., Reyes, M. L., & Bulik, C. M. (2009). Patterns and prevalence of disordered eating and weight control behaviors in women ages 25–45. https://doi.org/10.1007/BF03325116

Rodin, J., Silberstein, L., & Striegel-Moore, R. (1984). Women and weight: A normative discontent. *Nebraska Symposium on Motivation. Nebraska Symposium on Motivation, 32*, 267–307.

Rooney, J. M. J. (2019). *Development of the Multicultural Gender Role Scale for Asian American Women (MGRS-AAW)*. Columbia University.

Russell, C. J., & Keel, P. K. (2002). Homosexuality as a specific risk factor for eating disorders in men. *International Journal of Eating Disorders, 31*(3), 300–306. https://doi.org/10.1002/eat.10036

Schaefer, L. M., & Thompson, J. K. (2018). Self-objectification and disordered eating: A meta-analysis. *International Journal of Eating Disorders, 51*(6), 483–502. https://doi.org/10.1002/eat.22854

Schaumberg, K., Welch, E., Breithaupt, L., Hubel, C., Baker, J. H., Munn-Chernoff, M. A., Yilmaz, Z., Ehrlich, S., Mustelin, L., Ghaderi, A., Hardaway, J. A., Bulik-Sullivan, E. C., Hedman, A. M., Jangmo, A., Nilsson, I. A. K., Wiklund, C., Yao, S., Seidel, M., & Bulik, C. M. (2017). The science behind the Academy for Eating Disorders' nine truths about eating disorders. *European Eating Disorders Review, 25*(6), 432–450. https://doi.org/10.1002/erv.2553

Siegel, J. A., & Calogero, R. M. (2019). Conformity to feminine norms and self-objectification in self-identified feminist and non-feminist women. *Body Image, 28,* 115–118. https://doi.org/10.1016/j.bodyim.2019.01.005

Siegel, J. A., & Sawyer, K. B. (2020). "We don't talk about feelings or struggles like that": White men's experiences of eating disorders in the workplace. *Psychology of Men & Masculinities, 21*(4), 533–544. https://doi.org/10.1037/men0000253

Spence, J. T., Helmreich, R., & Stapp, J. (1975). Ratings of self and peers on sex role attributes and their relation to self-esteem and conceptions of masculinity and femininity. *Journal of Personality and Social Psychology, 32*(1), 29–39. https://doi.org/10.1037/h0076857

Springmann, M. L., Svaldi, J., & Kiegelmann, M. (2022). A qualitative study of gendered psychosocial processes in eating disorder development. *International Journal of Eating Disorders, 55*(7), 947–955.

Steele, S. M., Belvy, L., Veldhuis, C. B., Martin, K., Nisi, R., & Hughes, T. L. (2019). Femininity, masculinity, and body image in a community-based sample of lesbian and bisexual women. *Women & Health, 59*(8), 829–844.

Striegel-Moore, R. H., Rosselli, F., Perrin, N., DeBar, L., Wilson, G. T., May, A., & Kraemer, H. C. (2009). Gender difference in the prevalence of eating disorder symptoms. *International Journal of Eating Disorders, 42*(5), 471–474. https://doi.org/10.1002/eat.20625

Strong, S. M., Williamson, D. A., Netemeyer, R. G., & Geer, J. H. (2000). Eating disorder symptoms and concerns about body differ as a function of gender and sexual orientation. *Journal of Social and Clinical Psychology, 19*(2), 240–255.

Swami, V. (2015). Cultural influences on body size ideals: Unpacking the impact of Westernization and modernization. *European Psychologist, 20*(1). https://doi.org/10.1027/1016-9040/a000150

Swami, V., & Abbasnejad, A. (2010). Associations between femininity ideology and body appreciation among British female undergraduates. *Personality and Individual Differences, 48*(5), 685–687. https://doi.org/ 10.1016/j.paid.2009.12.017

Tiggemann, M., Martins, Y., & Kirkbride, A. (2007). Oh to be lean and muscular: Body image ideals in gay and heterosexual men. *Psychology of Men & Masculinity, 8*(1), 15–24. https://doi.org/10.1037/1524-9220.8.1.15

Till, C. (2011). The quantification of gender: Anorexia nervosa and femininity. *Health Sociology Review, 20*(4), 437–449. https://doi.org/ 10.5172/hesr.2011.20.4.437

Timko, C., Striegel-Moore, R. H., Silberstein, L. R., & Rodin, J. (1987). Feminity/masculinity and disordered eating in women: How are they related?. *International Journal of Eating Disorders, 6*(6), 701–712. https://doi.org/10.1002/1098-108X(198711)6:6<701::AID-EAT2260060603>3.0.CO;2-D

Tylka, T. L., & Wood-Barcalow, N. L. (2015). The Body Appreciation Scale-2: Item refinement and psychometric evaluation. *Body Image, 12*, 53–67. https://doi.org/10.1016/j.bodyim.2014.09.006

Udo, T., & Grilo, C. M. (2018). Prevalence and correlates of DSM-5-defined eating disorders in a nationally representative sample of U.S. adults. *Biological Psychiatry, 84*(5), 345–354. https://doi.org/10.1016/j.biopsych.2018.03.014

van Anders, S. (2015). Beyond sexual orientation: Integrating gender/sex and diverse sexualities via sexual configurations theory. *Archives of Sexual Behavior, 44,* 1177–1213. https://doi.org/10.1007/s10508-015-0490-8

Vasiliu, O. (2023). At the crossroads between eating disorders and body dysmorphic disorders—The case of bigorexia nervosa. *Brain Sciences, 13*(9), 1234. https://doi.org/10.3390/brainsci13091234

Wolf, N. (1991). *The beauty myth: How images of beauty are used against women.* Harper Perennial.

Chapter 10

Gender Identity

Kai Thomas

Introduction

The majority of research exploring the development and maintenance of anorexia nervosa (AN) has focused on cisgender individuals, whose gender identity aligns with their sex assigned at birth. However, the last decade has seen a growing interest in exploring eating disorders (EDs) in gender diverse people (i.e., people whose gender identity does not align with their sex assigned at birth; Ålgars et al., 2012; Ferrucci et al., 2022; Jones et al., 2016; Parker & Harriger, 2020). Worldwide estimates of the proportion of gender diverse people vary between 0.1 and 2% (Goodman et al., 2019); however, there are large methodological inconsistencies across population studies. An estimated 0.5% of the UK population (>16 years of age) identify with a gender that was different from their sex assigned at birth (Office for National Statistics, 2023). Similarly, in the US, 0.5% of adults identify as transgender, while rates are considerably higher in 13–17 year-olds at 1.4% (Herman et al., 2022).

This chapter will first synthesise the existing literature describing the prevalence and aetiology of AN in gender diverse populations. Proposed risk and protective factors for AN in these groups will be discussed alongside relevant theoretical models. Finally, the implications for future clinical practice and research will be presented. Throughout the chapter, the term 'gender diverse' is used to refer to people who identify with a gender identity that does not align with their sex assigned at birth. However, it is important to acknowledge that this term encompasses many identities and some that may be preferred include 'transgender', 'non-binary', and 'gender non-conforming'. Definitions of key terms are presented in Table 10.1.

The Prevalence of Anorexia Nervosa in Gender Diverse Populations

Research has demonstrated that gender diverse adults and youth are more likely to be diagnosed with an ED or engage in disordered eating behaviours and cognitions compared to their cisgender counterparts (Ålgars et al., 2012; Diemer et al., 2018; Duffy et al., 2016; Duffy et al., 2019; Ferrucci et al., 2022; Hartman-Munick

DOI: 10.4324/9781003468189-12

Table 10.1 Key terms related to gender identity.

Term	*Definition*
Gender identity	An internal sense and experience of gender, which may or may not be the same as one's sex assigned at birth.
Gender expression	External characteristics and behaviours socially defined as masculine, feminine, or neutral.
Transgender/gender diverse	An individual whose gender identity does not align with their sex assigned at birth.
Cisgender	An individual whose gender identity aligns with their sex assigned at birth.
Binary gender identity	A gender identity that is categorised as either man/boy or woman/girl.
Nonbinary gender identity	A gender identity that exists between or outside of the gender binary, e.g., not identifying exclusively as a man or woman. Other terms people may use to express their nonbinary gender identity include 'gender non-conforming', 'agender', 'genderqueer', and 'gender-fluid'.
Gender dysphoria	Psychological distress resulting from incongruence between one's gender identity and sex assigned at birth (American Psychiatric Association, 2013).
Trans man	An individual who was assigned female sex at birth but identifies and lives as a man.
Transmasculine	An individual who was assigned female sex at birth but whose gender identity is partially or fully aligned with masculinity.
Trans woman	An individual who was assigned male sex at birth but identifies and lives as a woman.
Transfeminine	An individual who was assigned male sex at birth but whose gender identity is partially or fully aligned with femininity.

et al., 2021; Jones et al., 2016; Jones et al., 2019; Nagata et al., 2020; Rasmussen et al., 2023). For example, in a large college student population, rates of ED diagnoses (AN or bulimia nervosa) in the past year were higher for gender diverse students compared to students who were cisgender women and men (17.6%, 1.8%, and 0.2%, respectively; Duffy et al., 2019). The high prevalence of EDs in gender diverse people reported in this study is in accordance with a recent meta-analysis, which found a prevalence of 17.7% across transgender men and women (Rasmussen et al., 2023). However, prevalence rates may differ substantially between studies based on the use of clinical validation of ED diagnoses. For example, in a community sample of gender diverse adults (Diemer et al., 2018), 4.7% reported receiving a diagnosis of AN or bulimia nervosa, while 7.4% self-reported AN or bulimia nervosa without receiving a diagnosis. Furthermore, in a large sample of gender diverse people accessing some form of gender-affirming care, only 2.4% had a clinical ED diagnosis (Ferrucci et al., 2022).

Very few studies have examined prevalence rates by ED diagnosis in gender diverse populations. In a study of over 10,000 gender diverse people accessing gender-affirming care, only 0.84% had a clinical diagnosis of AN, with unspecified feeding and EDs (1.37%) the most prevalent ED diagnosis (Ferrucci et al., 2022). Similar findings have been reported in gender diverse adolescents with diagnosed EDs. For example, Chaphekar et al. (2022) conducted a retrospective chart review of adolescents admitted to an inpatient ED medical unit across a 10-year period. They found gender diverse adolescents were more likely to have a diagnosis of atypical AN, captured under the other specified feeding and ED diagnosis, compared to their cisgender peers (70% vs. 31%, respectively). Furthermore, there was no difference in the prevalence of AN diagnoses across the two groups (Chaphekar et al., 2022). These findings suggest that, under current ED diagnostic frameworks, eating pathology displayed by gender diverse people may not align with typical ED presentations seen in cisgender women.

ED prevalence rates have also been found to differ across gender diverse identities. For example, Romano and Lipson (2022) reported the prevalence of a self-reported lifetime ED diagnosis to be highest in college students who identified as genderqueer/gender nonconforming (11.6%) or gender expansive (11.0%), compared to those who identified as trans men (9.6%) and trans women (4.0%). However, in a sample of gender diverse youth, Becerra-Culqui et al. (2018) found similar rates of lifetime ED diagnosis across transmasculine (4.3%) and transfeminine (4.2%) individuals. As well as gender identity, sex assigned at birth has also been found to impact ED prevalence rates. Diemer et al. (2018) found gender diverse people assigned female at birth were at greater risk of an ED than those assigned male at birth. Specifically, gender nonconforming participants assigned female at birth had the highest rates (9.7% diagnosed and 15% self-reported), followed by trans men assigned female sex at birth (4.1% and 6.1%), with trans women assigned male sex at birth (2.8% and 0.8%) and gender nonconforming participants assigned male at birth (0% and 5.5%) reporting the lowest rates. Research with gender diverse adolescents has also found those assigned female at birth to have higher rates of ED diagnoses (Feder et al., 2017) and AN symptoms (i.e., overevaluation of weight, fear of gaining weight, or recurrent behaviours to interfere with weight gain; Kerr et al., 2024), compared to those assigned male at birth. These findings suggest ED symptoms may be biologically driven, and/or influenced by environmental factors, such as sociocultural standards of body image for people assigned female at birth. Alternatively, Feder et al. (2017) propose greater engagement in ED behaviours in trans men compared to trans women may be explained by the potential for more physical changes to body and body shape as a result of ED behaviours in this group. Therefore, the function of disordered eating in alleviating gender dysphoria may differ among gender identities and sex assigned at birth.

Aetiology of ED Pathology in Gender Diverse Populations

Body Dissatisfaction and Gender Dysphoria

Although engagement in food restriction, compensatory behaviours, and body dissatisfaction are key features of eating pathology across cisgender and gender diverse people (Fairburn, 2008; Stice & Shaw, 2002; Witcomb et al., 2015), the underlying mechanisms driving ED symptoms may differ between these groups. A systematic review by Jones et al. (2016) found body dissatisfaction to be core to the distress some gender diverse people experience about their bodies, leading to engagement in disordered eating behaviours as a way of alleviating this distress. Restrictive eating and compensatory behaviours in gender diverse people may be used as a way to control pubertal development, including menstruation cessation and interruption of secondary sex characteristic development (e.g., Coelho et al., 2019; Diemer et al., 2018; Kamody et al., 2020; Romito et al., 2021). In addition, these behaviours may be used to achieve body characteristics that are more aligned with gender identity and alleviate symptoms of gender dysphoria (Ålgars et al., 2012). For example, gender diverse people assigned female at birth often report engaging in weight control behaviours and excessive exercise to achieve a more lean and muscular body, and suppress curves that reflect a stereotypically feminine body (Amodeo et al., 2022; Duffy et al., 2016; Nagata et al., 2020). For gender diverse people assigned male at birth, engagement in weight control behaviours may be used to appear more traditionally feminine, such as altering body shape to align with feminine body ideals and reducing facial and body hair growth (Ewan et al., 2014; Gordon et al., 2016; Murray et al., 2013; Winston et al., 2004).

Studies on EDs in nonbinary people, whose gender identity exists between or outside of the binary gender identity, are scarce compared to those with binary trans people. However, recent studies exploring eating pathology in nonbinary people have found thinness to be an important feature of their androgynous gender expression (Cusack & Galupo, 2021; Cusack et al., 2022a; Galupo et al., 2021). An androgynous body has been reported by nonbinary people as a way of achieving neutrality with respect to binary gender characteristics, as well as managing gender dysphoria, and potentially avoiding misgendering from others (Galupo et al., 2021). Engagement in dietary restriction and compensatory behaviours can therefore be tightly linked to how nonbinary people understand and experience their gender, as well as how they express this to others.

The literature described so far focuses heavily on the physical body and how this is linked to EDs among gender diverse people. However, many gender diverse people report their ED as being unrelated to their physical body (Duffy et al., 2016), and EDs are often reported to present prior to awareness of a gender diverse identity (Couturier et al., 2015; Duffy et al., 2016). Therefore, body dissatisfaction and gender dysphoria may be salient features of EDs for some gender diverse people, but not all. These findings demonstrate a variety of complex mechanisms that may underlie ED symptoms in gender diverse people, and the need to consider wider contextual factors.

Discrimination, Stigma, and Social Stressors

Gender diverse people experience high levels of discrimination and stigma (Truszczynski et al., 2022), which can impact significantly on their mental health and wellbeing (for systematic reviews, see Gosling et al., 2022; Mezza et al., 2024). Research with gender diverse populations has also demonstrated specific links between experiences of social stressors and overall ED risk. Experiences of discrimination, including harassment, rejection, and discrimination-based trauma symptoms, are associated with elevated levels of ED symptoms and body dissatisfaction in gender diverse youth and adults (Brewster et al., 2019; Brokjøb & Cornelissen, 2022; Tabaac et al., 2018; Urban et al., 2023; Watson et al., 2017). Elevated levels of ED symptoms have also been linked to internalised transphobia (Uniacke et al., 2021; Urban et al., 2023).

Unfortunately, research has repeatedly demonstrated that gender diverse people also experience discrimination, stigma, and a lack of understanding from healthcare professionals when accessing healthcare (Hobster & McLuskey, 2020). When internalised, these experiences can lead to psychological distress, as well as poorer physical health outcomes due to healthcare avoidance, less attendance at screenings, and delayed treatment (Drabish & Theeke, 2022). There also appear to be within-group differences in healthcare avoidance due to anticipated discrimination in the gender diverse population. For example, compared to transgender women, transgender men report greater healthcare avoidance, whereas nonbinary people report lower healthcare avoidance (Kcomt et al., 2020). Additionally, nonbinary people were less likely to share their gender identity within a healthcare setting compared to binary gender diverse people (Kcomt et al., 2020), suggesting gender diverse subgroups have unique experiences of accessing healthcare. Further, gender diverse people from ethnic minority backgrounds are found to experience greater healthcare avoidance compared to white gender diverse people, indicating that individuals from multiple marginalised backgrounds may experience an even greater exposure to healthcare discrimination and stigma (Kcomt et al., 2020). Similar findings are reported in ED treatment specifically, with research reporting multiple barriers to effective care for gender diverse populations. For example, Duffy et al. (2016) found negative experiences with clinicians to be a key theme within the ED treatment experiences of gender diverse people. This included dismissal, mistreatment, and a lack of awareness and competence around gender from clinicians, with some people reporting anticipation of mistreatment to be a barrier to effective care.

The Gender Minority Stress and Resilience (GMSR) model (Testa et al., 2015), based on the early work of Brooks (1981) and subsequent minority stress model (Meyer, 2003), has been proposed as a theoretical explanation for the significantly higher levels of mental health difficulties, including ED symptoms, in gender diverse people compared to their cisgender peers. This model proposes that gender diverse people experience unique stressors related to their minoritised identity which can contribute to psychological distress and subsequent mental health difficulties (Hendricks & Testa, 2012; Testa et al., 2015). The model includes a combination of interpersonal and intrapersonal stressors related to a gender minority identity. Interpersonal stressors captured in the model are caused by external sources which marginalise gender diverse people and/or threaten their safety, such as gender-related discrimination, victimisation, rejection, and non-affirmation of gender identity. These stressors are proposed to be related to mental health through the mediating pathway of intrapersonal stressors, which are subjective cognitions and emotions that occur in response to marginalisation and oppression. These are internalised transphobia, expectation and anticipation of negative interpersonal reactions, and concealment of their gender identity. Experiencing these gender-related stressors can result in high levels of psychological distress, potentially leading to the use of maladaptive coping strategies, including disordered eating (Copeland et al., 2015). The GMSR model also identifies two resilience factors, community connectedness and pride, which are posited to protect against the negative effects of minority stress on mental health and wellbeing.

Due to the heterogeneity of the gender diverse population, these social stressors must also be considered in the context of intersectionality. Intersectionality is a construct rooted in the work of Black feminist scholarship and practice (e.g., Crenshaw, 1989), which considers how multiple social identities, such as ethnicity, social class, and gender, can independently and interactively impact on risk and resilience to discrimination and disadvantage (Cole, 2009). Social identities should therefore be considered alongside hierarchies of power and privilege that exist in society, leading to greater health disparities for individuals who occupy multiple minoritised identities (Burke et al., 2023). Although research using intersectional approaches in this area is still in its infancy, findings so far suggest higher-than-expected ED risk for gender diverse people of colour, based on the additive impact of their minoritised gender identity and race/ethnicity (Egbert et al., 2024; Gordon et al., 2024). Heightened ED risk has also been found for trans men and/or gender expansive people who also identify with a sexual minority identity, compared to individuals who identify as heterosexual (Simone et al., 2022). However, further work is needed to examine the impact of intersecting gender diverse identities and other social minority identities on ED risk, such as those related to disability, social class, and neurodivergence.

Sociocultural Influences

The Tripartite Influence Model of body image and eating disturbance (Thompson et al., 1999a; Thompson et al., 1999b) proposes that three sociocultural influences (peers, family, and media) can impact on the risk of developing body dissatisfaction and eating pathology through two mediational processes: internalisation of appearance/body ideals and excessive social appearance comparison. For example, media portrayals of body ideals may be internalised as a personal standard by some individuals. Social comparisons with these unobtainable appearances can lead to body dissatisfaction and increased ED risk (Thompson & Stice, 2001).

The majority of research to date has focused on the impact of sociocultural norms on cisgender women; however, research over the last decade has increasingly focused on cisgender men's experience. In cisgender women and girls, a significant body of early research identified the 'thin ideal' as the ideal body type represented in the media (Polivy & Herman, 2002; Wiseman et al., 1992) and found it to be associated with increased body dissatisfaction and disordered eating (Grabe et al., 2008; Henrichs-Beck & Szymanski, 2017; Huang et al., 2021; Keery et al., 2004; Ozbek et al., 2023). However, recent research suggests this thinness-oriented appearance ideal in cisgender women is shifting towards an 'athletic ideal', characterised by a toned and thin body shape (Karazsia et al., 2017; Krug et al., 2020; Tiggemann & Zaccardo, 2015). A lean and muscular body is generally seen as the appearance ideal in cisgender men (Blond, 2008; Buote et al., 2011; Lavender et al., 2017; Leit et al., 2002). In line with the Tripartite Influence Model, thin and muscular internalisation, as well as appearance comparisons, have been found to predict disordered eating in cisgender men (Schaefer et al., 2021). There appear to be gender differences in cisgender populations when it comes to muscle-related behaviours, as cisgender men are more likely to engage in excessive muscle building activities and steroid use compared to cisgender women (Nagata et al., 2022a; Nagata et al., 2022b; Yager & McLean, 2020). These gender differences are also important to consider in the context of ED diagnostic criteria. For example, thinness-orientated disordered eating behaviours (e.g., restriction of caloric intake, compensatory behaviours like excessive exercise or purging) are consistent with DSM-5 criteria for AN (American Psychiatric Association, 2013). However, muscularity-orientated disordered eating behaviours are not represented in ED diagnostic criteria, which may be an important factor when considering the prevalence of EDs across genders (Muratore et al., 2022).

The Tripartite Influence Model may also be applicable to gender diverse people, as they are also found to internalise traditional gendered appearance ideals (Jones et al., 2016; Strübel et al., 2020). For example, internalisation of societal appearance ideals has been associated with body dissatisfaction, body monitoring, and disordered eating in both trans men (Velez et al., 2016) and trans women (Brewster et al., 2019; Comiskey et al., 2019). Levels of drive for thinness are comparable across trans men and trans women, and similar to levels reported by cisgender women (Witcomb et al., 2015). As drive for thinness is lower in cisgender men, these findings suggest female sex at birth and/or gender identity may increase risk for ED development due to exposure to and internalisation of sociocultural norms and ideals (Witcomb et al., 2015). Alternatively, trans men may over-evaluate thinness to reduce body fat and in turn, feminine secondary sex characteristics like hips and breasts (Ålgars et al., 2010; Velez et al., 2016). Alongside these behaviours, trans men report comparable muscularity-orientated body concerns to cisgender men (Amodeo et al., 2022; Strübel et al., 2020), suggesting they experience similar societal pressures. Qualitative findings demonstrate how conforming to societal ideals can be necessary for some gender diverse people who report feeling a need to prove their gender identity to others and themselves (Cusack et al., 2022a; Gordon et al., 2016; Pham et al., 2023). For example, ED symptoms may enable gender diverse people to 'pass' as cisgender (Anderson et al., 2020; e.g., a trans woman may want to be perceived as a cisgender woman in public) by altering their body shape and appearance to conform with cisgender appearance ideals. ED symptoms are strongly associated with being misgendered (Zamantakis & Lackey, 2022); therefore, engaging in these behaviours may reduce gender dysphoria by controlling gender expression.

The association between thin-ideal internalisation and disordered eating was recently extended from binary gender diverse people to nonbinary and gender non-conforming people (Romano & Lipson, 2022). Studies examining the experiences of nonbinary people are severely lacking; however, recent research has begun to explore the role of androgynous appearance ideals that exist outside of binary gendered appearance ideals and norms (Cusack & Galupo, 2021; Galupo et al., 2021). An androgynous body ideal has been found to be both affirming (Galupo et al., 2021) and detrimental to body image in nonbinary people (Cusack & Galupo, 2021). Therefore, further research is needed to understand how societal appearance ideals are experienced by nonbinary people, and the impact these have on their body image.

Resilience Factors

Research has identified both group and individual resilience factors for the development of EDs in gender diverse people. A recent systematic review of quantitative studies examining minority stress and mental health in gender diverse people found mixed findings for group-level resilience factors (Mezza et al., 2024). Mezza et al. (2024) reported community connectedness, a resilience factor highlighted in the GMSR model (Testa et al., 2015), to be mostly unrelated to poor mental health outcomes. However, social support appeared to be a more significant resilience factor. This may suggest gender diverse people may benefit more from support from others who do not share their minority identity, such as family members and peers (Mezza et al., 2024). In terms of resilience factors for EDs specifically, there is some evidence from gender diverse adolescents to suggest social support and connectedness with family and peers are related to lower levels of ED symptoms (Watson et al., 2017). However, there was inconclusive evidence for a buffering effect of community connectedness and pride in one's gender minority identity on disordered eating when examined in gender diverse adults (Muratore et al., 2022). Benefits of support and connectedness from others may vary according to factors such as the individual's personal network of support (e.g., people with less family and peer support may engage more with the gender diverse community) and their identity as a gender diverse person (e.g., gender diverse people who choose not to disclose their gender transition to others may experience less connectedness to the gender diverse community).

Many studies have reported that access to gender-affirming medical interventions (such as hormone therapy and surgeries) may alleviate ED symptoms and negative body image in gender diverse people (Becker et al., 2018; Fisher et al., 2014; Jones et al., 2018; Nowaskie et al., 2021; Owen-Smith et al., 2018; Rasmussen et al., 2023; Testa et al., 2017; Turan et al., 2018; van de Grift et al., 2017; van de Grift et al., 2018). It is suggested that gender-affirming hormone therapy may alleviate ED symptoms by reducing body dissatisfaction, anxiety symptoms, and perfectionism, and increasing self-esteem (Jones et al., 2018). Similar findings have been reported for gender-affirming surgeries, which are found to lead to fewer experiences of non-affirmation of gender identity from others (e.g., using incorrect pronouns), decreasing body dissatisfaction and ED symptoms (Testa et al., 2017). However, not all gender diverse people seek medical interventions during their transition, with some choosing to socially transition (e.g., use of a gender-affirming name, pronouns, clothing, hairstyle, etc.; Rafferty et al., 2020) without gender-affirming hormones and surgeries. Gender-affirming care, whether medical or non-medical, may help alleviate ED symptomatology by reducing the distress associated with gender incongruence in gender diverse people.

Implications for Future Clinical Research and Practice

Although there is an increasing clinical and research interest in ED treatment considerations for gender diverse people, there are currently no clinical guidelines and a dearth of evidence to guide clinical practice. As the aetiology of EDs is known to differ between gender diverse people and cisgender people, ED treatment approaches must consider these unique experiences to ensure support is accessible and efficient for all gender identities. Crucially, future research should directly involve gender diverse people with lived experience of EDs from the start (Papastavrou Brooks et al., 2023). Co-producing research from the design through to knowledge dissemination will ensure this work represents their priorities and experiences.

Qualitative studies with gender diverse people have highlighted how the interrelation between their EDs and gender identity has implications for their experiences of ED treatment (Duffy et al., 2016). For some gender diverse individuals, there is a clear link between their physical body and ED; whereas, for others, non-body related factors like anxiety and trauma are more strongly related to their ED (Duffy et al., 2016). Indeed, some gender diverse people find discussing their gender dysphoria with their clinician to be a helpful part of ED treatment, allowing them to explore new strategies for coping with their gender dysphoria, alleviating their ED symptoms (Cusack et al., 2022a). However, it is important that clinicians do not assume that an individual's gender identity is driving their ED symptoms. Although gender identity may play an important role for some gender diverse individuals, others report an over-emphasis on gender identity in ED treatment to be unhelpful for their ED recovery (Cusack et al., 2022a). Gender diverse people with EDs highlight the need for clinicians to take a 'whole person' approach, recognising them as an individual person beyond their ED and gender diverse identity (Smith & Harrop, 2024). Therefore, clinical ED approaches should be tailored to the individual and their needs, including the interplay between their gender identity and ED experience.

Gender diverse people report a lack of clinician understanding around their body image difficulties and how best to support these. For example, body discomfort specific to gender incongruence is unlikely to be overcome by typical cis-normative ED treatment approaches which emphasise positive body image (Duffy et al., 2016; McGregor et al., 2023). Instead, ED clinicians are being prompted to consider the concept of body neutrality, which promotes the functionality of the body, rather than its appearance (Perry et al., 2019). This approach may be particularly useful for gender diverse people as it suggests a more inclusive and realistic recovery goal. It also removes focus away from achieving acceptance of a body which is incongruent with one's gender identity, for which accessing gender-affirming interventions may be the individual's goal. Future research is needed to explore the efficacy of this approach when supporting gender diverse people who have lived experience of EDs.

Clinicians supporting gender diverse people with EDs should also consider the process of ED recovery and how this may exacerbate gender dysphoria for some individuals. Some gender diverse people report feeling conflicted between recovery from their ED and their gender expression (Harrop et al., 2023). As recovery from AN may require weight restoration, gender diverse individuals may experience an increase in gender dysphoria due to the re-emergence of secondary sex characteristics that have been suppressed by ED behaviours (Ewan et al., 2014). For individuals whose ED symptoms function as a way of managing gender dysphoria, access to gender-affirming medical interventions may reduce gender dysphoria, and in turn, reduce ED symptoms (Testa et al., 2017). However, access to gender-affirming medical care can be contingent on body mass index, negatively impacting the health of gender diverse people (Brownstone et al., 2021). Some gender diverse people are encouraged to lose weight in order to access this surgery, increasing the risk of developing ED symptoms (Brownstone et al., 2021). Individuals who experience malnutrition and underweight may be at increased risk of complications from surgery; however, Yesildemir and Akbulut (2023) argue gender-affirming surgery should not be cancelled for individuals with EDs. Instead, additional treatment should be offered before surgery to decrease ED symptoms, increase medical stability, and optimise post-surgical outcomes (Coleman et al., 2022). Therefore, there needs to be collaborative disciplinary approaches across ED and gender-affirming treatment providers to ensure the treatment and care provided is able to meet the needs of gender diverse people (Donaldson et al., 2018).

Many gender diverse people report a lack of inclusivity and transgender cultural competency of ED services and clinicians when receiving ED treatment (Duffy et al., 2016). Some individuals conceal their transgender status when accessing ED treatment to avoid discrimination and stigma; however, this can negatively impact the efficacy of the treatment, the development of a strong therapeutic relationship, as well as exploration of identity and how this is related to the ED (Duffy et al., 2016). Indeed, many people with AN report their ED as becoming integral to their identity (Marzola et al., 2015; Nordbø et al., 2006), helping to create a more coherent sense of self, increase feelings of self-worth, and provide a sense of achievement and success (McNamara & Parsons, 2016; Schmidt & Treasure, 2006). Therefore, environments which follow gender-affirming practices (e.g., correct pronoun use and use of gender-inclusive language, facility access, paperwork, etc.) and encourage exploration of identity within ED treatment can be helpful for promoting better ED treatment outcomes (Cusack et al., 2022b).

Previous studies often report gender diverse individuals being the main source of education on gender identity when interacting with clinicians (Duffy et al., 2016). This is likely due to the lack of formal education on supporting gender diverse individuals with EDs (Ferrucci et al., 2023). ED clinicians recognise a need for improved training in the area of gender identity and gender-affirming care, with many engaging in self-education around these topics to inform their work (Ferrucci et al., 2024). This may help explain why gender diverse people express a preference for working with clinicians who themselves are members of the LGBTQ+ community (Cusack et al., 2022b). LGBTQ+ clinicians may be able to share insight and understanding of identifying with a marginalised group, as well as a motivation to educate themselves on the specific needs of gender diverse people (Cusack et al., 2022b).

Increasingly, research has focused on validating ED screening measures with gender diverse populations. In a recent review, McGregor et al. (2023) summarised the studies that have examined the validity and reliability of a number of ED measures in gender diverse populations, such as the Eating Disorder Examination Questionnaire (EDE-Q; Fairburn & Beglin, 1994), the Eating Attitudes Test (EAT; Garner & Garfinkel, 1979), and the Sick, Control, One Stone, Fat, Food questionnaire (SCOFF; Morgan et al., 1999). For example, the EDE-Q, one of the most widely used self-report measures of ED symptoms, has been shown to demonstrate good validity and reliability in gender diverse people (Nagata et al., 2023). Qualitative data have also been collected to guide ED screener questions for clinicians working in both ED services and gender clinics (Donaldson et al., 2018). These questions were different for each setting, but those in ED clinics focused on exploring gender identity and the individuals' thoughts around their body and how it relates to gender. For gender clinicians, questions were instead targeted at gathering information around experiences of disordered eating more generally, as well as historical dieting or compensatory behaviours (Donaldson et al., 2018). Although validation of these measures is a positive step in ensuring ED measures are relevant for gender diverse people, they also have their limitations. The majority of research captures self-reported ED symptoms using measures which produce a global ED symptom score and/or subscales indicating engagement in certain behaviours/concerns. In order to comprehensively understand the presentations of ED symptoms in gender diverse people, further research is needed to explore measures that capture behaviours and concerns that may be unique to this group. For example, the underlying motivation to relieve gender dysphoria through dieting and compensatory behaviour may not be accurately captured in current ED assessments. These examinations should also be accurate and effective for people who identify with a broad array of gender diverse identities, to ensure we are identifying ED symptoms as early as possible.

Finally, when conducting ED research or clinical practice with gender diverse people, it is important to consider the multiple identities they may hold and how these may impact on their experience of the ED and its presentation. Recent research has started to explore the intersections of multiple marginalised social identities (e.g., ethnic and sexual minority identity) on ED risk (Austin et al., 2012; Burke et al., 2023; Burke et al., 2020; Calzo et al., 2017; Diemer et al., 2015; Egbert et al., 2024; Gordon et al., 2024). These studies highlight disparities in ED risk between individuals who identify with two minoritised identities compared to those who identify with one (Egbert et al., 2024). However, the intersections between other facets of identity (such as neurodivergence, disability status) and their impact on ED risk require further examination in gender diverse populations. For example, research demonstrates an epidemiological overlap between gender diversity and autism (Cooper et al., 2018; Strang et al., 2014; van der Miesen et al., 2018; Warrier et al., 2020), with elevated risk for EDs reported in both gender diverse (Duffy et al., 2019) and autistic people (Tchanturia et al., 2017; Westwood et al., 2017). Initial evidence suggests an additive effect of being gender diverse and autistic on ED risk (Strauss et al., 2021), but there is a lack of understanding around how these identities intersect to influence ED aetiology. Therefore, future research is needed to explore the unique and shared mechanisms underlying EDs in gender diverse and autistic people, to inform adaptations to ED treatment and screening. Overall, these findings highlight the importance of using intersectionality-informed approaches in ED treatment to consider the unique experiences of individuals from various social identity groups and the impact their identity may have on their experience of an ED.

References

Ålgars, M., Alanko, K., Santtila, P., & Sandnabba, N. K. (2012). Disordered eating and gender identity disorder: A qualitative study [Article]. *Eating Disorders*, *20*(4), 300–311. https://doi.org/10.1080/10640266.2012.668482

Ålgars, M., Santtila, P., & Sandnabba, N. K. (2010). Conflicted gender identity, body dissatisfaction, and disordered eating in adult men and women. *Sex Roles*, *63*(1), 118–125. https://doi.org/10.1007/s11199-010-9758-6

American Psychiatric Association, D.-T. F. (2013). *Diagnostic and statistical manual of mental disorders: DSM-5™* (5th ed.). American Psychiatric Publishing, Inc. https://doi.org/10.1176/appi.books.9780890425596

Amodeo, A. L., Esposito, C., Antuoni, S., Saracco, G., & Bacchini, D. (2022). Muscle dysmorphia: What about transgender people? *Culture, Health & Sexuality*, *24*(1), 63–78. https://doi.org/10.1080/13691058.2020.1814968

Anderson, A. D., Irwin, J. A., Brown, A. M., & Grala, C. L. (2020). "Your picture looks the same as my picture": An examination of passing in transgender communities. *Gender Issues*, *37*(1), 44–60. https://doi.org/10.1007/s12147-019-09239-x

Austin, S. B., Nelson, L. A., Birkett, M. A., Calzo, J. P., & Everett, B. (2012). Eating disorder symptoms and obesity at the intersections of gender, ethnicity, and sexual orientation in US high school students. *American Journal of Public Health*, *103*(2), e16–e22. https://doi.org/10.2105/AJPH.2012.301150

Becerra-Culqui, T. A., Liu, Y., Nash, R., Cromwell, L., Flanders, W. D., Getahun, D., Giammattei, S. V., Hunkeler, E. M., Lash, T. L., Millman, A., Quinn, V. P., Robinson, B., Roblin, D., Sandberg, D. E., Silverberg, M. J., Tangpricha, V., & Goodman, M. (2018). Mental health of transgender and gender nonconforming youth compared with their peers. *Pediatrics*, *141*(5), e20173845. https://doi.org/10.1542/peds.2017-3845

Becker, I., Auer, M., Barkmann, C., Fuss, J., Möller, B., Nieder, T. O., Fahrenkrug, S., Hildebrandt, T., & Richter-Appelt, H. (2018). A cross-sectional multicenter study of multidimensional body image in adolescents and adults with gender dysphoria before and after transition-related medical interventions. *Archives of Sexual Behavior*, *47*(8), 2335–2347. https://doi.org/10.1007/s10508-018-1278-4

Blond, A. (2008). Impacts of exposure to images of ideal bodies on male body dissatisfaction: A review. *Body Image*, *5*(3), 244–250. https://doi.org/https://doi.org/10.1016/j.bodyim.2008.02.003

Brewster, M. E., Velez, B. L., Breslow, A. S., & Geiger, E. F. (2019). Unpacking body image concerns and disordered eating for transgender women: The roles of sexual objectification and minority stress. *Journal of Counseling Psychology*, *66*(2), 131–142. https://doi.org/10.1037/cou0000333

Brokjøb, L. G., & Cornelissen, K. K. (2022). Internalizing minority stress: Gender dysphoria, minority stress, and psychopathology in a norwegian transgender population. *Psychology of Sexual Orientation and Gender Diversity*, *9*(3), 272–286. https://doi.org/10.1037/sgd0000480

Brooks, V. R. (1981). *Minority stress and lesbian women*. Lexington Books. https://cir.nii.ac.jp/crid/1130282271372632320

Brownstone, L. M., DeRieux, J., Kelly, D. A., Sumlin, L. J., & Gaudiani, J. L. (2021). Body mass index requirements for gender-affirming surgeries are not empirically based. *Transgend Health*, *6*(3), 121–124. https://doi.org/10.1089/trgh.2020.0068

Buote, V. M., Wilson, A. E., Strahan, E. J., Gazzola, S. B., & Papps, F. (2011). Setting the bar: Divergent sociocultural norms for women's and men's ideal appearance in real-world contexts. *Body Image*, *8*(4), 322–334. https://doi.org/https://doi.org/10.1016/j.bodyim.2011.06.002

Burke, N. L., Hazzard, V. M., Schaefer, L. M., Simone, M., O'Flynn, J. L., & Rodgers, R. F. (2023). Socioeconomic status and eating disorder prevalence: At the intersections of gender identity, sexual orientation, and race/ethnicity. *Psychological Medicine*, *53*(9), 4255–4265. https://doi.org/10.1017/S0033291722001015

Burke, N. L., Schaefer, L. M., Hazzard, V. M., & Rodgers, R. F. (2020). Where identities converge: The importance of intersectionality in eating disorders research. *International*

Journal of Eating Disorders, *53*(10), 1605–1609. https://doi.org/https://doi.org/10.1002/eat.23371

Calzo, J. P., Blashill, A. J., Brown, T. A., & Argenal, R. L. (2017). Eating disorders and disordered weight and shape control behaviors in sexual minority populations. *Current Psychiatry Reports*, *19*(8), 49. https://doi.org/10.1007/s11920-017-0801-y

Chaphekar, A. V., Vance, S. R., Garber, A. K., Buckelew, S., Ganson, K. T., Downey, A., & Nagata, J. M. (2022). Transgender and other gender diverse adolescents with eating disorders requiring medical stabilization. *Journal of Eating Disorders*, *10*(1), 199. https://doi.org/10.1186/s40337-022-00722-7

Coelho, J. S., Suen, J., Clark, B. A., Marshall, S. K., Geller, J., & Lam, P.-Y. (2019). Eating disorder diagnoses and symptom presentation in transgender youth: A scoping review. *Current Psychiatry Reports*, *21*(11), 107. https://doi.org/10.1007/s11920-019-1097-x

Cole, E. R. (2009). Intersectionality and research in psychology. *American Psychologist*, *64*(3), 170–180. https://doi.org/10.1037/a0014564

Coleman, E., Radix, A. E., Bouman, W. P., Brown, G. R., de Vries, A. L. C., Deutsch, M. B., Ettner, R., Fraser, L., Goodman, M., Green, J., Hancock, A. B., Johnson, T. W., Karasic, D. H., Knudson, G. A., Leibowitz, S. F., Meyer-Bahlburg, H. F. L., Monstrey, S. J., Motmans, J., Nahata, L., . . . Arcelus, J. (2022). Standards of care for the health of transgender and gender diverse people, version 8. *International Journal of Transgender Health*, *23*(sup1), S1–S259. https://doi.org/10.1080/26895269.2022.2100644

Comiskey, A., Parent, M. C., & Tebbe, E. A. (2019). An inhospitable world: Exploring a model of objectification theory with trans women. *Psychology of Women Quarterly*, *44*(1), 105–116. https://doi.org/10.1177/0361684319889595

Cooper, K., Smith, L. G. E., & Russell, A. J. (2018). Gender identity in autism: Sex differences in social affiliation with gender groups. *Journal of Autism and Developmental Disorders*, *48*(12), 3995–4006. https://doi.org/10.1007/s10803-018-3590-1

Copeland, W. E., Bulik, C. M., Zucker, N., Wolke, D., Lereya, S. T., & Costello, E. J. (2015). Does childhood bullying predict eating disorder symptoms? A prospective, longitudinal analysis. International Journal of Eating Disorders, *48*(8), 1141–1149. https://doi.org/10.1002/eat.22459

Couturier, J., Pindiprolu, B., Findlay, S., & Johnson, N. (2015). Anorexia nervosa and gender dysphoria in two adolescents. *International Journal of Eating Disorders*, *48*(1), 151–155. https://doi.org/https://doi.org/10.1002/eat.22368

Crenshaw, K. (1989). Mapping the margins: Intersectionality, identity politics, and violence against women of color. *Stanford Law Review*, *43*(6), 1241.

Cusack, C. E., & Galupo, M. P. (2021). Body checking behaviors and eating disorder pathology among nonbinary individuals with androgynous appearance ideals. *Eating and Weight Disorders - Studies on Anorexia, Bulimia and Obesity*, *26*(6), 1915–1925. https://doi.org/10.1007/s40519-020-01040-0

Cusack, C. E., Iampieri, A. O., & Galupo, M. (2022a). "I'm still not sure if the eating disorder is a result of gender dysphoria": Trans and nonbinary individuals' descriptions of their eating and body concerns in relation to their gender. *Psychology of Sexual Orientation and Gender Diversity*, *9*(4), 422–433. https://ovidsp.ovid.com/ovidweb.cgi?T=JS&CSC=Y&NEWS=N&PAGE=fulltext&D=psyc21&AN=2022-25381-001 https://libkey.io/libraries/777/openurl?genre=article&aulast=Cusack&issn=2329-0382&title=Psychology+of+Sexual+Orientation+and+Gender+Diversity&atitle=%22I%27m+still+not+sure+if+the+eating+disorder+is+a+result+of+gender+dysphoria%22%3A+Trans+an

d+nonbinary+individuals%27+descriptions+of+their+eating+and+body+concerns+in+relation+to+their+gender.&volume=9&issue=4&spage=422&epage=433&date=2022&doi=10.1037%2Fsgd0000515&pmid=&sid=OVID:psycdb

Cusack, C. E., Levenson, N. H., & Galupo, M. P. (2022b). "Anorexia wants to kill me, dysphoria wants me to live": Centering transgender and nonbinary experiences in eating disorder treatment. *Journal of LGBTQ Issues in Counseling*, *16*(3), 265–284. https://doi.org/10.1080/26924951.2022.2054492

Diemer, E. W., Grant, J. D., Munn-Chernoff, M. A., Patterson, D. A., & Duncan, A. E. (2015). Gender identity, sexual orientation, and eating-related pathology in a national sample of college students. *Journal of Adolescent Health*, *57*(2), 144–149. https://doi.org/10.1016/j.jadohealth.2015.03.003

Diemer, E. W., White Hughto, J. M., Gordon, A. R., Guss, C., Austin, S. B., & Reisner, S. L. (2018). Beyond the binary: Differences in eating disorder prevalence by gender identity in a transgender sample. *Transgender Health*, *3*(1), 17–23. https://doi.org/10.1089/trgh.2017.0043

Donaldson, A. A., Hall, A., Neukirch, J., Kasper, V., Simones, S., Gagnon, S., Reich, S., & Forcier, M. (2018). Multidisciplinary care considerations for gender nonconforming adolescents with eating disorders: A case series. *International Journal of Eating Disorders*, *51*(5), 475–479. https://doi.org/https://doi.org/10.1002/eat.22868

Drabish, K., & Theeke, L. A. (2022). Health impact of stigma, discrimination, prejudice, and bias experienced by transgender people: A systematic review of quantitative studies. *Issues in Mental Health Nursing*, *43*(2), 111–118. https://doi.org/10.1080/01612840.2021.1961330

Duffy, M. E., Henkel, K. E., & Earnshaw, V. A. (2016). Transgender clients' experiences of eating disorder treatment. *Journal of LGBT Issues in Counseling*, *10*(3), 136–149. https://doi.org/10.1080/15538605.2016.1177806

Duffy, M. E., Henkel, K. E., & Joiner, T. E. (2019). Prevalence of self-injurious thoughts and behaviors in transgender individuals with eating disorders: A national study. *Journal of Adolescent Health*, *64*(4), 461–466. https://doi.org/https://doi.org/10.1016/j.jadohealth.2018.07.016

Egbert, J., Luke, A., & Qeadan, F. (2024). Intersectionality of demographic characteristics in self-reported anorexia nervosa, bulimia nervosa, and probable eating disorders among college students. *International Journal of Eating Disorders*, *57*(1), 132–145. https://doi.org/https://doi.org/10.1002/eat.24090

Ewan, L. A., Middleman, A. B., & Feldmann, J. (2014). Treatment of anorexia nervosa in the context of transsexuality: A case report. *International Journal of Eating Disorders*, *47*(1), 112–115. https://doi.org/https://doi.org/10.1002/eat.22209

Fairburn, C. G. (2008). *Cognitive behavior therapy and eating disorders*. Guilford Publications. https://books.google.co.uk/books?id=KRvAlB3l8-MC

Fairburn, C. G., & Beglin, S. J. (1994). Assessment of eating disorders: Interview or self-report questionnaire? *International Journal of Eating Disorders*, *16*(4), 363–370. https://doi.org/https://doi.org/10.1002/1098-108X(199412)16:4<363::AID-EAT2260160405>3.0.CO;2-#

Feder, S., Isserlin, L., Seale, E., Hammond, N., & Norris, M. L. (2017). Exploring the association between eating disorders and gender dysphoria in youth. *Eating Disorders*, *25*(4), 310–317. https://doi.org/10.1080/10640266.2017.1297112

Ferrucci, K. A., Lapane, K. L., & Jesdale, B. M. (2022). Prevalence of diagnosed eating disorders in US transgender adults and youth in insurance claims. *International Journal of Eating Disorders*, *55*(6), 801–809. https://doi.org/https://doi.org/10.1002/eat.23729

Ferrucci, K. A., Lapane, K. L., Jesdale, B. M., McPhillips, E., & Dubé, C. E. (2024). Eating disorder specialist views on gender competency and education for treating gender minority patients. *The Journal of Behavioral Health Services & Research*, *51*(2), 232–249. https://doi.org/10.1007/s11414-023-09864-1

Ferrucci, K. A., McPhillips, E., Lapane, K. L., Jesdale, B. M., & Dubé, C. E. (2023). Provider perceptions of barriers and facilitators to care in eating disorder treatment for transgender and gender diverse patients: A qualitative study. *Journal of Eating Disorders*, *11*(1), 36. https://doi.org/10.1186/s40337-023-00760-9

Fisher, A. D., Castellini, G., Bandini, E., Casale, H., Fanni, E., Benni, L., Ferruccio, N., Meriggiola, M. C., Manieri, C., Gualerzi, A., Jannini, E., Oppo, A., Ricca, V., Maggi, M., & Rellini, A. H. (2014). Cross-sex hormonal treatment and body uneasiness in individuals with gender dysphoria. *The Journal of Sexual Medicine*, *11*(3), 709–719. https://doi.org/10.1111/jsm.12413

Galupo, M. P., Cusack, C. E., & Morris, E. R. (2021). "Having a non-normative body for me is about survival": Androgynous body ideal among trans and nonbinary individuals. *Body Image*, *39*, 68–76. https://doi.org/https://doi.org/10.1016/j.bodyim.2021.06.003

Garner, D. M., & Garfinkel, P. E. (1979). The eating attitudes test: An index of the symptoms of anorexia nervosa. *Psychological Medicine*, *9*(2), 273–279. https://doi.org/10.1017/S0033291700030762

Goodman, M., Adams, N., Corneil, T., Kreukels, B., Motmans, J., & Coleman, E. (2019). Size and distribution of transgender and gender nonconforming populations: A narrative review. *Endocrinology and Metabolism Clinics of North America*, *48*(2), 303–321. https://doi.org/https://doi.org/10.1016/j.ecl.2019.01.001

Gordon, A. R., Austin, S., Krieger, N., White Hughto, J. M., & Reisner, S. L. (2016). "I have to constantly prove to myself, to people, that I fit the bill": Perspectives on weight and shape control behaviors among low-income, ethnically diverse young transgender women. *Social Science & Medicine*, *165*, 141–149. https://ovidsp.ovid.com/ovidweb.cgi?T=JS&CSC=Y&NEWS=N&PAGE=fulltext&D=psyc15&AN=2016-42585-016 https://libkey.io/libraries/777/openurl?genre=article&aulast=Gordon&issn=0277-9536&title=Social+Science+%26+Medicine&atitle=%22I+have+to+constantly+prove+to+myself%2C+to+people%2C+that+I+fit+the+bill%22%3A+Perspectives+on+weight+and+shape+control+behaviors+among+low-income%2C+ethnically+diverse+young+transgender+women.&volume=165&issue=&spage=141&epage=149&date=2016&doi=10.1016%2Fj.socscimed.2016.07.038&pmid=&sid=OVID:psycdb

Gordon, A. R., Beccia, A. L., Egan, N., & Lipson, S. K. (2024). Intersecting gender identity and racial/ethnic inequities in eating disorder risk factors, symptoms, and diagnosis among U.S. college students: An intersectional multilevel analysis of individual heterogeneity and discriminatory accuracy. *International Journal of Eating Disorders*, *57*(1), 146–161. https://doi.org/https://doi.org/10.1002/eat.24089

Gosling, H., Pratt, D., Montgomery, H., & Lea, J. (2022). The relationship between minority stress factors and suicidal ideation and behaviours amongst transgender and gender non-conforming adults: A systematic review. *Journal of Affective Disorders*, *303*, 31–51. https://doi.org/https://doi.org/10.1016/j.jad.2021.12.091

Grabe, S., Ward, L. M., & Hyde, J. S. (2008). The role of the media in body image concerns among women: A meta-analysis of experimental and correlational studies. *Psychological Bulletin, 134*(3), 460–476. https://doi.org/10.1037/0033-2909.134.3.460

Harrop, E. N., Hecht, H. K., Harner, V., Call, J., & Holloway, B. T. (2023). "How do I exist in this body…that's outside of the norm?" Trans and nonbinary experiences of conformity, coping, and connection in atypical anorexia [Article]. *International Journal of Environmental Research and Public Health, 20*(2), Article 1156. https://doi.org/10.3390/ijerph20021156

Hartman-Munick, S. M., Silverstein, S., Guss, C. E., Lopez, E., Calzo, J. P., & Gordon, A. R. (2021). Eating disorder screening and treatment experiences in transgender and gender diverse young adults. *Eating Behaviors, 41*, 101517. https://doi.org/https://doi.org/10.1016/j.eatbeh.2021.101517

Hendricks, M. L., & Testa, R. J. (2012). A conceptual framework for clinical work with transgender and gender nonconforming clients: An adaptation of the minority stress model. *Professional Psychology: Research and Practice, 43*(5), 460–467. https://doi.org/10.1037/a0029597

Henrichs-Beck, C. L., & Szymanski, D. M. (2017). Gender expression, body–gender identity incongruence, thin ideal internalization, and lesbian body dissatisfaction. *Psychology of Sexual Orientation and Gender Diversity, 4*(1), 23–33. https://doi.org/10.1037/sgd0000214

Herman, J. L., Flores, A. R., & O'Neill, K. K. (2022). *How many adults and youth identify as transgender in the United States?* T. U. S. o. L. The Williams Institute.

Hobster, K., & McLuskey, J. (2020). Transgender patients' experiences of health care. *British Journal of Nursing, 29*(22), 1348–1353. https://doi.org/10.12968/bjon.2020.29.22.1348

Huang, Q., Peng, W., & Ahn, S. (2021). When media become the mirror: A meta-analysis on media and body image. *Media Psychology, 24*(4), 437–489. https://doi.org/10.1080/15213269.2020.1737545

Jones, B. A., Haycraft, E., Bouman, W. P., Brewin, N., Claes, L., & Arcelus, J. (2018). Risk factors for eating disorder psychopathology within the treatment seeking transgender population: The role of cross-sex hormone treatment. *European Eating Disorders Review, 26*(2), 120–128. https://doi.org/https://doi.org/10.1002/erv.2576

Jones, B. A., Haycraft, E., Murjan, S., & Arcelus, J. (2016). Body dissatisfaction and disordered eating in trans people: A systematic review of the literature. *International Review of Psychiatry, 28*(1), 81–94. https://doi.org/10.3109/09540261.2015.1089217

Jones, B. A., Pierre Bouman, W., Haycraft, E., & Arcelus, J. (2019). Gender congruence and body satisfaction in nonbinary transgender people: A case control study. *International Journal of Transgenderism, 20*(2–3), 263–274. https://doi.org/10.1080/15532739.2018.1538840

Kamody, R. C., Yonkers, K., Pluhar, E. I., & Olezeski, C. L. (2020). Disordered eating among trans-masculine youth: Considerations through a developmental lens. *LGBT Health, 7*(4), 170–173. https://doi.org/10.1089/lgbt.2019.0354

Karazsia, B. T., Murnen, S. K., & Tylka, T. L. (2017). Is body dissatisfaction changing across time? A cross-temporal meta-analysis. *Psychological Bulletin, 143*(3), 293–320. https://doi.org/10.1037/bul0000081

Kcomt, L., Gorey, K. M., Barrett, B. J., & McCabe, S. E. (2020). Healthcare avoidance due to anticipated discrimination among transgender people: A call to create trans-affirmative environments. *SSM - Population Health, 11*, 100608. https://doi.org/https://doi.org/10.1016/j.ssmph.2020.100608

Keery, H., van den Berg, P., & Thompson, J. K. (2004). An evaluation of the Tripartite Influence Model of body dissatisfaction and eating disturbance with adolescent girls. *Body Image, 1*(3), 237–251. https://doi.org/https://doi.org/10.1016/j.bodyim.2004.03.001

Kerr, J. A., Paine, J., Thrower, E., Hoq, M., Mollica, C., Sawyer, S. M., Azzopardi, P. S., & Pang, K. C. (2024). Prevalence of eating disorder symptoms in transgender and gender diverse adolescents presenting for gender-affirming care. *Journal of Adolescent Health, 74*(4), 850–853. https://doi.org/https://doi.org/10.1016/j.jadohealth.2023.11.396

Krug, I., Selvaraja, P., Fuller-Tyszkiewicz, M., Hughes, E. K., Slater, A., Griffiths, S., Yee, Z. W., Richardson, B., & Blake, K. (2020). The effects of fitspiration images on body attributes, mood and eating behaviors: An experimental ecological momentary assessment study in females. *Body Image, 35*, 279–287. https://doi.org/https://doi.org/10.1016/j.bodyim.2020.09.011

Lavender, J. M., Brown, T. A., & Murray, S. B. (2017). Men, muscles, and eating disorders: An overview of traditional and muscularity-oriented disordered eating. *Current Psychiatry Reports, 19*(6), 32. https://doi.org/10.1007/s11920-017-0787-5

Leit, R. A., Gray, J. J., & Pope Jr, H. G. (2002). The media's representation of the ideal male body: A cause for muscle dysmorphia? *International Journal of Eating Disorders, 31*(3), 334–338. https://doi.org/https://doi.org/10.1002/eat.10019

Marzola, E., Abbate-Daga, G., Gramaglia, C., Amianto, F., & Fassino, S. (2015). A qualitative investigation into anorexia nervosa: The inner perspective. *Cogent Psychology, 2*(1), 1032493. https://doi.org/10.1080/23311908.2015.1032493

McGregor, K., McKenna, J. L., Barrera, E. P., Williams, C. R., Hartman-Munick, S. M., & Guss, C. E. (2023). Disordered eating and considerations for the transgender community: A review of the literature and clinical guidance for assessment and treatment. *Journal of Eating Disorders, 11*(1), 75. https://doi.org/10.1186/s40337-023-00793-0

McNamara, N., & Parsons, H. (2016). 'Everyone here wants everyone else to get better': The role of social identity in eating disorder recovery. *British Journal of Social Psychology, 55*(4), 662–680. https://doi.org/https://doi.org/10.1111/bjso.12161

Meyer, I. H. (2003). Prejudice, social stress, and mental health in lesbian, gay, and bisexual populations: Conceptual issues and research evidence. *Psychological Bulletin, 129*(5), 674–697. https://doi.org/10.1037/0033-2909.129.5.674

Mezza, F., Mezzalira, S., Pizzo, R., Maldonato, N. M., Bochicchio, V., & Scandurra, C. (2024). Minority stress and mental health in European transgender and gender diverse people: A systematic review of quantitative studies. *Clinical Psychology Review, 107*, 102358. https://doi.org/https://doi.org/10.1016/j.cpr.2023.102358

Morgan, J. F., Reid, F., & Lacey, J. H. (1999). The SCOFF questionnaire: Assessment of a new screening tool for eating disorders. *BMJ, 319*(7223), 1467–1468. https://doi.org/10.1136/bmj.319.7223.1467

Muratore, L. A., Flentje, A., Schuster, D., & Capriotti, M. R. (2022). Disordered eating and body dissatisfaction in transgender and gender-expansive adults: An evaluation and integration of the gender minority stress and resilience and tripartite influence models. *Behavior Therapy, 53*(5), 869–886. https://doi.org/https://doi.org/10.1016/j.beth.2022.02.006

Murray, S. B., Boon, E., & Touyz, S. W. (2013). Diverging eating psychopathology in transgendered eating disorder patients: A report of two cases. *Eating Disorders*, *21*(1), 70–74. https://doi.org/10.1080/10640266.2013.741989

Nagata, J. M., Compte, E. J., McGuire, F. H., Brown, T. A., Lavender, J. M., Murray, S. B., Capriotti, M. R., Flentje, A., Lubensky, M. E., Lunn, M. R., & Obedin-Maliver, J. (2023). Investigating the factor structure and measurement invariance of the Eating Disorder Examination-Questionnaire (EDE-Q) in a community sample of gender minority adults from the United States. *International Journal of Eating Disorders*, *56*(8), 1570–1580. https://doi.org/https://doi.org/10.1002/eat.23978

Nagata, J. M., Ganson, K. T., & Austin, S. B. (2020). Emerging trends in eating disorders among sexual and gender minorities. *Current Opinion in Psychiatry*, *33*(6). https://journals.lww.com/co-psychiatry/fulltext/2020/11000/emerging_trends_in_eating_disorders_among_sexual.8.aspx

Nagata, J. M., Ganson, K. T., Griffiths, S., Mitchison, D., Garber, A. K., Vittinghoff, E., Bibbins-Domingo, K., & Murray, S. B. (2022a). Prevalence and correlates of muscle-enhancing behaviors among adolescents and young adults in the United States. *International Journal of Adolescent Medicine and Health*, *34*(2), 119–129. https://doi.org/doi:10.1515/ijamh-2020-0001

Nagata, J. M., Hazzard, V. M., Ganson, K. T., Austin, S. B., Neumark-Sztainer, D., & Eisenberg, M. E. (2022b). Muscle-building behaviors from adolescence to emerging adulthood: A prospective cohort study. *Preventive Medicine Reports*, *27*, 101778. https://doi.org/https://doi.org/10.1016/j.pmedr.2022.101778

Nordbø, R. H. S., Espeset, E. M. S., Gulliksen, K. S., Skårderud, F., & Holte, A. (2006). The meaning of self-starvation: Qualitative study of patients' perception of anorexia nervosa. *International Journal of Eating Disorders*, *39*(7), 556–564. https://doi.org/https://doi.org/10.1002/eat.20276

Nowaskie, D. Z., Filipowicz, A. T., Choi, Y., & Fogel, J. M. (2021). Eating disorder symptomatology in transgender patients: Differences across gender identity and gender affirmation. *International Journal of Eating Disorders*, *54*(8), 1493–1499. https://doi.org/https://doi.org/10.1002/eat.23539

Office for National Statistics. (2023). *Gender identity by age and sex, England and Wales: Census 2021*. Retrieved from https://www.ons.gov.uk/peoplepopulationandcommunity/culturalidentity/genderidentity/articles/genderidentityageandsexenglandandwalescensus2021/2023-01-25

Owen-Smith, A. A., Gerth, J., Sineath, R. C., Barzilay, J., Becerra-Culqui, T. A., Getahun, D., Giammattei, S., Hunkeler, E., Lash, T. L., Millman, A., Nash, R., Quinn, V. P., Robinson, B., Roblin, D., Sanchez, T., Silverberg, M. J., Tangpricha, V., Valentine, C., Winter, S., . . . Goodman, M. (2018). Association between gender confirmation treatments and perceived gender congruence, body image satisfaction, and mental health in a cohort of transgender individuals. *The Journal of Sexual Medicine*, *15*(4), 591–600. https://doi.org/10.1016/j.jsxm.2018.01.017

Ozbek, S., Greville, J., & Hooper, N. (2023). The thin-ideal across two cultural contexts: The role of body image inflexibility and the fear of negative evaluation. *Psychology of Popular Media*. Advance online publication. https://doi.org/10.1037/ppm0000464

Papastavrou Brooks, C., Kafle, E., Butt, N., Chawner, D., Day, A., Elsby-Pearson, C., Elson, E., Hammond, J., Herbert, P., Jenkins, C. L., Johnson, Z., Keith-Roach, S. H., Papasileka, E., Reeves, S., Stewart, N., Gilbert, N., & Startup, H. (2023). Co-producing principles to guide health research: An illustrative case study from an eating disorder research clinic. *Research Involvement and Engagement*, *9*(1), 84. https://doi.org/10.1186/s40900-023-00460-3

Parker, L. L., & Harriger, J. A. (2020). Eating disorders and disordered eating behaviors in the LGBT population: A review of the literature. *Journal of Eating Disorders*, *8*(1), 51. https://doi.org/10.1186/s40337-020-00327-y

Perry, M., Watson, L., Hayden, L., & Inwards-Breland, D. (2019). Using body neutrality to inform eating disorder management in a gender diverse world. *The Lancet Child & Adolescent Health*, *3*(9), 597–598. https://doi.org/10.1016/S2352-4642(19)30237-8

Pham, A., Kerman, H., Albertson, K., Crouch, J. M., Inwards-Breland, D. J., & Ahrens, K. R. (2023). Understanding the complex relationship between one's body, eating, exercise, and gender-affirming medical care among transgender and nonbinary adolescents and young adults [Article]. *Transgender Health*, *8*(2), 149–158. https://doi.org/10.1089/trgh.2021.0112

Polivy, J., & Herman, C. P. (2002). Causes of eating disorders. *Annual Review of Psychology*, *53*, 187–213. https://doi.org/https://doi.org/10.1146/annurev.psych.53.100901.135103

Rafferty, J. R., Donaldson, A. A., & Forcier, M. (2020). Primary care considerations for transgender and gender-diverse youth. *Pediatrics in Review*, *41*(9), 437–454. https://doi.org/10.1542/pir.2018-0194

Rasmussen, S. M., Dalgaard, M. K., Roloff, M., Pinholt, M., Skrubbeltrang, C., Clausen, L., & Kjaersdam Telléus, G. (2023). Eating disorder symptomatology among transgender individuals: A systematic review and meta-analysis. *Journal of Eating Disorders*, *11*(1), 84. https://doi.org/10.1186/s40337-023-00806-y

Romano, K. A., & Lipson, S. K. (2022). Weight misperception and thin-ideal overvaluation relative to the positive functioning and eating disorder pathology of transgender and nonbinary young adults. *Psychology of Sexual Orientation and Gender Diversity*, *9*(4), 446–453. https://doi.org/10.1037/sgd0000524

Romito, M., Salk, R. H., Roberts, S. R., Thoma, B. C., Levine, M. D., & Choukas-Bradley, S. (2021). Exploring transgender adolescents' body image concerns and disordered eating: Semi-structured interviews with nine gender minority youth [Article]. *Body Image*, *37*, 50–62. https://doi.org/10.1016/j.bodyim.2021.01.008

Schaefer, L. M., Rodgers, R. F., Thompson, J. K., & Griffiths, S. (2021). A test of the tripartite influence model of disordered eating among men. *Body Image*, *36*, 172–179. https://doi.org/https://doi.org/10.1016/j.bodyim.2020.11.009

Schmidt, U., & Treasure, J. (2006). Anorexia nervosa: Valued and visible. A cognitive-interpersonal maintenance model and its implications for research and practice. *British Journal of Clinical Psychology*, *45*(3), 343–366. https://doi.org/https://doi.org/10.1348/014466505X53902

Simone, M., Hazzard, V. M., Askew, A. J., Tebbe, E. A., Lipson, S. K., & Pisetsky, E. M. (2022). Variability in eating disorder risk and diagnosis in transgender and gender diverse college students. *Annals of Epidemiology*, *70*, 53–60. https://doi.org/https://doi.org/10.1016/j.annepidem.2022.04.007

Smith, E. K., & Harrop, E. N. (2024). "That's not at all what I needed" trans adults' perspectives on trans-affirming primary care and eating disorders. *Social Science & Medicine*, *348*, 116836. https://doi.org/https://doi.org/10.1016/j.socscimed.2024.116836

Stice, E., & Shaw, H. E. (2002). Role of body dissatisfaction in the onset and maintenance of eating pathology: A synthesis of research findings. *Journal of Psychosomatic Research*, *53*(5), 985–993. https://doi.org/https://doi.org/10.1016/S0022-3999(02)00488-9

Strang, J. F., Kenworthy, L., Dominska, A., Sokoloff, J., Kenealy, L. E., Berl, M., Walsh, K., Menvielle, E., Slesaransky-Poe, G., Kim, K.-E., Luong-Tran, C., Meagher, H., & Wallace, G. L. (2014). Increased gender variance in autism spectrum disorders and attention deficit hyperactivity disorder. *Archives of Sexual Behavior*, *43*(8), 1525–1533. https://doi.org/10.1007/s10508-014-0285-3

Strauss, P., Cook, A., Watson, V., Winter, S., Whitehouse, A., Albrecht, N., Wright Toussaint, D., & Lin, A. (2021). Mental health difficulties among trans and gender diverse young people with an autism spectrum disorder (ASD): Findings from trans pathways. *Journal of Psychiatric Research*, *137*, 360–367. https://doi.org/https://doi.org/10.1016/j.jpsychires.2021.03.005

Strübel, J., Sabik, N. J., & Tylka, T. L. (2020). Body image and depressive symptoms among transgender and cisgender adults: Examining a model integrating the tripartite influence model and objectification theory. *Body Image*, *35*, 53–62. https://doi.org/https://doi.org/10.1016/j.bodyim.2020.08.004

Tabaac, A., Perrin, P. B., & Benotsch, E. G. (2018). Discrimination, mental health, and body image among transgender and gender-non-binary individuals: Constructing a multiple mediational path model. *Journal of Gay & Lesbian Social Services*, *30*(1), 1–16. https://doi.org/10.1080/10538720.2017.1408514

Tchanturia, K., Adamson, J., Leppanen, J., & Westwood, H. (2017). Characteristics of autism spectrum disorder in anorexia nervosa: A naturalistic study in an inpatient treatment programme. *Autism*, *23*(1), 123–130. https://doi.org/10.1177/1362361317722431

Testa, R. J., Habarth, J., Peta, J., Balsam, K., & Bockting, W. (2015). Development of the gender minority stress and resilience measure. *Psychology of Sexual Orientation and Gender Diversity*, *2*(1), 65–77. https://doi.org/10.1037/sgd0000081

Testa, R. J., Rider, G. N., Haug, N. A., & Balsam, K. F. (2017). Gender confirming medical interventions and eating disorder symptoms among transgender individuals. *Health Psychology*, *36*(10), 927–936. https://doi.org/10.1037/hea0000497

Thompson, J. K., Coovert, M. D., & Stormer, S. M. (1999a). Body image, social comparison, and eating disturbance: A covariance structure modeling investigation. *International Journal of Eating Disorders*, *26*(1), 43–51. https://doi.org/https://doi.org/10.1002/(SICI)1098-108X(199907)26:1<43::AID-EAT6>3.0.CO;2-R

Thompson, J. K., Heinberg, L. J., Altabe, M., & Tantleff-Dunn, S. (1999b). Exacting beauty: Theory, assessment, and treatment of body image disturbance. *American Psychological Association*. https://doi.org/10.1037/10312-000

Thompson, J. K., & Stice, E. (2001). Thin-ideal internalization: Mounting evidence for a new risk factor for body-image disturbance and eating pathology. *Current Directions in Psychological Science*, *10*(5), 181–183. https://doi.org/10.1111/1467-8721.00144

Tiggemann, M., & Zaccardo, M. (2015). "Exercise to be fit, not skinny": The effect of fitspiration imagery on women's body image. *Body Image*, *15*, 61–67. https://doi.org/https://doi.org/10.1016/j.bodyim.2015.06.003

Truszczynski, N., Singh, A. A., & Hansen, N. (2022). The discrimination experiences and coping responses of non-binary and trans people. *Journal of Homosexuality*, *69*(4), 741–755. https://doi.org/10.1080/00918369.2020.1855028

Turan, Ş., Aksoy Poyraz, C., Usta Sağlam, N. G., Demirel, Ö. F., Haliloğlu, Ö., Kadıoğlu, P., & Duran, A. (2018). Alterations in body uneasiness, eating attitudes, and psychopathology before and after cross-sex hormonal treatment in patients with female-to-male gender dysphoria. *Archives of Sexual Behavior*, *47*(8), 2349–2361. https://doi.org/10.1007/s10508-018-1189-4

Uniacke, B., Glasofer, D., Devlin, M., Bockting, W., & Attia, E. (2021). Predictors of eating-related psychopathology in transgender and gender nonbinary individuals. *Eating Behaviors*, *42*, 101527. https://doi.org/https://doi.org/10.1016/j.eatbeh.2021.101527

Urban, B., Knutson, D., Klooster, D., & Soper, J. (2023). Social and contextual influences on eating pathology in transgender and nonbinary adults. *Eating Disorders*, *31*(4), 301–319. https://doi.org/10.1080/10640266.2022.2135715

van de Grift, T. C., Elaut, E., Cerwenka, S. C., Cohen-Kettenis, P. T., De Cuypere, G., Richter-Appelt, H., & Kreukels, B. P. C. (2017). Effects of medical interventions on gender dysphoria and body image: A follow-up study. *Psychosomatic Medicine*, *79*(7). https://journals.lww.com/psychosomaticmedicine/fulltext/2017/09000/effects_of_medical_interventions_on_gender.14.aspx

van de Grift, T. C., Elfering, L., Greijdanus, M., Smit, J. M., Bouman, M.-B., Klassen, A. F., & Mullender, M. G. (2018). Subcutaneous mastectomy improves satisfaction with body and psychosocial function in trans men: Findings of a cross-sectional study using the BODY-Q chest module. *Plastic and Reconstructive Surgery*, *142*(5). https://journals.lww.com/plasreconsurg/fulltext/2018/11000/subcutaneous_mastectomy_improves_satisfaction_with.4.aspx

van der Miesen, A. I. R., Hurley, H., Bal, A. M., & de Vries, A. L. C. (2018). Prevalence of the wish to be of the opposite gender in adolescents and adults with autism spectrum disorder. *Archives of Sexual Behavior*, *47*(8), 2307–2317. https://doi.org/10.1007/s10508-018-1218-3

Velez, B. L., Breslow, A. S., Brewster, M. E., Cox Jr, R., & Foster, A. B. (2016). Building a pantheoretical model of dehumanization with transgender men: Integrating objectification and minority stress theories. *Journal of Counseling Psychology*, *63*(5), 497–508. https://doi.org/10.1037/cou0000136

Warrier, V., Greenberg, D. M., Weir, E., Buckingham, C., Smith, P., Lai, M.-C., Allison, C., & Baron-Cohen, S. (2020). Elevated rates of autism, other neurodevelopmental and psychiatric diagnoses, and autistic traits in transgender and gender-diverse individuals. *Nature Communications*, *11*(1), 3959. https://doi.org/10.1038/s41467-020-17794-1

Watson, R. J., Veale, J. F., & Saewyc, E. M. (2017). Disordered eating behaviors among transgender youth: Probability profiles from risk and protective factors. *International Journal of Eating Disorders*, *50*(5), 515–522. https://doi.org/https://doi.org/10.1002/eat.22627

Westwood, H., Mandy, W., & Tchanturia, K. (2017). Clinical evaluation of autistic symptoms in women with anorexia nervosa. *Molecular Autism*, *8*(1), 12. https://doi.org/10.1186/s13229-017-0128-x

Winston, A. P., Acharya, S., Chaudhuri, S., & Fellowes, L. (2004). Anorexia nervosa and gender identity disorder in biologic males: A report of two cases. *International Journal of Eating Disorders*, *36*(1), 109–113. https://doi.org/https://doi.org/10.1002/eat.20013

Wiseman, C. V., Gray, J. J., Mosimann, J. E., & Ahrens, A. H. (1992). Cultural expectations of thinness in women: An update. *International Journal of Eating Disorders*, *11*(1), 85–89. https://doi.org/10.1002/1098-108X(199201)11:1<85::AID-EAT2260110112>3.0.CO;2-T

Witcomb, G. L., Bouman, W. P., Brewin, N., Richards, C., Fernandez-Aranda, F., & Arcelus, J. (2015). Body image dissatisfaction and eating-related psychopathology in trans individuals: A matched control study. *European Eating Disorders Review*, *23*(4), 287–293. https://doi.org/https://doi.org/10.1002/erv.2362

Yager, Z., & McLean, S. (2020). Muscle building supplement use in Australian adolescent boys: Relationships with body image, weight lifting, and sports engagement. *BMC Pediatrics*, *20*(1), 89. https://doi.org/10.1186/s12887-020-1993-6

Yesildemir, O., & Akbulut, G. (2023). Gender-affirming nutrition: An overview of eating disorders in the transgender population. *Current Nutrition Reports*, *12*(4), 877–892. https://doi.org/10.1007/s13668-023-00504-w

Zamantakis, A., & Lackey, D. (2022). Dying to be (A)Gendered: An exploratory content analysis of trans/nonbinary people's experiences with eating disorders [Article]. *Sociological Inquiry*, *92*(S1), 870–893. https://doi.org/10.1111/soin.12425

Chapter 11

Global and Cultural Perspectives

Christopher Paul Szabo

> I write this chapter as a clinician, providing a personal perspective shaped by decades of work with sufferers. Whatever I have learned from the literature, they have been my best teachers.
>
> (Szabo, 2019)

Introduction

Anorexia nervosa (AN) is a diagnostic entity within a group of conditions "Feeding and eating disorders" in the 5th edition of the Diagnostic and Statistical Manual of Mental Disorders (DSM-5; American Psychiatric Association, 2013) and "Feeding or eating disorders" in the 11th Revision of the International Classification of Diseases (ICD 11; World Health Organization, 2019). Common to the diagnosis, using either system, are fundamental features which characterize the disorder. These are: *restriction* (of food intake relative to energy requirements with low body weight), *fear* (of weight gain), disturbance of *perception* (related to weight/shape) together with undue influence of weight and shape on *self-evaluation*. The criteria do not speak to motivation but describe a dietary process that is initiated and accompanied by concerns/preoccupations, driven by misperception together with a singular/excessive focus on specific aspects of being (related to weight and shape) that, in the mind of the sufferer, define them. In this regard, one might say that the illness is the identity of the sufferer (a more detailed discussion of "identity" to follow). AN can also become a person's social identity, in which others perceive the individual primarily through this lens; and yet, a key aspect of AN is the "*…persistent lack of recognition of the seriousness of the current low body weight*" (APA, 1993). This raises a fundamental issue, namely: can AN truly be considered a disorder of "identity", or are its identity-related features simply a consequence of the dietary process, as highlighted by the "Minnesota Starvation Experiment" (Baker & Keramidas, 2013)? We will return to this question later.

Further, when considered culturally (i.e., Western versus non-Western), the meaning or intent of AN may not be consistent: not only are eating disorders,

DOI: 10.4324/9781003468189-13

generally, more prevalent in Western society (Szabo, 2015) but the form may also differ in non-Western societies and not conform to diagnostic criteria as per either the DSM-5 or ICD 11. A study on rural secondary-school girls in Ghana was particularly interesting insofar as those diagnosed with AN did not have "*a morbid fear of fatness nor a pervasive need to be slim*" (Bennett et al., 2004). The contention of Bennett et al. (2004) was thus that "*morbid self-starvation*" (p. 316) was the core issue in AN with cultural context impacting how it manifests. Van den Heuvel et al. (2023) interpreted these findings to suggest "*that weight concern may in fact be a Western cultural variant of [AN]*" (p. 8). Hence, what emerges is that the "identity" of the sufferer will vary by culture and that Western understanding, whilst helpful generally, may not be relevant specifically, i.e., within a non-Western setting. In this regard the DSM-5 appears increasingly aligned with such thinking insofar as having replaced *culture-bound syndrome* with the term *cultural concepts of distress* which "*...refers to ways cultural groups experience, understand and communicate suffering*" and ultimately "*...acknowledges that all forms of distress are locally shaped.*" (APA, 2013).

Identity

The American Psychological Association's Dictionary of Psychology defines "identity" as: "an individual's sense of self defined by (a) a set of physical, psychological, and interpersonal characteristics that are not wholly shared with any other person and (b) a range of affiliations (e.g., ethnicity) and social roles" (APA, n.d.). The definition suggests that a continuous sense of self derives from a range of factors such as memories, goals, values, expectations, and body image.

However, given the impact of the starvation process, leading to a starvation state which so profoundly affects the sufferer (Baker & Keramidas, 2013), how is the "personal identity" projected into the social space as a "social identity" to be understood? It should be emphasized that the most recent iteration of the DSM (DSM-5; APA, 2013) no longer describes an absolute value of weight in the diagnostic criteria. In fact, the powerful and pervasive impact of starvation on all aspects of functioning, i.e., physical, psychological, and cognitive, is nowhere to be found diagnostically. This is likely because all who starve are not necessarily suffering from AN. This may also be the case with the removal of amenorrhea as a diagnostic criterion since it is not unique to anorexia nervosa. Hence, as much as low weight would appear to be a central feature of AN, the condition is potentially better understood as a mindset that operates irrespective of the physical. Seen in this way, the physical might represent a manifest presentation of an underlying "disease" (i.e., a mindset) whose symptoms and signs signal the recognizable "illness" that evokes response – both social and medical. But, in relation to the definition of identity – how does one begin to understand the patient, and they themselves, whilst in the grip of starvation, imposing itself on the sufferer as it does? And, where body image is distorted and denial of severity of illness are inherent to the presentation, does the sufferer have any concept of individual identity or concern for how they project themselves in society, i.e., their "social identity"? Clearly the illness state contaminates perception and thus identity, and yet there is a new identity on display – a very powerful and disturbing one. This brings one to the notion of "communication", another way to understand AN, i.e., the body as a vehicle, a somatic representation of intra-psychic distress. Certainly, it is reasonable to surmise that *the condition arises from emotional distress which is ultimately communicated non-verbally*. Not talking, and not eating – both, very powerful.

So, what is the identity of the sufferer? To elaborate further on the aforementioned starvation study of the 1950s (Baker & Keramidas, 2013), it was demonstrated that physically healthy and psychologically normal men, when starved, will present in stereotypical ways related to thoughts, behaviors, and emotions. The men participating in the study were all volunteers who took part in the study as an alternative to military service (Garner, 1997, pp. 153–154). Through the findings of the study, it came to be understood that much of what one sees clinically in AN is a function of the nutritional state, i.e., identity is consumed by and subsumed in the starvation process.

In their bid to be something, someone different – as often stated – the sufferers paradoxically become the same due to the powerful, homogenizing impact of starvation. The pursuit of an individual identity has led to being subsumed in the general identity of the condition. Hence, when one speaks of "social identity", it is important to consider what "personal identity" is being consciously or subconsciously projected socially versus the one experienced by others.

George Devereux's notion of an "ethnic disorder", as cited by Richard Gordon (1990, pp. 5–11) can be invoked here. Devereux described how "*...certain disorders become a core expression of the stresses and tensions of a particular culture or historical period...*" (Gordon, 1990). In this sense, *ethnic* reflects *culture* in terms of meaning, further noting that Devereux's conceptualization of an "ethnic disorder" was ultimately applied to schizophrenia, although initially in relation to a range of conditions that have been viewed as "culture bound syndromes", e.g., Amok or Koro, a term which the DSM-5 (APA, 1993, p. 758) has reasoned is no longer appropriate. Gordon (1990) described a range of criteria noted by Devereux that would "*...qualify a particular syndrome as an ethnic disorder...*" going on to use these criteria in relation to eating disorders and AN specifically. In doing so, he invoked "hysteria", a presentation amongst 19th century females, as representing a particular form of female identity during those times but with several shared characteristics with AN, e.g., "*control over unmanageable personal distress*"; "*socially patterned*"; generating both "*repugnance and fascination*"; in essence, a somatic representation of intra-psychic distress. This highlights an important consideration – that *social identity* within the context of AN will be influenced by culture.

The Cultural Dimension – Africa

It has been noted that AN is uncommon within an African context (Szabo, 2015; van den Heuvel et al., 2023). However, this may have to do with limited data, or culture-specific presentations that preclude a diagnosis based on DSM and ICD criteria, as weight concerns may be absent (as reported by Bennett et al., 2004). In addition, the two case scenarios presented by Bennett et al. (2004) revealed a religious motivation behind self-starvation as in: atonement for sin and assisting with focus for prayer.

Notwithstanding the relative paucity of cases of AN in the African context (van den Heuvel et al., 2023), there are a range of community-based studies that have suggested (using Western-derived screening instruments, with some validated for use in an African context; e.g., Szabo & Allwood, 2004b) that based on the prevalence of abnormal eating attitudes, which potentially reflect existing eating disorders or risk for eating disorders, there was a risk they would emerge in greater numbers in an African context. Lee (1996, p. 23) argued that the culture of *modernity* is the culture to which eating disorders are bound. It was noted that societies with "*…industrial capitalism, urbanization, immigration, abundance of food, rising population weight, advanced information technology, proliferation of body orientated advertisements, decreased birth rate and changing roles of women*" may be associated with the emergence of eating disorders. Lee (1996) was specifically reflecting on Chinese people in Hong Kong. However, this appeared to be the emerging scenario in South Africa, i.e., spreading and emerging modernity related to political change. The first democratic elections in 1994 heralded a post-apartheid South Africa with the country coming to represent a "culture in transition". This phenomenon has been explored as a risk factor for the emergence of eating disorders, associated with possible identity struggles, and is covered fully in the book "Eating Disorders and Cultures in Transition" edited by Nasser, Katzman, and Gordon (2001). The central thrust of Nasser's position (Nasser & Di Nicola, 2001, p. 172) is that the body is a potential vehicle for expression of identity with "*the nature of eating psychopathology being potentially susceptible to economic or political forces*" further noting that "*'neurosis' has a habit of taking different shapes and forms in response to changing societies*". It is not clear that such a theory has been conclusively borne out in the South African context, notwithstanding the emergence of cases (Szabo et al., 1995) and various community-based studies appearing to support the contention that one could anticipate greater numbers over time (Szabo & Holland, 1997; Szabo & Allwood, 2004a; Szabo & Allwood, 2004b). A qualitative study noted that eating disorders in black, South African females may take the form of an "*atypical, purging form of eating disorder which fails to qualify for anorexia nervosa*" (Morris & Szabo, 2013, p. 341). This study thus provided a potential basis for the paucity of AN cases reported in the African context. Moreover, it is possible that culturally-sanctioned rituals of remedial purging and social overeating may also contribute to under-recognition of eating disorders. Of significance, Morris and Szabo (2013), found that the greater the exposure of black, adolescent females to their white, westernized counterparts, the greater the experience of "acculturative stress" (where they were in the minority) with thinness described "*as a means to construct a more coherent sense of identity*" (p. 340). Hence, proximity to Western body image ideals appeared to impact on attitudes toward thinness. The suggestion was that traditional values and expectations in the home provided a counterbalance notwithstanding the stress of differing cultural expectations in different settings. It should be noted that the study by Morris and Szabo (2013) involved a sample of Zulu adolescents in an urban setting. An earlier study by Szabo and Allwood (2006) reported that the drive for thinness was significantly less amongst a rural sample of Zulu adolescent females compared to a diverse group of urban black female adolescents, with the desire to be larger more prevalent in the rural sample. The suggestion was that the rural setting appeared to confer protection against the development of eating disorders. A lack of comparative data amongst other black ethnic groups in South Africa precludes generalizing these findings to all black South African adolescent females. It is important to note that there are 11 official languages in South Africa (Afrikaans, English, *Ndebele, Xhosa, Zulu, Pedi, Sotho, Tswana, Swazi, Venda, Tsonga)*; nine of these (italicized) specifically relate to black South Africans, which supports the idea that "there is no single 'Culture of South Africa'" (South African History Online, n.d.).

Whilst South Africa might represent an atypical African scenario in terms of its multi-cultural and racially/ethnically diverse population, van den Heuvel et al. (2023) cite a range of African data related to the prevalence of anorexia nervosa (Tanzania, Ghana, Kenya, Burkina Faso, and Nigeria) providing evidence that AN "*...is a rare disorder, with atypical forms more frequently observed*" (p. 8). Whilst one cannot view "Africa" as a culturally homogenous continent, comprising as it does a vast array of peoples defined by language and culture (aside from borders, which some may regard as artificial) (Gbenyenye, 2016) – there does appear to be a consistent finding regarding the comparatively low prevalence of AN.

Although modernization is a priority for South Africa post-1994 (as an illustration of an African scenario) (The World Bank, 2018), the question is to what extent this has taken place in a meaningful way (DBSA, n.d.) and whether modernization – such as it has been – has impacted traditional values of the black, South African population who comprise 81.4% of the population (South African Government, n.d.). This may have implications for the emergence of eating disorders, and specifically when considering AN and identity in this setting.

The Meaning of Size – Bigger Is Better?

Over two decades ago it had been suggested that the incidence of eating disorders may be leveling off or declining in Western countries (Gordon, 2001) at a time that eating disorders were emerging in non-Western settings with highly developed economies such as Hong Kong and Singapore. However, more recent data from both the United Kingdom (Trafford et al., 2023) and Australia (Hay et al., 2023) suggest otherwise, with increasing rates noted in both of these Western, developed-world settings. This does not appear to be the case for Africa. Aside from there being less prevalence data (van den Heuvel et al., 2023), why might this be and what are the implications in terms of "personal identity", "social identity" and AN? What is the meaning of self-starvation in an African context? To some extent, the Ghanaian study of Bennett et al. (2004) provided some explanation, i.e., control and self-efficacy in response to specific stressors, or aligned with religious beliefs. Another possibility is that the meaning of body size in an African context (specifically amongst black females) differs to that in a Western one.

Research related to obesity in the South African context noted that black mothers and their daughters (compared to other South African ethnic groups, i.e., white and mixed ancestry) associated a bigger body size with beauty, respect, and happiness (Mchiza et al., 2011). Draper, Davidowitz and Goedecke (2016) demonstrated that most participants in their study of black South African women in a low-income setting had positive perceptions of being overweight or obese. This has been echoed in research by Bosire et al. (2020) who have noted how "socio-cultural norms" amongst black South African women in an urban-poor setting attribute bigger bodies to beauty and wealth. Finally, a systematic review of body size preferences for black women and adolescent girls living in Africa found that most of the studies reviewed documented a preference for normal or overweight body sizes with *only some* indicating a preference for underweight (Pradeilles et al., 2022).

There might be an urban/rural divide in a South African setting. For example, a slimmer body size preference was observed for urban dwelling adolescent females of all races and a larger body size preference was noted for black rural dwelling adolescents (Szabo & Allwood, 2006). Pradeilles et al. (2022) noted a tendency for larger body size preference amongst black women, and where there was body dissatisfaction it was related to slimness thus promoting weight gain, i.e., a larger size was desirable whereas slimness was not. Aside from beauty and wealth, larger body size also denotes health insofar as being underweight is generally associated with illness, and more specifically HIV/AIDS and Tuberculosis, i.e., being underweight may indeed lead to stigmatization. However, in a modernizing South Africa, with rapid urbanization this may change (Predeilles et al., 2022). In essence, the cited literature as well as the study of Bennett et al. (2004) and the review of van den Heuvel et al. (2023) suggest that body size can have a different meaning in an African setting compared with a Western setting. Hence, to some extent the issue of AN and identity is significantly impacted by culture and therefore any broad generalizations need to be regarded cautiously given that meaning appears to be context-specific. Moreover, the paucity of AN cases in an African context makes any interpretation of meaning, specifically in relation to identity, difficult. In relation to a larger size – albeit defined as "obese" – the associated meaning is much clearer.

Beyond Size – the Skin

It has been stated that the skin "…*acts as an interface for political, cultural and social identity*" (Jacobs et al., 2016, p. 69). Within this context, the phenomenon of "skin lightening" is germane, i.e., to change skin color from darker to lighter, with lighter shades deemed more desirable, not only in Africa but globally. To achieve this end, skin lightening products are used, with a reported 35% of South African women using such products (National Toxicology Program, 2009). A study of African and Indian women in a specific South African city (Durban) reported such usage amongst 32.2% of the population (Dlova et al., 2014). Use of such products is not confined to South Africa, with data for other African countries documenting that 25% of women in Bamako, Mali, 52% in Dakar, Senegal, and 77% in Lagos, Nigeria make use of skin lighteners (National Toxicology Program, 2009; cited by Jacobs et al., 2016, p. 68). It should be emphasized that the use of skin lighteners may cause irreversible damage to the skin, specifically a condition known as *exogenous ochronosis,* whereby chronic use leads to paradoxical hyperpigmentation, which is distressing to the user (Jacobs et al., 2016; Lazar et al., 2023).

Skin-lightening may function to enhance self-esteem (Hamed et al., 2010). It could be that the paucity of AN cases in the African context relates to the culture-specific nature of somatic representations and manifestations of self-esteem. Is it possible that the skin may serve as a proxy for body dissatisfaction in an African setting, whereas thinness is more likely to serve this purpose in a Western setting?

Conclusion

If "social identity", within the context of AN, is about being seen in a certain way – a way that is understood to communicate and convey emotional suffering – the presentation of AN accomplishes that in a Western setting. Yet, in a non-Western setting, would there be an attribution of the same meaning? Seemingly not, based on the limited data from Africa, which suggest something more deeply personal and less social, as well as being potentially stigmatizing in relation to being understood to be potentially infected with a communicable or transmissible disease. At one level, this may explain the paucity of AN cases, as does the preference for a larger body size in an African context, which emerges from the obesity literature. At another level, one may be witnessing the powerful role of culture in mediating "illness" presentation, i.e., culture shapes the presentation of underlying disease, which may present completely differently in an African context. This raises the question – what is the "disease"? Regarding AN, it is not clear to me that this has been understood generally, notwithstanding decades of research which led Touyz et al. (2023) to raise the question as to what kind of illness AN is, more specifically within the context of the ongoing search for a cure. However, within an African context – with specific reference to black women and girls – it begs the question as to whether this would be of any relevance in relation to AN where identity or communication issues, within a cultural context, may manifest differently, e.g., as a Conversion Disorder (Functional Neurological Symptom Disorder) (APA, 2013). South African data in this regard have described the predominance of females, of black African ethnicity, with social factors being causative and contributing to the presentation (Naidoo & Bhigjee, 2021). As an idiom of distress, as a manifestation of such an identity, one might question the extent to which AN in an African setting is of relevance where presentations of intra-psychic distress may take different somatic forms.

References

American Psychological Association. (n.d.). Just-world Identity. In *APA dictionary of psychology*. Retrieved April 27, 2024, from https://dictionary.apa.org/identity

American Psychiatric Association. (2013). *Diagnostic and statistical manual of mental disorders* (5th ed.). https://doi.org/10.1176/appi.books.9780890425596

Baker, D. B., & Keramidas, N. (2013). The psychology of hunger. *Monitor on Psychology, 44*(9). https://www.apa.org/monitor/2013/10/hunger

Bennett, D., Sharpe, M., Freeman, C., & Carson, A. (2004). Anorexia nervosa among female secondary school students in Ghana. *British Journal of Psychiatry, 185*, 312–317.

Bosire, E. N., Cohen, E., Erzse, A., Goldstein, S. J., Hofman, K. J., & Norris, S. A. (2020). "I'd say I'm fat, I'm not obese": Obesity normalisation in urban-poor South Africa. *Public Health Nutrition, 23*(9), 1515–1526.

Calvo, F., Karras, B. T., Phillips, R., Kimball, A. M., & Wolf, F. (2003). Diagnoses, syndromes, and diseases: A knowledge representation problem. In *AMIA Annual Symposium Proceedings* (Vol. 2003, p. 802). American Medical Informatics Association.

DBSA. (n.d.) What steps should South Africa take to modernise infrastructure? Retrieved May 11, 2024, from https://www.dbsa.org/article/what-steps-should-south-africa-take-modernise-infrastructure

Dlova, N., Hamed, S. H., Tsoka-Gwegweni, J., Grobler, A., & Hift, R. (2014). Women's perceptions of the benefits and risks of skin-lightening creams in two South African communities. *Journal of Cosmetic Dermatology, 13*(3), 236–241.

Draper, C. E., Davidowitz, K. J., & Goedecke, J. H. (2016). Perceptions relating to body size, weight loss and weight-loss interventions in black South African women: A qualitative study. *Public Health Nutrition, 19*(3), 548–556.

Garner, D. M. (1997). Psychoeducational principles in treatment. In D. M. Garner & P. E. Garfinkel (Eds.), *Handbook of treatment for eating disorders* (2nd ed., pp. 153–154). Guilford Press.

Gbenenye, E. M. (2016). African colonial boundaries and nation-building. *Inkanyiso, 8*(2), 117–124.

Gordon, R. A. (1990). *Anorexia and bulimia: Anatomy of a social epidemic*. Basil Blackwell.

Gordon, R. A. (2001). Eating disorders East and West: A culture-bound syndrome unbound. In M. Nasser, M. A. Katzman, & R. A. Gordon (Eds.), Eating disorders and cultures in transition (pp. 1–16). Brunner-Routledge.

Hamed, S. H., Tayyem, R., Nimer, N., & AlKhatib, H. S. (2010). Skin-lightening practice among women living in Jordan: Prevalence, determinants, and user's awareness. *International Journal of Dermatology, 49*(4), 414–420.

Hay, P., Aouad, P., Le, A., Marks, P., Maloney, D., Touyz, S., & Maguire, S. (2023). Epidemiology of eating disorders: Population, prevalence, disease burden and quality of life informing public policy in Australia—A rapid review. *Journal of Eating Disorders*, *11*(1), 23.

Jacobs, M., Levine, S., Abney, K., & Davids, L. (2016). Fifty shades of African lightness: A bio-psychosocial review of the global phenomenon of skin lightening practices. *Journal of Public Health in Africa*, *7*(2), 552. https://doi.org/10.4081/jphia.2016.552

Lazar, M., De La Garza, H., & Vashi, N. A. (2023). Exogenous ochronosis: Characterizing a rare disorder in skin of color. *Journal of Clinical Medicine*, *12*(13), 4341. https://doi.org/10.3390/jcm12134341

Lee, S. (1996). Reconsidering the status of anorexia nervosa as a Western culture-bound syndrome. *Social Science & Medicine*, *42*(1), 21–34.

Littman, L. (2018). Rapid-onset gender dysphoria in adolescents and young adults: A study of parental reports. *PloS One*, *13*(8), e0202330. https://doi.org/10.1371/journal.pone.0202330

Mchiza, Z. J., Goedecke, J. H., & Lambert, E. V. (2011). Intra-familial and ethnic effects on attitudinal and perceptual body image: A cohort of South African mother-daughter dyads. *BMC Public Health*, *11*, 433.

Morris, P. F., & Szabo, C. P. (2013). Meanings of thinness and dysfunctional eating in black South African females-a qualitative study: Original. *African Journal of Psychiatry*, *16*(5), 338–342.

Naidoo, L., & Bhigjee, A. I. (2021). The spectrum of functional neurological disorders: A retrospective analysis at a tertiary hospital in South Africa. *South African Journal of Psychiatry*, *27*, a1607. https://doi.org/10.4102/sajpsychiatry.v27i0.1607

Nasser, M., & Di Nicola, V. (2001). Changing bodies, changing cultures: An intercultural dialogue on the body as the final frontier. In M. Nasser, M. A. Katzman, & R. A. Gordon (Eds.), Eating disorders and cultures in transition (pp. 171–187). Brunner-Routledge.

National Toxicology Program. (2009). Nomination profile: Hydroquinone. Available from: https://ntp.niehs.nih.gov/ntp/noms/support_docs/hydroquinone_may2009.pdf

Nasser, M., Katzman, M., & Gordon, R. (2003). *Eating disorders and cultures in transition*. Routledge.

Pradeilles, R., Holdsworth, M., Olaitan, O., Irache, A., Osei-Kwasi, H. A., Ngandu, C. B., & Cohen, E. (2022). Body size preferences for women and adolescent girls living in Africa: A mixed-methods systematic review. *Public Health Nutrition*, *25*(3), 738–759.

South African Government. (n.d.). *People of South Africa*. Retrieved 11 May, 2024, from https://www.gov.za/about-sa/south-africas-people#

Swartz, L. (1998). *Culture and mental health: A Southern African view*. Oxford University Press Southern Africa.

Szabo, C. P., Berk, M., Tlou, E., & Allwood, C. W. (1995). Eating disorders in black South African females. *South African Medical Journal*, *85*(6), 588–590.

Szabo, C. P., & Hollands, C. (1997). Abnormal eating attitudes in secondary-school girls in South Africa-a preliminary study. *South African Medical Journal*, *87*(4), 524–530.

Szabo, C. P., & Allwood, C. W. (2004). A cross-cultural study of eating attitudes in adolescent South African females. *World Psychiatry*, *3*(1), 41.

Szabo, C. P., & Allwood, C. W. (2004). Application of the Eating Attitudes Test (EAT-26) in a rural, Zulu speaking, adolescent population in South Africa. *World Psychiatry*, *3*(3), 169.

Szabo, C. P., & Allwood, C. W. (2006). Body figure preference in South African adolescent females: A cross cultural study. *African Health Sciences*, *6*(4), 201–206.

Szabo, C. P. (2015). Prevalence and incidence of eating disorders in underrepresented countries. In L. Smolak & M. P. Levine (Eds.), The Wiley handbook of eating disorders (pp. 79–92). John Wiley & Sons, Ltd.

Szabo, C. P. (2019). Eating disorders, risk and management: A personal journey and a South African and African perspective. *Global Psychiatry*, *2*(2), 121–134.

The World Bank. (2018, October 19). *South Africa's efforts to modernize, improve urban management boosted.* https://www.worldbank.org/en/news/press-release/2018/10/19/south-africas-efforts-to-modernize-improve-urban-management-boosted

Trafford, A. M., Carr, M. J., Ashcroft, D. M., Chew-Graham, C. A., Cockcroft, E., Cybulski, L., ... & Mok, P. L. (2023). Temporal trends in eating disorder and self-harm incidence rates among adolescents and young adults in the UK in the 2 years since onset of the COVID-19 pandemic: A population-based study. *The Lancet Child & Adolescent Health*, *7*(8), 544–554.

Touyz, S., Bryant, E., Dann, K. M., Polivy, J., Le Grange, D., Hay, P., ... & Maguire, S. (2023). What kind of illness is anorexia nervosa? Revisited: Some preliminary thoughts to finding a cure. *Journal of Eating Disorders*, *11*(1), 221.

van den Heuvel, L. L., Van der Merwe, C. A., Jordaan, G. P., & Szabo, C. P. (2023). Eating disorders in Africa. In P. Robinson, T. Wade, B. Herpertz-Dahlmann, F. Fernandez-Aranda, J. Treasure, & S. Wonderlich (Eds.), Eating disorders. Springer. https://doi.org/10.1007/978-3-030-97416-9_17-1

World Health Organization. (2019). *International statistical classification of diseases and related health problems* (11th ed.). https://icd.who.int/https://www.sahistory.org.za/article/people-and-culture-south-africa#

Part III

Reflections and Recovery

Lived Experience and Looking Forward

Chapter 12

Where the Secret Lies

A Deep Glimpse into the 'Lived Eating Disorder Experience'

Lili Clark and SiennaMarísa Brown

Introduction

In the context of psychology, researchers and clinicians often turn to lived experience as a window into understanding disorders or conditions from the inside. Ultimately, what is being sought is insight, to be told a coherent story of what occurs when the limited omniscient Self struggles to narrate, no longer knows its characters, or becomes lost within life circumstances. After all, without cohesion—without a sense of past, present, or future—are not such experiences inherently disordered? Indeed, narrative theory posits that narrative is a foundational human strategy for making sense of the elements that make up one's experience; for example, time, process, and change. In doing so, narrative offers power over banalities, familiarity during change, and understanding despite novelty. Narrative differs from other forms of discourse in that it not only explains and expresses but illustrates a style unique to human thinking. To such ends, narrative identity proposes that an individual forms their identity through the act of integrating life experiences into an evolving story that they use to make sense of circumstances, generate a feeling of unity, and foster purpose in life. By knitting together past, present, and potential future, narrative identity serves to provide temporal, causal, thematic, and cultural coherence to understandings of lived experience.

Humans find narrative comforting in that it provides structure to life's randomness by allowing people to declare a known beginning; for instance, 'Once upon a time' (English); 'Listen to tell it and tell it to teach it' (Chilean); because, 'I've told you what's coming' (Moroccan). In doing so, narratives comfort because they offer closure that is otherwise perpetually elusive (i.e., 'And they all lived happily ever after' (English); 'Disaster there, feast here' (Georgian). Accordingly, this chapter offers two empirical, narrative accounts—'vignettes'—of lived experience with eating disorders (ED), specifically severe and enduring EDs (SE-ED). The perspectives critically differ in terms of ED type, race and ethnicity, cultural background, trauma history, and access to medical or therapeutic healthcare. The following vignettes serve to provide a deeper glimpse into the kaleidoscope of evolving etiologies and meanings behind 'the lived eating disorder experience.' Within ED contexts, lived experience encourages mental health research and

DOI: 10.4324/9781003468189-15

treatment to adopt informed and representative therapeutic approaches. We've told you what's coming.

Vignette 1: Memory-Eater

Background: Lili is a white, cis-gendered, middle-class female, born to college-educated parents in a Western, Educated, Industrialized, Rich, and Democratic (WEIRD) country, who developed severe anorexia nervosa (AN) at the age of 11 and recovered at the age of 21. A recipient of the highest level of the Hathaway Merit Scholarship, she completed university during ED treatment and went straight into recovery and her PhD at the University of Edinburgh. She has now successfully passed her viva.

Once upon a time, a father of a little girl would often remark how 'there's no one happier than Lili.' This child was jubilant, outgoing, athletic, and loved nothing more than to have fun—swimming, soccer, theater, art—no one had more of an appetite for life than this kid whose first word was 'tah-dah!' School for Lili was an effortless activity that felt like a hobby done with friends, rather than mandated learning. This was a child who was never stressed nor scared nor uncertain about who she was or what she was doing. She developed a fearless reputation for standing up to bullies within her first decade—it didn't matter if it meant going up against a peer, opposing a city council, or challenging a state senator at a town hall Q&A. But something wicked happened during an otherwise perfect autumn, in an altogether sleepy little town, safe in a warm and loving home. If you asked her parents, they would say it was as if waking into a nightmare—something so hard to believe and so unreal about the night they lost their daughter. Were these medieval times, when folklore made sense for science, arguments may have been made that this child was a changeling whose body got snatched. Over the next ten years, as the life was sucked out of her, one might even be inclined to blame an invisible vampire. It must be something else that saw a happy child eat dinner the day before with no signs of distress yet wake up refusing to eat any breakfast. From the outside, AN can appear this simple, clear, and orderly. Clinically, it is a disorder made of hard lines, and obvious symbols—in this case, a child unfurling as a skull and crossbones.

In my experience with AN, it crept up slowly, like a season changing or falling asleep, and occurred long before the rapid presentation of highly restrictive eating. From the inside, I remember starting to struggle to paint pictures in my head when reading; words stayed trapped on pages instead of forming new worlds. My comprehension was not impacted, nor my semi-photographic memory, but rather there suddenly was no joy in the task I adored. That, for me, was the first sign of something shifting in how I understood things, in how I experienced myself. I could no longer enter imaginary lives with ease; I became bound to the island of my own reality. It was then that I started to be concerned about the inconsistency of my reflections in various forms of matter—mirrors, windows, photos, shadows, and through the eyes of others. I found it perplexing and frustrating that I could wear the same outfit, stand in the same place at the same time of day, and come to see myself differently every time. It was as if my memory was no longer trustworthy, as if the narrator of my life had gone rouge and left me in the wrong story, lost in life. This occurred 6 months before any bodysnatching.

During this period, I found myself delving deeper into my mind, sifting through memories, trying to make sense of this sudden change in my way of interpretation of being. It had felt as if a new door had appeared in the room of my psyche, blocking my thoughts' usual paths. Upon opening this door, I discovered an empty, cavernous space that seemed hungry with anticipation, not for information or experience, but for me, in a form I didn't understand. It was then that I truly grasped the concept of time—not the mundane passage of hours, but the gnawing expanse of a lifetime. This new awareness flooded me with fears of missteps or mistakes that could derail my entire future. The contrast was stark for mere weeks ago; I had never considered any day beyond tomorrow. Perhaps unsurprisingly, this oppressively blank mental space of potential became a wellspring for extreme academic perfectionism and test anxiety. The creative abundance and vast expanse of a near-century felt paralyzing rather than exhilarating. At 11 years old, I wanted to stop reading because the story I was living felt like it was unraveling.

I needed to pause time long enough to understand the changes to my experience, regain my bearings of understanding, and learn how to manage this entirely new life. We call it 'growing up' but I think adults forget that, at the time, this can feel like the end of everything. I didn't know it was merely the close of 'childhood,' because up until then, that was only my entire life—a life I cherished deeply. So, in many ways, restricting food felt surprisingly natural and intuitive, as if I were doing the right thing to preserve my existence. It seemed as logical as drinking water when thirsty or resting when tired. Despite appearances, my desire to pause time wasn't rooted in a fear of sexual maturation, contrary to what Bruch and others often argue as causes of EDs. Although, I think, as someone nearing thirty, one may be free to admit that puberty is, at best, a biological indignity, social injustice, and deeply intimate self-betrayal to any inkling of free will. At worst, it's awkward, moist, and overly fleshy—all of which does little to limit any overwhelm one may feel from the existential weight of their newly realized potential future. For me, restricting was about trying to understand life, in time, to live it—what was the new spare room for? Why did it resist being filled yet demand nothing else?

It turns out that is textbook starvation—a gnawing presence of absence whose repellent void offers the smoothest, purest, most addictive feeling of invincibility because if nothing satisfies then I could satisfy by wanting for nothing. This surprising side effect was wholly welcomed, though unexpected. I found myself less sensitive to external criticism or perception. True, I was still walking into an iron maiden of my own making, but I viewed my poniards of self-criticism as constructive, pre-emptively protective. Besides, the self-inflicted hurt of starvation and excessive exercise didn't matter because I felt invigorated and well-rested to combat the world. I no longer cared for friends or company; isolation felt like independence—calming, certain, and simple. Reading's lost appeal became replaced with consuming numbers and constant calculations. Calories substituted stories, measurements offered escapes, and self-narrative was now found in the skeleton of a relentless structured routine. I felt powerful. Any social or testing anxiety slipped away as my weight decreased. Above all, I felt mature and capable, as if I could handle whatever came next—like how I felt before the changes in my reading occurred, but now even sharper and stronger. The noise and raw nerves that were building in my mind, worries about the future, settled. Now, all the rooms of my psyche were open and my thoughts were clear to wander unobstructed by walls and mysterious doors. I believed I had hacked nature and matured without the social and biological treachery of adolescence.

Suffice it to say, starvation is not subtle—try as one might to hide such, eventually, time comes to collect the debt energy owes life's antagonism regarding perpetual motion. In this case, time came in the form of ED treatment at both pediatric and adult in-patient levels. The true distress of treatment for me, however, was that I didn't understand what was 'wrong' with me and why, whatever I was, warranted these new external restrictions. To have my agency and bodily privacy stripped from me; my genuine questions and all elements of my personality be pathologized; my natural food preferences demonized; and my intelligence about myself and my needs doubted was enraging and traumatic. Daily, I was weighed, measured, drained for blood, force-fed food I had no say in (hand to God, I've never liked cheese), denied access to the movement I've always used for thinking things through. I observed clinicians watching me, taking notes on my actions or inactions, recording my interactions with the other 'anorexics.' Their EDs felt foreign. They described having an anorexic voice; they identified as being anorexics. I had no ED voice. I felt no attachment to this personified entity of 'Ed' nor did I identify with the concept of recovery. Both notions made my lip curl at their conceptual saccharine simplicity and valorization of processes that felt otherwise natural and obvious. Yet being surrounded by multiple EDs became far more damaging to my wellbeing than having just one because, in treatment, any semblance of identity or meaning in my life got reduced to the diagnosis. In treatment, I could only see EDs, learn about EDs, and witness my physical body become valued as if it were the only part of me that was worth saving to others. Overall, my treatment experiences resembled Captain Hook's interactions with Peter Pan—like a lion in a cage tormented by a sparrow that would otherwise be ignored were he allowed to be in nature (Barrie, 2021). I pushed back against various forms of treatment because it was prescriptive 'restriction'—I was limited in what I could have access to read, when and what I could eat, how I could move, and what I could say. 'It's not you, it's the ED.' But what happens if it was me? Am I not enough? What if it was monstrous to witness and a bear to treat because it wasn't something or someone else? It was my voice, my desires, my actions, me, mine, sharpened with life's biting desire for understanding.

The ED for me came from this and recovery occurred through the same vein. I 'recovered' because, after a decade of severe malnutrition with no appetite and with a heart that was finally failing, I suddenly felt hungry. Not for time, this time, but for peanut butter. It was an unapologetically rapacious hunger that I could not explain after having spent half my life feeling nothing. As my body was starting to shut down, and I was unnervingly peaceful about dying, I asked my parents for a toasted bagel, with smooth peanut butter, and fresh strawberry jam. It was the first time I asked for food, let alone for bread and peanut butter. My folks were in genuine shock, and horribly torn—on one side they wanted nothing more than to feed me, yet on the other, both were deeply concerned that providing drastically rich nourishment might actually kill me due to refeeding syndrome. In all honesty, I rather hoped it would, I saw the entire thing as a last supper. Maybe they felt that knife's edge as well because they risked the bagel. I ate through tears, and not out of fear of calories or tomorrow's weight gain or measurement changes, but out of pure contentment. It tasted like the hug my dad gave me when I bolted into his arms after my first day in kindergarten.

At long last, time finally stopped. It just felt good to savor what tasted like childhood. I wanted my mother's roast chicken because it's October and I'm deliciously exhausted after our last soccer game; my father's blueberry pancakes because it's a morning in May and we are going rock-hopping up canyon; my sibling's naan because we are dancing in the warm kitchen during a cold January; the family turkey because that means the house is full of laughter and Christmas lights; my grandpa's carrots from the garden because he is still alive; my grandmother's birthday carrot cakes because she is still alive; and peanut butter because I am still alive. I wasn't eating for food but for memory. I was eating to keep access to the life and the people I love so very much. I finished the entire bagel and looked at my parents, who were shocked at not having to battle with me to finish a meal, and I asked if I could have another in the morning.

It has been eight years since I had my second, and final, round of treatment for medical stabilization from severe AN. I did not require nor desire clinical psychotherapy for treating the ED. It left like it arrived, through death's door in my family's home, where the scythe of my spine, that I used to watch with grotesque fascination as it slithered across my stomach threateningly, turned into a smile at the release of this riddle. The empty room in my mind sighed softly, because here, here was a deep part of me that I could see, touch, and finally reach to fulfill. It was a simple desire to understand that almost killed me through starvation, and it was this haunting appetite that saved me. Haunting, holding both pursuit and dwelling in its linguistic capacity, is what it's like to have an ED. That's the cost of pausing time; in my desire to maintain the goodness of my life at the start of this, I cast myself out of its heaven. As a result of this sin against nature's progression, whilst I do feel at home in my body now and my ability to escape into story returned quickly in recovery, I don't feel at home anywhere anymore nor with anyone. With AN, I lost my childhood, my adolescence, my early adulthood, and the feeling of home with my loved ones. My family's heart and home remain ghostly in ways no one seems to talk about when they offer soporific speeches dripping in maudlin metaphors and thought-terminating cliches in treatment centers. But it is understandable for a haunting to remain as it is the shadow to living. My parents lost the child they knew, and then the child they didn't know almost died on them not once, nor twice, but three times in a decade. The young adult that came back to them has echoes of the Lili they first lost, but I never fully returned to them, to home, nor to myself.

Vignette 2: Caged Bird

Background: Sienna is a cisgender, Afro-Latina female who was born to college-educated parents in a suburban household in a WEIRD country. After receiving private primary and secondary education, she secured a merit-based, full-tuition scholarship for higher education from which she graduated summa cum laude. She earned a master's degree from the University of Oxford and is quickly approaching the successful completion of her PhD. She has experienced various forms of undiagnosed and untreated severe feeding and EDs throughout her life. She also bears a complex trauma history.

> *A word after a word after a word is power.*
>
> (Margaret Atwood, 1981)

From an early age, I understood myself and my world through the language of others. I was raised with the legend of the birth of my sibling. My sibling experienced a premature birth that physically and emotionally traumatized our mother and father. In contrast, my birth was relatively less traumatic with slightly fewer complications. Despite the four years separating my and my sibling's births, and the following years during which we both thrived, my sibling's premature birth somehow dictated how caregivers behaved toward and described the two of us. For example, my sibling was positioned as 'vulnerable' and was more likely to be protected, whilst I was positioned as 'headstrong' and was frequently neglected. In terms of 'roles,' my sibling was a 'miracle,' and I was evidently born to be their domestique. In terms of food and eating, my sibling's preferences were framed as 'particular' (i.e., 'eating like a bird') and mine were framed as 'problematic' (i.e., 'picky eating').

As a child, I exhibited selective ('picky') eating and food-specific sensory sensitivities (i.e., Avoidant Restrictive Food Intake Disorder [ARFID]). Around four years old, I failed to eat the appropriate amount or diversity of food necessary to maintain appropriate nutrition. I ate a limited variety of food, refused new and unknown foods, rejected foods with certain textures or odors and tastes, and was repulsed by the mixing of foods. During mealtimes, I experienced significant difficulty tolerating the noise of my own chewing in my ears, including the chewing and slurping sounds of others around me. Frustrated by my 'stubbornness,' my parents presented me as a 'problem' for my primary care provider to 'fix.' In response, my pediatrician suggested that my parents re-introduce lower textured foods, like puréed fruits and vegetables (i.e., 'baby food'), to my diet and encourage the use of divided plates. Though some measures were taken to lessen the daily impact of sensory-related restrictive eating and poor nutritional intake, caregivers never considered my behaviors as 'serious' and would instead verbally and emotionally abuse me to 'discourage me from being a problem.' As a result, disturbances in my relationship with eating and food continued.

At five years old, I was enrolled in a private elementary school that provided a full-day kindergarten educational program. Scheduled opportunities for snacks throughout the day afforded students time to replenish their energy, as well as a chance to socialize with their peers. Unlike lunch, students ate their snacks inside the classroom at their assigned desks and away from friends. Despite experiencing difficulties during mealtimes, I did not hesitate bringing baby food to eat at school. At the time, I was happy to have found a small selection of 'safe foods' I could manage that allowed for a sort of respite from ridicule at home. Nonetheless, the first day I brought baby food into my kindergarten class, I was inundated with questions and comments from peers that further positioned my limited food preferences as 'abnormal' or 'atypical.' Although I initially felt confident in my decision to pack palatable food preferences, I did not expect my choice to bring more attention to my 'otherness' (i.e., multicultural heritage) and further alienate me as a 'problem' at the predominantly white private school. Most memorably, my kindergarten teacher sometimes placed me in 'time out' during recess—intentionally removing me from the friends I struggled to make in the first place—to 'encourage' me to 'act my age' and to eat foods that were, in their opinion, 'appropriate.' When I reported feeling distressed by my teacher's punishments and classmates' jeers to adults, caregivers echoed the importance of taking 'brave bites' to challenge my 'problematic' eating behaviors. Feeling stuck in a series of unspeakable experiences anchored in inadequate language that simultaneously restricted and shaped my reality, I started to search for answers in books. Perhaps through the language of others I could not only better understand my perception of the world, but my position in it, as well.

The adage 'No one can take knowledge away from you' provided rhythm and speed to my understanding of the world. Raised with bedtime stories and television shows like Reading Rainbow, I developed a passion to discover new words, if not new worlds, through the written word. To better comprehend the pattern of words assigned to my actions and emotions, I began studying vocabulary from children's books like Junie B. Jones. I used an illustrated children's dictionary to understand who the characters were and why people behaved toward them the way they did. Fascinated by the profound power of language and the transformative force of the written word, my interest developed into a passion for pronunciation, grammatical forms and functions, syntactic peculiarities, and variant spellings. Eventually, I advanced to referencing a worn, decades-old dictionary that I hid under my bed for late-night investigations into the vernacular. I was convinced if I understood why I existed, or at least found the correct words to explain my experiences, perhaps I might become less of a 'problem.' The terms habitually used to describe me were consistently incongruent with my self-view; however, my self-view was regularly rejected. With an improved vocabulary, I hoped to free myself from an ouroboric cycle of inadequate and unaccepted language. However, attempting to understand others and redefine myself through shared language was not a welcome practice. When my parents started using the dictionary as a tool for punishment, it became clear I was barred from seeing my Self outside of the gaze of those who 'chose' who I was, or who I could ever be.

Left to navigate the unintended consequences of being born into my sibling's legend, the development of my vocabulary spearheaded an inadvertent quest into my personal lore. When I was in my mother's womb, I was to be named 'Maya' after acclaimed renaissance poet and storyteller, Maya Angelou. Desperate to understand the idea behind that decision and why I was ultimately not her namesake, when I was around seven years old, I began reading collections of Angelou's work and became increasingly intrigued by verse and song. Angelou confronted problems through innovative and incisive commentary characterized by the rhythm of prose and poetry. Her words evoked emotion and made me feel capable of transforming my Self through conversation. Throughout the process of attempting to harness communication as a guide to becoming less of a 'problem,' I started associating physiological (felt) sensations (e.g., discomfort) with certain emotions, like despair.

At the age of eight, my habitual diet—comprising a few preferred and/or accepted foods and persistent refusal of new foods—continued to fail to meet my nutritional needs. The feeding problems I experienced evolved into escaping mealtimes and eventually contributed to severe gastrointestinal problems. All day, every day, I felt 'heavy' and 'out of place'; these felt experiences were associated with physiological (e.g., swelling) and psychosocial (i.e., anxiety, difficulty maintaining friendships) problems, but consistently lacked a preoccupation with food, eating, or body image. Nevertheless, no matter whom I turned to for help, the language I used was rejected and the distress I experienced was neglected. Over time, I began to feel the unspeakable realities—like anxiety, isolation, and neglect—in my body, in my gut. Inexplicably, my abdomen held the compounding 'weight' of otherwise unspeakable traumas. By the age of 10, the 'discomfort' enveloped my body and progressed into unrecognized and untreated body dysmorphia, dermatillomania, and trichotillomania—a period of 11 months during which I pulled out all my eyelash and eyebrow hairs.

As feeding difficulties continued, people making comments comparing mine and my sibling's mealtime behaviors progressed into punishment—like being coerced to eat excessive amounts of preferred foods during mealtimes to correct 'problematic' feeding habits. In response, my body inadvertently changed in weight, size, and shape, and I began to experience episodes of severe nausea and vomiting (i.e., cyclic vomiting syndrome) that eventually caught the attention of caregivers. Upon consulting my pediatric clinician, caregivers received firm guidance regarding 'controlling' my eating habits. At 11 years old, I was measured head-to-toe with a soft tape measure, shown on clinical growth and BMI-for-age charts how I was 'overweight,' and instructed to keep a food diary. In a matter of minutes, I was professionally positioned as a 'problem' projected to be at risk of further, more severe health complications in adulthood. Unfortunately, my parents decided such medical guidance 'confirmed' my behaviors as 'attention-seeking' and punished me for being 'problematic' by never again taking me to a physician for issues regarding feeding and eating. Over the next three years, caregivers began to vigilantly monitor the types and quantities of food I ate and comment more on the idiosyncrasies between me and my sibling, especially those surrounding mealtime behaviors and food preferences.

At the age of 14, I began high school at the same time my sibling moved away to university. During this transition, caregivers frequently discussed how my sibling and I had different types of potential ('room for improvement' versus 'great expectations') as well as body shapes ('petite' compared to 'voluptuous'). The labeling was socially reinforced and felt awkward. How could others' language describe me, especially when my own language always seemed to fall short? Was there a lack of communication or a problem with comprehension? Overwhelmed by an onerous cascade of felt experiences, I began challenging perceptions of my Self through my physicality to create 'balance' or meaning where there was otherwise none. Despite still lacking medical or therapeutic guidance on how to adequately and appropriately approach food and eating, through the language of others (and a high school Health course video depicting EDs) I learned I could manipulate weight, size, and shape through certain eating habits and exercise regimens. Based on the knowledge I gained, evidently bulimia nervosa (BN) simultaneously allowed for caregivers to visually witness preferred mealtime behaviors and created an opportunity to 'let go' (i.e., emesis) of the uncomfortable 'weight' (i.e., satiety) I felt in my gut. When I decided to intentionally engage in BN behaviors, I almost immediately felt balanced, if not 'in tune,' with the emotions and experiences I embodied but could not otherwise communicate. I began experiencing rapid, significant weight loss and, at one time, lost 30lbs in a little over a week. The BN behaviors I engaged in, and the changes my body endured, were not noticed by parents, but were recognized by one high school guidance counselor who detected I was wearing excessive layers of uniform clothing (i.e., five shirts and two pairs of pants) to school. Much to my dismay, I was told to disclose my ED to my parents within 24 hours or risk immediate expulsion. Unfortunately, I was neither referred to a clinician nor encouraged to seek mental healthcare; rather, I was threatened by the school and then punished at home.

Reinforced by familial abuse and neglect, as well as normalized discrimination that cemented the pillars of my educational career, BN behaviors became a long-term coping mechanism that helped me manage day-to-day experiences, as well as periods of transition and/or prolonged uncertainty. Severe and enduring BN (SE-BN) functioned as an active attempt to combat my Problematic Self—to minimize factors of myself that, as explained to me by others, made me a bad or 'problematic' person. I had no idea of how to reduce or reshape my Problematic Self into something less harmful, thus the ED acted as a sort of driver's license—a psychosomatic permit to get from point A ('unworthy') to point B ('worthy'). I did not identify with ED behaviors; rather, disordered eating acted as more of a mechanism to minimize the impact of adverse lived experiences on my life. Disordered eating habits ebbed between presentations (SE-BN, AN-binge eating/purging type, adult ARFID) and eventually contributed to severe cardiovascular and orthopedic problems and continued throughout my adolescence into young adulthood. Furthermore, traumatic experiences in young adulthood solidified a felt sense of emotional stability through a focus on manipulated physicality.

From 22 to 27 years old, SE-BN behaviors vacillated in intensity as I struggled to independently redefine myself through a worldview unsullied by abuse and neglect. At 27, I was clinically administered controlled doses of a therapeutic psychedelic that helped to restore brain plasticity and promote cognitive flexibility. Thereupon, in conjunction with psychological support, I no longer feel like the EDs I experienced are a practical psychosomatic mechanism able to 'correct' or 'control' sensory issues or to 'balance' embodied traumas. The shift in my psychological script impacted my eating habits and expedited my 'recovery' from severe disordered eating. Though my experiences remain rejected by people close to me, I now have the language and capacity to understand and affirm my lived experiences. Now, I radically accept my Self. Now, I sing my song.

Conclusion

It is not only a dearth of evidence (and persistent underfunding) that makes EDs complex and challenging to treat; it is also the ways in which information is interpreted. EDs simplify priorities in life, they are clarifying because they are deadly and deadly because they are not sufficiently understood clinically. Failing to focus on, or deeply understand, the assortment of meanings and motivations behind EDs critically impacts how clinicians and researchers make sense of, and decide to treat, individuals living with EDs. As researchers interpret data, particularly qualitative data from individuals with EDs, close attention must be paid to not only the literal what but the nuanced why through which experience comes to the surface as language and becomes shared. Narrative can help bridge the gap between experience and understanding because it transforms isolated accounts into complementary histories—collective narratives—that promote contextual understanding.

Indeed, deeply understanding EDs is neither a simple nor a straightforward endeavor. Both authors, in their positions as researchers of EDs who have lived experience with EDs, struggled to shape their experiences with available language—from visual vernacular to expert jargon—as it failed to articulate the complexities of their diverse perspectives. hooks (1990) describes how personal recovery becomes challenging as the individual is intertwined with words, making language a 'place of struggle' to find one's 'voice.' This becomes particularly difficult when needs or wants are historically dismissed, ignored, or unrecognized (e.g., 'That's just your ED talking'). Indeed, both authors experience the consequences of what Pascual (2001) observes in the life narratives of EDs where, '...when one assigns to women that which is imprecise, it amounts to maintaining them in a position of marginality, to reserving them the place of the unsayable' (p.343).

Scott (1992) states that experience is neither the source of explanation nor the definitive evidence for understanding, but rather the subject of clarification itself. A line from Shakespeare's Much Ado About Nothing followed the authors through their reflection and construction of this chapter: 'Are you yet living?' (1.1.117). Whilst its reference began in jest, we found ourselves asking it, with deepening sincerity, as a point of reflection in assessing what is meant by the concept and phrase 'lived experience' in the context of EDs, self, and identity. Often, researchers who are simultaneously academic experts and have lived experience of their area of interest face scrutiny and trivialization of their work, despite possessing the 'first-hand perspective' so often sought for 'quality' research. Regularly, their professional expertise is reduced to their ED experience and their ED experience is reduced to a professional liability. Whilst we echo Charland et al.'s (2013) position that EDs are an affective dedication to a meaningfully resolute idea, our lived experience 'passion' becomes better translated by the poet Adrienne Rich (2016) who affirms: 'This is the oppressor's language yet I need it to talk to you.'

There is a pressing need to conduct informed, ethical evaluations of how identification with EDs, even throughout recovery, can impact individuals with lived experience. It is essential to question whether individuals with lived experience are being holistically valued or merely utilized as sources of knowledge that further research agendas. If identification with EDs is already pathologized as a manifestation of the disorder's 'ego-syntonic presence,' what are researchers seeking from those with lived experience? In the pursuit to integrate individuals with lived experience into research and practice, are individuals being asked to restructure their life narratives around EDs? In doing so, does ethical risk arise in the form of qualitative procrustean errors? Moreover, are the interests behind such practices critically considered?

In striving to answer these concerns, research efforts must endeavor to reduce the potential hermeneutical injustice and iatrogenic harm that may arise in clinical settings where lived experience—the individual's capacity as a 'knower'—may be discounted or distrusted (see Fricker, 2007). Quite frankly, if one would like to better understand EDs and their relationship to self and identity, look not to caricatures of Dr Jekyll and Mr. Hyde, but refer to Shelley's Frankenstein to witness how souls starved of both hope and fear have such a love and anger within them that 'if denied one they indulge the other.' If EDs are unintended consequences of the human condition (as we seem to be the only species that develop them), research and practice cannot continue to deny how such complex, at times confounding, behaviors require monstrosity and monstrous responsibility in order to exist and persist. Must one restrict their potential to safely navigate identity and self? Must one continuously deny their needs, wants, and agency to be more palatable to others? The authors advocate for research that fosters an emancipatory praxis, aiming not only to comprehend and transform the relational dynamics of EDs, but to also address stigma, inequality, and promote ethical practices (hooks, 1994). Building upon the recommendations and protections suggested by Musić et al. (2022) and Wade et al. (2022), there are ample opportunities to generate specific guidelines for the inclusion of lived experience in ED research to thus ensure such contributions, involvement, collaborations, and insight are not denigrated in the research process.

In sum, what makes EDs terrifyingly complex is that they are intimately familiar. They may be considered disorders of the self and identity because true horror is what happens when the familiar becomes unspeakable. Identity is, pragmatically speaking, a structure or set of rules that an individual creates and evolves to provide sense and meaning to their life. Identity is an intimate social ritual in that it encapsulates a series of hidden and nested behaviors through which others come to recognize another. EDs, with their extensive rules and patterns, are easy to mistake as forms of identity. Thus, it is inappropriate to minimize these disorders and equate them as a sort of pathological organization. Rather, from the lived-experience perspective, EDs manifest as an exposed armature in the cathedral of oneself that reveals the rawest features—the metaphysical pillars holding up the vaulted ceilings of Self. To better understand and improve the clinical treatment of EDs, researchers and clinicians must gain a better understanding of the individual narrative. Disorders of the self are not a monolith. Indeed, lived experience represents a valuable source of knowledge, but it is crucial to acknowledge such 'knowing' as an extension of the individual that requires a radically humanizing approach which supports agency, belonging, and competence. For many, lived experience is not simply lived but an ongoing process of living. This continuance provides a meaningful context that may imbue empirical data with vitality, transforming it from an armature of facts into a dynamic body of actionable knowledge that holds clinical systems accountable.

References

Atwood, M. (1981). Spelling. In *True stories* (pp. 63–64). Simon & Schuster.

Barrie, J. M. (2021). *Peter Pan* [Ebook]. Duncan Research. https://www.gutenberg.org/files/16/16-h/16-h.htm

Charland, L. C., Hope, T., Stewart, A., & Tan, J. (2013). Anorexia nervosa as a passion. *Philosophy, Psychiatry, & Psychology, 20*(4), 353–365. https://doi.org/10.1353/ppp.2013.0049

Fricker, M. (2007). *Epistemic injustice: Power and the ethics of knowing*. Oxford University Press.

hooks, b. (1990). *Yearning: Race, gender, and cultural politic*. South End Press.

hooks, b. (1994). *Teaching to transgress: Education as the practice of freedom*. Routledge.
Musić, S., Elwyn, R., Fountas, G., Gnatt, I., Jenkins, Z. M., Malcolm, A., Miles, S., Neill, E., Simpson, T., Yolland, C. O., & Phillipou, A. (2022). Valuing the voice of lived experience of eating disorders in the research process: Benefits and considerations. *Australian and New Zealand Journal of Psychiatry*, *56*(3), 216–218. https://doi.org/10.1177/00048674211998794
Pascual, N. (2001). Depathologizing anorexia: The risks of life narratives. *Style*, *35*(2), 341–352. http://www.jstor.org/stable/10.5325/style.35.2.341
Rich, A. (2016). *Collected Poems: 1950-2012*. WW Norton & Company.
Scott, J. (1992). Experience. In J. Butler & J. W. Scott (Eds.), *Feminists theorize the political*. Routledge.
Shakespeare, W. (n.d.). *Much Ado About Nothing*. Project Gutenberg. https://www.gutenberg.org/ebooks/1519
Wade, C., Akanksha Mimi Malhotra, McGuire, P., Vincent, C., & Fowler, A. (2022). Action on patient safety can reduce health inequalities. *BMJ. British Medical Journal* (Clinical Research Ed.), e067090–e067090. https://doi.org/10.1136/bmj-2021-067090

Chapter 13

Rediscovering the Self

Anorexia, Identity, and the Path Forward

Marc O. Williams and John R.E. Fox

Why Identity Matters

Across this edited volume, leading academics, clinicians, and experts by experience have offered scholarly insights into the complex interactions between anorexia nervosa (AN) and the sense of self. Considering the self is crucial in understanding AN, which continues to present an enigma for many clinicians and clients, as reflected in the relatively modest outcomes of current treatment models. For example, in a rapid review on eating disorder outcomes, Miskovic-Wheatley et al. (2023) found that, while the literature generally shows reasonable outcomes for eating disorders, the outcomes for AN are poorer. These authors highlighted that there are still high levels of relapse (longer term) and, worryingly, a high risk of mortality for AN despite evidence-based treatments.

One promising avenue for progress lies in developing our understanding of how AN and identity influence one another in ways that may worsen outcomes. As argued by Kinderman et al. (2006) and Higbed and Fox (2010), psychological difficulties and identity cannot be meaningfully separated, as humans are fundamentally meaning-making beings. People with lived experience of AN inevitably understand their distress through the lens of their own identity and narrative, as articulated powerfully in Chapter 12. This core idea lies at the heart of this book, with contributors examining the interplay between AN and the self from multiple perspectives. In this concluding chapter, we will draw together the overarching themes that emerge across the book's chapters to explore how these insights might guide future research, theory, and treatment development.

Limits of Current Approaches

Conventional treatment approaches for AN, such as CBT for eating disorders (CBT-E), have contributed significantly to improving care. While CBT-E does recognise the central importance of identity in driving AN – where the central issue is seen as a sense of self narrowly fixated upon body weight, shape, and their control (Fairburn et al., 2003) – in clinical practice and in real-world service contexts, identity-focused elements receive scant attention. As discussed in Chapter

DOI: 10.4324/9781003468189-16

7, CBT-E also tends to address emotion regulation indirectly rather than making it a central focus, despite emotion processing difficulties being deeply interwoven with identity problems in AN. This is important, because the *lost emotional self* (Oldershaw et al., 2019) described in Chapter 2 suggests that without active work to recognise, tolerate, and transform maladaptive emotions, identity reconstruction work may stall or remain superficial.

The reality is that many people presenting at eating disorder services have already undergone a process of weaving AN into their identities; by that stage, there are such substantial barriers to identity reconstruction – things that emerge or intensify as a result of AN, such as social isolation and emotional and social difficulties – that a therapy focused primarily on weight restoration will often come unstuck. Relapse in AN is common, as is the lament from patients that, while they might appear to have recovered on the outside, the AN is still very much resident in their thinking and anxieties about food, weight, and shape. As one patient noted of her inpatient treatment for AN, "It just feels like the physical perspective is a little too ... out of perspective in comparison to the mental, because to me the mental problems are what have caused physical problems and it doesn't seem to be working that way in terms of recovery" (P3; Colton & Pistrang, 2004, p. 312). There is a risk that, without addressing the underlying identity-based aspects of AN, those who do demonstrate conventional markers of treatment success – such as weight restoration – remain in a state of pseudorecovery (Keski-Rahkonen & Tozzi, 2005).

One of the editors (MW) has noted in his time working across various eating disorder outpatient services – both child and adolescent – that the clinical focus on physical safety frequently captures attention away from the underlying psychology of the illness, as well as the social dynamics that emerge between individuals with AN, their treatment teams, and their families. While prioritising physical safety is often appropriate, it is difficult to see how shifting attention constantly to the physical could result in anything more than a physical recovery. The deeper, identity and relationship-based change that must occur for lasting remission becomes lost amid urgent and, often, panic-driven responses to ensure physical safety. In many ways, this response from clinicians and services runs in parallel with the individual's own diversion from their emotions by focusing on anorexic concerns such as eating, weight, and shape.

This book has argued over various chapters that the underlying psychological aspects require attention, as clinicians and services need to engage with these aspects in order for identity beyond AN to flourish. Some newer treatments, such as MANTRA, do include work to explore pro-AN beliefs and values that maintain the illness. While this can be a helpful template, an entire-service approach is needed where the physical aspect is seen for what it is: a consequence of psychological and identity chaos and confusion and, in some ways, a distraction from a hidden world of anxieties and preoccupations.

How Anorexia Nervosa Interferes with Identity

One of the main themes cutting across the various chapters is the core identity confusion that operates as a central vulnerability to developing AN. A fragile sense of self is vulnerable to AN as the illness comes to provide a focus and identity for the person (Chapters 2, 4, and 6). Chapters 1 and 2 discuss how AN is a massively disruptive factor within adolescent identity development and this disruption can often continue across teenage and early adult life.

This can be significantly damaging to self-development and can continue well into adulthood, where the individual comes to define themselves increasingly in terms of the AN (e.g., "I am anorexic"). Chapter 6 proposes that this lack of self is a significant risk factor for developing longstanding AN, as the longer someone defines themselves via their AN the stronger it will become. Moreover, the sheer presence of AN within one's life also limits the opportunity for self-development away from the eating disorder (e.g., avoiding social events for the fear of food).

One of the editors (JF) worked on a Specialist Eating Disorders Unit (SEDU) for many years and there were multiple examples of this process in play. People often came to the ward at very low weights and, as a result, would have long admissions to regain weight. Although these admissions were often life-saving, it did also mean that patients would miss many of the experiences that would help shape their identities (e.g., going to university, socialising with friends, having and losing relationships, and so on). This was further compounded by the fact that many patients would often have multiple admissions and it was a difficult sight to see, as a clinician, that often patients going through this type of revolving door admission onto the unit did not have any sense of who they would be without AN. As O'Connell (2020) reflected on their own experience of AN, "As I moved through treatment, I learned new ways of doing anorexia, living up to the SEDU's implicit expectations of how 'an anorexic' behaves and how anorexia manifests psychologically" (p. 165). This framing resonates with the theme in this book that AN is not simply an illness to be treated but also an identity that is enacted and defended, which complicates both motivation and recovery. Treatments and treatment teams that do not acknowledge this risk entrenching the illness further.

The ego-syntonic nature of AN is clear to see here. Individuals with AN frequently extol its benefits and their desire to engage in AN-related behaviours. Both of the editors have commonly heard from their patients that AN can provide them with a sense of self-worth, pride, and purpose. Without AN, one often hears, "I don't know who I would be anymore". As discussed in several chapters, AN is commonly seen by patients as providing control, discipline, uniqueness, or safety. Ambivalence toward AN, therefore, is not simply resistance or defiance; it is best understood as a signal that alternative identities feel less coherent or less acceptable than the anorexic identity. This may be especially true for those with longstanding presentations and whose AN developed early on in life, when the illness has woven its way into the very fabric of their identity.

Rebuilding Identity through Social Connection

A key argument of Chapter 8 is that recovery from AN can be facilitated when individuals start to form new, meaningful social identities, by joining communities that affirm different values, identities, and relationships. Through new connections and experiences, people learn what they enjoy or dislike, discover who they relate to or who they don't, and gradually develop a fuller sense of who they are, what they are good at, and what they find challenging.

A crucial part of this self-development is facilitated via our emotions, as they provide near-instant feedback on experiences and interactions, allowing us to learn and grow from them. As described by Damasio (2003), emotions form a bridge between bodily states and conscious awareness. It is this mapping of emotion, both physical and psychological, that allows for the development of an autobiographical self – a coherent sense of being a continuous person with a personal identity shaped by meaningful experiences. It is via individual emotional states, such as anger, fear, and sadness, that we mark out the significant "chapters" of our personal life story (e.g., Fox et al., 2012).

However, as discussed in Chapter 7, it is a fairly established finding within AN research that there are significant difficulties with emotions and high levels of alexithymia (difficulty identifying and describing one's emotions). Furthermore, difficulties in recognising and expressing emotions will often make building meaningful relationships challenging as this leads to challenges with intimacy and feelings of inauthenticity. Not only does this prevent the self-learning from emotion feedback loops, but it also leaves the person feeling at constant risk of rejection. This results in a further withdrawal into AN-defined self and engaging with the anorexic voice, as described in Chapter 4.

Sociocultural Pressures, Trauma, and Belonging

A key feature of the discussion over Chapters 3, 5, and 9 is that these intra- and inter-personal difficulties are further compounded by social trauma, such as rejection and bullying by peers. It is the clinical experience of both editors that one of the pervasive factors in AN, beyond the specifics of weight and eating difficulties, is that clients often describe a sense of disconnection and loneliness. It is this lack of any meaningful social/group membership that further influences the course of the AN (Chapter 8). The slow but steady takeover of the self by AN is exacerbated by the widespread internalisation of societal norms, such as the thin-ideal, rigid gender roles that prioritise appearance and caretaking over assertiveness, and socialisation discouraging women from setting boundaries (Chapter 9). In many ways, the descent into AN is reinforced by the toxic expectations of femininity in 21st-century Western society. Chapter 9 also highlights that, while AN is less common in men, traditional masculine norms can still shape risk, as men who internalise traditionally feminine appearance ideals may also be at elevated risk, further demonstrating problems with the pressure to conform to narrow, culturally defined standards of attractiveness.

Alongside pressures relating to femininity and the thin-ideal, gender identity also intersects with AN (Chapter 10). Some gender-diverse individuals may rely on AN behaviours, such as attempting to attain a body type more congruent with their gender identity. Restrictive eating, for example, may be employed to suppress secondary sexual characteristics or to achieve a body more aligned with one's gender identity, including, for some, an androgynous appearance. More broadly, gender minority status itself may act as a chronic social stressor, and being a sexual minority introduces additional sociocultural stressors for some people, which may motivate disordered eating as a coping strategy. These aspects are seldom considered in treatment, yet they help explain the particular draw that AN may hold for specific demographics of society.

AN varies in prevalence and presentation across cultures. Chapter 11 discussed the role of acculturation to Western body ideals, leading to body dissatisfaction and identity conflict. Nonetheless, rural settings and traditional cultural values may act as protective factors by offering alternative body ideals and resisting Western thinness norms. These findings highlight that treatment should be culturally sensitive, understanding AN not (just) in terms of individual identity but also broader sociocultural identity.

Chapter 5 explores the role of autism, which is known to be relatively common in AN. Autism intersects with identity in key ways: communication differences, understanding of emotions, and sensory sensitivities may complicate self-understanding. Furthermore, autistic individuals report engaging in camouflaging – masking autistic traits to "fit in" – which may over time intensify emotional exhaustion and feelings of inauthenticity or identity confusion. AN, for some, may become a coping strategy for managing overwhelm and negative emotions linked to autistic experiences. Neurodiversity-aware approaches are needed that allow autistic individuals to make sense of their autism and to develop a positive, integrated sense of identity.

Final Reflections and Future Directions

Several research priorities emerge across the chapters in this book. It is commonplace to track eating disorder symptomatology over treatment with the use of measures such as the Eating Disorder Examination Questionnaire (EDE-Q) (Carter et al., 2001). If identity development is truly a mechanism for recovery, this should presumably precede any (lasting) change in such measures of disordered eating. While there are measures that allow for tracking motivational changes during treatment, it would be helpful to develop measures to track identity development beyond AN as a key outcome of interest. This would allow for research to examine the benefits of focusing on identity development in therapeutic approaches, whether these do in fact lead to identity changes, and whether this is associated with recovery. Researchers have already begun to examine specific techniques that could foster identity development in those with AN; Koskina & Schmidt (2019) detail a case study in which work on identity development – which involved discussing a role model and experimenting with embodying another "self" congruent with one's values – was considered a "turning point" by a young woman with AN (p. 5). This work may be particularly needed for those with more longstanding illness, where alternative identities beyond the AN may have eroded over time. More work is clearly needed to understand the prevalence of AN in gender-diverse and neurodivergent individuals, and to address the interaction between AN and sociocultural expectations of femininity, and more broadly to understand the role of sociocultural identity as a risk and protective factor for AN. For each of these examples, there is a case to be made that developing a positive identity, where one can feel proud and valuable within one's social group and find a way toward authentic self-expression, may be important in AN. In embracing these priorities, we hope the field can move toward treatments that not only restore weight but also nourish the self.

References

Carter, J. C., Stewart, D. A., & Fairburn, C. G. (2001). Eating disorder examination questionnaire: Norms for young adolescent girls. *Behaviour Research and Therapy*, *39*(5), 625–632.

Colton, A., & Pistrang, N. (2004). Adolescents' experiences of inpatient treatment for anorexia nervosa. *European Eating Disorders Review: The Professional Journal of the Eating Disorders Association*, *12*(5), 307–316.

Damasio, A. (2003). Feelings of emotion and the self. *Annals of the New York Academy of Sciences*, *1001*(1), 253–261.

Fairburn, C. G., Cooper, Z., & Shafran, R. (2003). Cognitive behaviour therapy for eating disorders: A "transdiagnostic" theory and treatment. *Behaviour Research and Therapy*, *41*(5), 509–528.

Fox, J.R.E, Federici, A. & Power, M. (2012). Emotions and Eating Disorders. In Fox, J. and Power, M. Eating and its Disorders. Wiley Series in Clinical Psychology. Wiley - Blackwell: Chichester.

Higbed, L., & Fox, J. R. (2010). Illness perceptions in anorexia nervosa: A qualitative investigation. *British Journal of Clinical Psychology*, *49*(3), 307–325.

Keski-Rahkonen A, Tozzi F (2005). The process of recovery in eating disorder sufferers' own words: an Internet-based study. Int J Eat Disord. 37, Suppl:S80-6, discussion S87-9. doi: 10.1002/eat.20123.

Kinderman, P., Setzu, E., Lobban, F., & Salmon, P. (2006). Illness beliefs in schizophrenia. *Social Science & Medicine*, *63*(7), 1900–1911.

Koskina, A., & Schmidt, U. (2019). Who am I without anorexia? Identity exploration in the treatment of early stage anorexia nervosa during emerging adulthood: A case study. *The Cognitive Behaviour Therapist*, *12*, e32.

Miskovic-Wheatley, J., Bryant, E., Ong, S. H., Vatter, S., Le, A., Touyz, S., & Maguire, S. (2023). Eating disorder outcomes: Findings from a rapid review of over a decade of research. *Journal of Eating Disorders*, *11*(1), 85.

O'Connell, L. J. (2020). Being and doing anorexia nervosa: An exploration of diagnosis, identity-work, and performance of illness. PhD thesis, University of Essex.

Oldershaw, A., Startup, H., & Lavender, T. (2019). Anorexia nervosa and a lost emotional self: A psychological formulation of the development, maintenance, and treatment of anorexia nervosa. *Frontiers in Psychology*, *10*, Article 219. https://doi.org/10.3389/fpsyg.2019.00219

Index

For Product Safety Concerns and Information please contact our EU representative GPSR@taylorandfrancis.com Taylor & Francis Verlag GmbH, Kaufingerstraße 24, 80331 München, Germany